30 MINUTES OR LESS COOKBOOK

Sunset

minutes
or less cookbook

By the Editors of Sunset Books

SUNSET BOOKS INC. MENLO PARK, CA 94025

Sunset Books Inc.
Director, Sales & Marketing: Richard A. Smeby
Editorial Director: Bob Doyle
Production Director: Lory Day
Art Director: Vasken Guiragossian
Group Marketing Manager: Becky Ellis

Staff for this book:
Developmental Editor: Linda J. Selden
Recipe Development and Text: Catherine Alioto,
  Beth Allen, Andrew Baker, Paula Freschet,
  Jean Galton, Karyn Lipman, Lori Longbotham,
  Cynthia Scheer
Copy Editor: Rebecca LaBrum
Design: Robin Weiss
Photography: Noel Barnhurst
Food Stylist: Andrea Lucich
Assistant Food Stylists: Kim Konecny, Chris Lasack,
  Mirna Osorio
Production Coordinator: Patricia S. Williams

ISBN 0-376-02009-1 (Hardcover edition)
ISBN 0376-02010-5 (Softcover edition)
Library of Congress Catalog Card Number:
97-60842
Printed in the United States

For additional copies of *30 Minutes or Less
Cookbook* or any other Sunset book, call
1-800-526-5111.

Front Cover:
Simple Sukiyaki (page 71).

Frontispiece:
Roasted Honey-Wine Game Hens with New
Potatoes (page 105).

Table of Contents

Cooking with More Ingenuity than Time

Time-pressed cooks are making a hopeful discovery: it is becoming easier all the time to bring delicious meals to the table in a hurry, every night of the week. The cynical might look for the explanation in the proliferation of fast-food and carry-out shops. But as anyone who has explored that option knows, discerning diners soon tire of such fare. Better to take a fresh look at the possibilities for creating quick meals in your own kitchen—a wide variety of time-saving food products, are as close as your supermarket.

SUPERMARKET STRATEGY

Before starting work on this cookbook, our recipe developers surveyed the aisles of their supermarkets. In virtually every department, they found something to celebrate. Quick-cooking meats, poultry, and fish and shellfish abound. Fruits and vegetables rival a midsummer farmer's market for variety and freshness—and they're available in ever more convenient, ready-to-use forms. In-store bakeries offer an upgraded, extended selection of breads and rolls, and wonderful artisan-style loaves from local bakers now find their way onto the supermarket shelves.

Supermarket delicatessens have also augmented their offerings. Alongside the familiar coleslaws and potato salads, you're now likely to find cumin-spiked hummus to enjoy with crackers or pita crisps, chewy tabbouleh to mound atop crisp baby romaine leaves for a refreshing summer supper, and elegant cheeses to present with fruit for an effortless dessert.

What about high-quality packaged, bottled, canned, and frozen foods? You can stock your pantry and freezer with a dazzling variety of these products, from flavored olive oils to designer mustards and quick-cooking grains. Call on these ingredients to brighten a straightforward side dish or complement a favorite entrée. And if you'd like to enhance your meal with just the right wine, the supermarket can help there, as well—the selection is often admirable.

USING OUR RECIPES

You've probably observed more than once that getting food ready to cook often takes as long, or longer than the actual cooking. For that reason, we've designed our recipes to take advantage of ingredients that can be ready to use with a minimum of effort.

Pork with Orange-Cranberry Sauce (page 78) is a good example. You can purchase the chief ingredient, boneless pork chops, in exactly the form you need. The sauce is made from pantry staples such as canned beef broth, dried cranberries, frozen orange juice concentrate, and Dijon mustard. Altogether, you can prepare and cook this sparkling dish in about 25 minutes—so quickly and smoothly that if you want to serve rice or pasta with the pork, you should probably start boiling the cooking water while you're pounding the chops.

As the above example shows, preparation and cooking often overlap, when minutes count. That's why the time indicated at the start of each recipe is an *overall* time; it combines both the time needed to prepare the ingredients and the time the dish takes to cook.

The recipes are written in step-by-step form, letting you see when there's a pause in the preparation—a moment when you can begin cooking a vegetable or mixing a salad to round out your meal.

Aside from the desserts in the last chapter, all the recipes in this book are main dishes. They range from family fare such as sturdy vegetable soups and ample sandwiches to more elegant choices, such as butterflied beef and lamb roasts or Cornish game hens you can present as the entrée for an impromptu dinner party. Many recipes include suggestions for completing a menu with simple side dishes.

GETTING ORGANIZED FOR EFFICIENT COOKING

Cooking with an eye on the clock takes more than shopping savvy. If you feel you may be taking unnecessary steps as you move around the kitchen, take a critical look at the organization of your work and storage spaces. Then, when possible, group utensils and staple ingredients near where you use them.

Most meal preparation revolves around three areas: refrigerator, range, and sink. Try to keep plastic bags, foil, and storage containers handy to the refrigerator; spoons, spatulas, pans, and pot holders within easy reach of the range; and cutting board, colander, knives, and cleanup materials near the sink.

Keep your kitchen equipment in good condition. Sharp knives are a must. Position your food processor conveniently. Think about the various tasks for which you'll use the processor, and perform the less messy ones first—you might not have to wash the work bowl in between steps. Make the most of your microwave for small jobs such as melting or softening butter, warming tortillas, and making broth from bouillon cubes.

Though it can't always be avoided, inventing menus on a day-to-day basis isn't very time efficient. If you rely heavily on last-minute planning, you'll too often find yourself tapping your toe in the supermarket checkout line, when you'd rather be home with dinner in the works. To cut the time you spend at the grocery store and to spare yourself frustration, plot out several weeknight meals at once; then do most of the shopping in a single trip.

Start by sitting down with the weekly supermarket advertisements. Meat, poultry, seafood, and produce specials may well inspire menu ideas. Especially in the produce department, such good buys are often at the peak of seasonal perfection. You may also spot pantry items you need to restock (see page 236 for a list suggesting staple foods to keep on hand).

Consider the layout of the store where you do most of your shopping. If you organize your list to correspond to the order of the various departments, you're likely to reach the checkout stand a little sooner.

When you choose a main dish, think about the process of cooking the entire meal. Ultimately, you'll gain a useful sense of how to have everything ready at once. For instance, take a look at Crusty Mexican Chicken (page 96). After the first step, the chicken bakes for 15 minutes. This is a good time to begin steaming rice or a green vegetable to serve alongside. Once that job is under way, go on to make the sauce for the chicken (step 2).

Shrewd cooks also gain time by cooking ahead. If you roast a chicken for a Sunday dinner, for example, you may well have enough leftover meat for Chicken, Corn & Chile Polenta with Bacon (page 109) on Monday night.

COOKING WITH AN EYE TOWARD GOOD NUTRITION

More and more cooks are selecting recipes not just for good taste and quick preparation, but also for healthful eating. This means choosing plenty of fresh fruits and vegetables. Besides providing essential nutrients, these foods bring contrasting texture and glowing color to your dinner plate, without adding unwanted fat.

Another strategy for eating more healthfully is to increase your consumption of grains, legumes, and fat-free breads. Take advantage of couscous and quick-cooking grains such as rice, barley, bulgur, and polenta; explore the ever-increasing variety of canned beans on your grocer's shelves.

Thanks to the nutrition labels now found on virtually every packaged food, it's easier than ever to make low-fat choices when you select prepared foods. To limit fat in your diet, look at both the calorie count and the number of calories from fat per serving on the label. Choose foods with a big difference between those two numbers.

ABOUT OUR NUTRITIONAL DATA

For each recipe in this book there is a nutritional analysis stating calorie count; grams of total fat and saturated fat; milligrams of cholesterol and sodium; grams of carbohydrates, fiber, and protein; and milligrams of calcium and iron. Generally, the analysis applies to a single serving, based on the number of servings given for that recipe and the amount of each ingredient. If a range is given for the number of servings and/or the amount of an ingredient, the analysis is based on the average of the figures given.

The nutritional analysis does not include optional ingredients or those for which no specific amount is stated. If an ingredient is listed with a substitution, the information was calculated using the first choice.

Chapter One

SALADS

Taco Salad with Chipotle Cream

30 MINUTES

Chipotle chiles—smoked red jalapeños—add a deliciously fiery accent to the dressing for this cold beef salad. We call for canned chipotles packed in adobado sauce (a tomato-based sauce); you'll find them in the Mexican food section of well-stocked supermarkets.

- ¼ cup honey
- ¼ cup lime juice
- 2 to 3 teaspoons minced canned chipotle chiles in adobado sauce
- 1 tablespoon Dijon mustard
- 2 cloves garlic, minced or pressed
- ½ teaspoon ground cumin
- ¼ teaspoon ground allspice
- ¼ teaspoon salt
- ¼ cup sour cream
- ¼ cup chopped cilantro
- 12 cups (about 10 oz.) shredded iceberg lettuce
- ¾ to 1 pound cooked roast beef or steak, shredded
- ½ cup shredded sharp Cheddar cheese
- 2 medium-size tomatoes (about 12 oz. *total*), cut into wedges
- 1 large avocado (about 8 oz.), pitted, peeled, and sliced
- 1 cup corn chips or tortilla chips

1. In a small bowl, whisk honey, lime juice, chiles, mustard, garlic, cumin, allspice, and salt to blend smoothly. Whisk in sour cream until smooth. Stir in cilantro; set aside.

2. Divide lettuce equally among 4 wide, rimmed bowls. Top evenly with beef. Decoratively arrange cheese, tomatoes, avocado, and corn chips on each salad. Drizzle with dressing.

MAKES 4 SERVINGS.

PER SERVING: 516 calories, 26 g total fat, 8 g saturated fat, 65 mg cholesterol, 1,532 mg sodium, 48 g carbohydrates, 5 g fiber, 29 g protein, 288 mg calcium, 6 mg iron

Antipasto Salad

30 MINUTES

To make this salad, you serve a traditional Italian appetizer assortment—roasted peppers, savory cold meats, and cheese—atop a bed of mixed greens in a tangy red wine vinaigrette. Serve with crusty Italian bread or breadsticks; offer clusters of grapes and almond biscotti for dessert.

- ¼ cup red wine vinegar
- 2 tablespoons olive oil
- 2 tablespoons drained capers
- 1 tablespoon lemon juice
- ¼ teaspoon black pepper
- 8 to 12 ounces thinly sliced cold meats, such as salami, mortadella, and roast beef (choose 2 or 3 kinds)
- 12 cups (about 10 oz.) mixed salad greens, rinsed and crisped
- 1 large yellow bell pepper (about 8 oz.), seeded and cut into short, wide strips

- ½ cup firmly packed fresh basil leaves, chopped
- 1 jar (7 to 12 oz.) roasted red peppers, drained and patted dry
- 2 ounces Parmesan cheese, cut into thin shavings; or 2 ounces provolone cheese, cut into thin strips
- 1 can (about 2 oz.) anchovies, drained well (optional)
- Basil sprigs

Antipasto Salad

1. In a small bowl, whisk vinegar, oil, capers, lemon juice, and black pepper to blend; set aside.

2. Cut sliced meats into short strips about ¼ inch wide (or cut each slice in half).

3. In a shallow serving bowl, mix greens, bell pepper, and chopped basil. Drizzle three-fourths of the dressing over greens; mix well. Decoratively arrange meats, roasted peppers, cheese, and anchovies (if desired) over greens. Drizzle with remaining dressing. Garnish with basil sprigs.

MAKES 4 SERVINGS.

PER SERVING: 488 calories, 35 g total fat, 12 g saturated fat, 66 mg cholesterol, 1,916 mg sodium, 17 g carbohydrates, 3 g fiber, 24 g protein, 275 mg calcium, 4 mg iron

Indian-spiced Garbanzo Beans with Cucumber & Cabbage Slaw

30 MINUTES

This aromatic meatless specialty features some favorite Indian spices—cumin, coriander, and red pepper. A touch of sour cream cools and enriches the dish. Serve with warm pocket breads; offer wedges of cantaloupe or watermelon for dessert.

- 6 cups (about 9 oz.) shredded cabbage
- 1 medium-size cucumber (about 8 oz.), halved and thinly sliced
- 2 tablespoons lemon juice
- 1 tablespoon olive oil
- 2 tablespoons butter or margarine
- 1 large red bell pepper (about 8 oz.), seeded and cut into thin strips
- 1 large onion (about 8 oz.), halved and thinly sliced
- 1 tablespoon ground cumin
- 1 teaspoon ground coriander
- ½ teaspoon salt (or to taste)
- ⅛ teaspoon ground red pepper (cayenne)
- 2 cans (about 15 oz. *each*) garbanzo beans, rinsed and drained
- ½ cup chopped cilantro
- ½ cup sour cream

1. In a large bowl, combine cabbage, cucumber, lemon juice, and oil; mix well.

2. Melt butter in a wide nonstick frying pan over medium-high heat. Add bell pepper, onion, cumin, coriander, salt, and ground red pepper. Cook, stirring often, until onion is soft and beginning to brown (about 7 minutes). Add beans and ¼ cup water. Cook, stirring often, until beans are heated through (about 3 minutes); add water, 1 tablespoon at a time, if pan appears dry.

3. Remove pan from heat and stir in three-fourths of the cilantro. Spoon bean mixture over cabbage. Sprinkle with remaining cilantro. Offer sour cream to add to taste.

MAKES 4 SERVINGS.

PER SERVING: 353 calories, 19 g total fat, 8 g saturated fat, 28 mg cholesterol, 606 mg sodium, 37 g carbohydrates, 10 g fiber, 11 g protein, 155 mg calcium, 5 mg iron

Indian-spiced Garbanzo Beans with Cucumber & Cabb

Smoked Salmon & Cheese Salad

20 MINUTES

This attractive entrée goes together quickly and offers some delicious surprises: succulent smoked salmon, piquant Gorgonzola cheese, and crunchy nuts and croutons. For variety, substitute other fish, such as smoked trout or sardines, for the salmon.

5 tablespoons olive oil

3 tablespoons white wine vinegar

1 teaspoon Dijon mustard

3 ounces thinly sliced smoked salmon, cut into ½-inch-wide strips

⅔ cup crumbled Gorgonzola cheese

1½ cups purchased plain or seasoned croutons

12 cups (about 10 oz.) bite-size pieces romaine lettuce, rinsed and crisped

⅓ cup thinly sliced green onions

¼ cup salted roasted almonds, coarsely chopped

1. In a large bowl, whisk oil, vinegar, and mustard to blend.

2. To dressing, add salmon, cheese, croutons, lettuce, and onions. Mix well. Sprinkle with almonds.

MAKES 4 SERVINGS.

PER SERVING: 372 calories, 31 g total fat, 8 g saturated fat, 24 mg cholesterol, 651 mg sodium, 12 g carbohydrates, 3 g fiber, 13 g protein, 178 mg calcium, 2 mg iron

Smoked Salmon & Cheese Salad

Smoked Trout & Onion Salad

30 MINUTES

Red onion rings, mellowed and crisped by soaking in ice water and vinegar, are a crunchy surprise in this salad of romaine lettuce and smoked trout.

1 medium-size red onion (about 6 oz.), thinly sliced

¼ cup distilled white vinegar

¼ cup sour cream

1 tablespoon lemon juice

2 teaspoons prepared horseradish

1 tablespoon chopped fresh dill

1 large head romaine lettuce (about 1¼ lbs.), separated into leaves, rinsed, and crisped

12 ounces smoked trout, boned, skinned, and cut or torn into ½-inch pieces

Dill sprigs (optional)

1. Place onion slices in a deep bowl and add enough cold water to cover. With your hands, squeeze slices until they are almost limp. Drain, rinse, and drain again.

2. Return onion to bowl and add vinegar and about 2 cups each ice cubes and water. Let stand until onion is crisp (about 15 minutes); drain well. Remove onion from bowl.

3. While onion is soaking, in a small bowl, whisk sour cream, lemon juice, horseradish, and chopped dill to blend smoothly; set aside.

4. Line each of 4 individual plates with 2 or 3 large lettuce leaves. Cut remaining lettuce crosswise into ¼-inch-wide strips.

5. In a large bowl, gently mix lettuce strips, trout, and onion. Add dressing and mix gently but thoroughly. Divide salad equally among lettuce-lined plates; garnish with dill sprigs, if desired. Serve immediately.

MAKES 4 SERVINGS.

PER SERVING: 240 calories, 12 g total fat, 4 g saturated fat, 29 mg cholesterol, 911 mg sodium, 9 g carbohydrates, 3 g fiber, 24 g protein, 85 mg calcium, 2 mg iron

Corn Cobb Salad

25 MINUTES

Like the traditional Cobb salad, this tempting entrée features a variety of colorful ingredients arranged spoke-fashion on the serving platter. But this variation on the classic dish is meatless: fresh-cut corn, cherry tomatoes, roasted cashews, and tangy feta, all served on a bed of vinaigrette-dressed spinach, take the place of the usual chicken, bacon, and blue cheese.

⅓ cup olive oil

3 tablespoons red wine vinegar

1 tablespoon Dijon mustard

1 tablespoon minced shallot or red onion

1 cup (about 4 oz.) crumbled feta cheese

2 medium-size ears corn (*each* about 8 inches long)

9 ounces packaged triple-washed spinach

½ cup salted roasted cashews

1 cup tiny bite-size cherry tomatoes

1 very small red onion (about 4 oz.), halved and thinly sliced

1. In a shallow bowl, whisk oil, vinegar, mustard, and shallot to blend. Stir in ¼ cup of the cheese; set aside.

2. Remove and discard husks and silk from corn. In a shallow bowl, hold one ear of corn upright, and, with a sharp knife, cut kernels from cob. Then, using blunt edge of knife, scrape juice from cob into another shallow bowl. Repeat with remaining ear of corn. Discard cobs. Stir corn juice into dressing.

3. To assemble salad, remove and discard any coarse stems from spinach. Then, in a wide serving bowl, combine spinach and half the dressing. Mound corn, remaining ¾ cup cheese, cashews, and tomatoes in separate sections atop spinach; place onion in center. Offer remaining dressing to add to taste.

MAKES 4 TO 6 SERVINGS.

PER SERVING: 349 calories, 27 g total fat, 7 g saturated fat, 24 mg cholesterol, 497 mg sodium, 21 g carbohydrates, 4 g fiber, 9 g protein, 184 mg calcium, 2 mg iron

Spinach & Shrimp Salad with Tri-mustard Dressing

15 MINUTES

Two kinds of prepared mustard and a pinch of dry mustard go into the dressing for this fresh shrimp salad. If you prefer an even spicier dressing, add additional dry mustard. Serve with crisp-crusted French rolls or a hot loaf of sourdough bread.

- 10 **ounces packaged triple-washed baby spinach**
- 1 **pound shelled, deveined cooked shrimp (31 to 40 per lb.); leave tails on, if desired**
- 6 **tablespoons olive oil**
- ¼ **cup balsamic or red wine vinegar**
- 2 **teaspoons Dijon mustard**
- 2 **teaspoons honey mustard**
- ¼ **teaspoon salt**
- ⅛ **teaspoon dry mustard blended with 1 tablespoon cold water**
- ¼ **cup mayonnaise**
- 1 **tablespoon minced shallot or red onion**

1. Remove and discard any coarse stems from spinach. Then arrange spinach in a wide salad bowl and top with shrimp.

2. In a 1- to 1½-quart pan, combine oil, vinegar, Dijon mustard, honey mustard, salt, and dry mustard mixture. Bring to a boil over medium heat (about 3 minutes), stirring constantly. Remove pan from heat and whisk in mayonnaise and shallot.

3. Pour hot dressing over salad; mix well. Serve immediately.

MAKES 4 SERVINGS.

PER SERVING: 417 calories, 33 g total fat, 5 g saturated fat, 229 mg cholesterol, 585 mg sodium, 5 g carbohydrates, 2 g fiber, 26 g protein, 119 mg calcium, 6 mg iron

Crab Salad with Avocado Dressing

20 MINUTES

Looking for an elegant dish for quick entertaining? Serve a crisp green salad enhanced by a tart avocado dressing and topped with fresh crab. Alongside, serve warm baguettes with plenty of sweet butter.

- 12 **ounces cooked crabmeat**
- 2 **medium-size firm-ripe avocados (about 12 oz. *total*)**
- ½ **cup sour cream**
- ½ **cup lemon juice**
- ⅛ **teaspoon ground red pepper (cayenne)**
- 12 **cups (about 10 oz.) shredded butter or iceberg lettuce**
- ¼ **cup thinly sliced green onions**
- 2 **large tomatoes (about 1 lb. *total*), thinly sliced**
  Lemon slices

1. Pick through crab and discard any bits of shell; set aside.

2. Halve and pit avocados; scoop flesh from skins into a blender or food processor. Add sour cream, lemon juice, and red pepper. Whirl until smoothly puréed.

3. In a large bowl, combine lettuce and onions.

4. Divide avocado dressing among 4 wide, shallow individual plates; spread dressing out to rims of plates. Mound lettuce mixture equally on plates; top equally with tomatoes, then with crab. Garnish with lemon slices.

MAKES 4 SERVINGS.

PER SERVING: 291 calories, 18 g total fat, 6 g saturated fat, 98 mg cholesterol, 280 mg sodium, 15 g carbohydrates, 4 g fiber, 21 g protein, 142 mg calcium, 2 mg iron

Chinese Chicken Salad

30 MINUTES

This Chinese chicken salad is a refreshing twist on the old favorite. Like the classic recipe, it's made with chicken and noodles, but nothing is deep-fried—the chicken is lean shredded breast, and the noodles are boiled and bursting with flavor from a gingery dressing. You'll find cellophane noodles in the Asian food section of well-stocked supermarkets.

- 4 to 5 ounces cellophane noodles (*saifun;* made from bean or yam, not rice)
- 1 package (about 6 oz.) frozen Chinese pea pods, thawed
- ½ cup seasoned rice vinegar
- 3 tablespoons soy sauce
- 4 teaspoons minced fresh ginger
- 1 tablespoon sugar
- 1 tablespoon dry mustard blended with 1 tablespoon cold water
- 1 tablespoon Oriental sesame oil
- 6 cups (about 5 oz.) mixed salad greens, rinsed and crisped
- ½ cup finely chopped cilantro
- 1 tablespoon vegetable oil
- 2 large red or yellow bell peppers (about 1 lb. *total),* seeded and chopped
- 1 cup thinly sliced red onion
- 2 tablespoons lemon juice
- 2 cloves garlic, thinly sliced
- 3 cups shredded cooked chicken breast

1. In a 4- to 5-quart pan, bring about 2 quarts water to a boil over high heat. Stir in noodles; reduce heat and boil gently for 5 minutes. Remove pan from heat and let stand until noodles are tender to bite (5 to 10 minutes). Transfer to a strainer to drain. Leaving noodles in strainer, snip them with scissors into smaller strands; then stir in pea pods. Set aside to drain.

2. In a small bowl, whisk vinegar, soy sauce, ginger, sugar, mustard mixture, and sesame oil to blend. Set aside.

3. In a large bowl, combine greens and two-thirds of the cilantro. Transfer to a large platter.

4. Heat vegetable oil in a wide frying pan over medium-high heat. Add bell peppers, onion, lemon juice, and garlic. Cook, stirring often, until onion is soft (about 5 minutes); add water, 1 tablespoon at a time, if pan appears dry. With a slotted spoon, transfer onion mixture to bowl used to mix greens. Mix in chicken.

5. Shake noodles and pea pods in strainer to remove any remaining water; then return to noodle cooking pan and mix with a third of the dressing. Mound noodle mixture on greens; top with chicken mixture. Drizzle with remaining dressing. Sprinkle with remaining cilantro.

MAKES 6 SERVINGS.

PER SERVING: 315 calories, 8 g total fat, 1 g saturated fat, 60 mg cholesterol, 977 mg sodium, 36 g carbohydrates, 2 g fiber, 25 g protein, 61 mg calcium, 2 mg iron

Chicken Caesar

30 MINUTES

Chicken breasts baked in a coating of Parmesan cheese are served warm, on a bed of greens tossed with crisp croutons and a zesty garlic dressing. If you like, make the dressing with minced canned anchovies in place of anchovy paste.

½ cup grated Parmesan cheese

¼ teaspoon pepper

¼ teaspoon salt

4 boneless, skinless chicken breast halves (about 6 oz. *each*)

¼ cup olive oil

2 tablespoons lemon juice

½ teaspoon anchovy paste

½ teaspoon Dijon mustard

1 clove garlic, minced or pressed

12 cups (about 10 oz.) bite-size pieces romaine lettuce, rinsed and crisped

2 cups purchased plain or seasoned croutons

Lemon slices (optional)

1. In a shallow bowl, combine ¼ cup of the cheese, pepper, and salt. Rinse chicken and pat dry. Turn each piece in cheese mixture to coat completely. Pat any remaining coating on chicken.

2. Arrange chicken in a lightly oiled 9- by 13-inch baking pan. Bake in a 450° oven until meat in thickest part is no longer pink; cut to test (15 to 17 minutes). Let cool slightly.

3. Meanwhile, in a large bowl, whisk oil, lemon juice, anchovy paste, mustard, and garlic to blend. Add lettuce, remaining ¼ cup cheese, and croutons; toss to coat. Divide salad among 4 individual plates.

4. Cut each chicken breast diagonally into 5 strips; carefully arrange one sliced breast atop each salad. Garnish with lemon slices, if desired.

MAKES 4 SERVINGS.

PER SERVING: 440 calories, 21 g total fat, 5 g saturated fat, 107 mg cholesterol, 586 mg sodium, 14 g carbohydrates, 2 g fiber, 47 g protein, 199 mg calcium, 3 mg iron

Olive-Pecan Chicken Slaw

30 MINUTES

Crunchy toasted pecans and sweet apples are popular for snacks and simple desserts—and they're great in salads, too, as this winning main-dish slaw proves. Another time, you might try it with toasted almonds or walnuts in place of pecans, or with another favorite apple variety. Serve with hot buttermilk biscuits.

1 tablespoon butter or margarine

½ cup pecan halves

½ cup mayonnaise

2 tablespoons lemon juice

1 teaspoon Dijon mustard

½ teaspoon sugar

¼ teaspoon pepper

1 medium-size Red Delicious apple (about 6 oz.), cored and diced

2 cups shredded cabbage

1½ cups shredded cooked chicken

1 jar (about 2 oz.) diced pimentos, drained

1 can (about 2¼ oz.) sliced ripe olives, drained

¼ cup thinly sliced celery

Salt

1. Melt butter in a small frying pan over medium heat. Add pecans and stir occasionally until nuts are a darker brown (about 5 minutes). Drain on paper towels.

2. While nuts are toasting, combine mayonnaise, lemon juice, mustard, sugar, and pepper in a large bowl. Beat to blend smoothly.

3. To dressing, add apple, cabbage, chicken, pimentos, olives, and celery; mix well. Season to taste with salt; sprinkle with pecans.

MAKES 4 SERVINGS.

PER SERVING: 472 calories, 40 g total fat, 7 g saturated fat, 71 mg cholesterol, 416 mg sodium, 14 g carbohydrates, 3 g fiber, 17 g protein, 57 mg calcium, 2 mg iron

Olive-Pecan Chicken Slaw

Creamy Tarragon-Turkey Salad

30 MINUTES

Reminiscent of a classic Waldorf salad, this main-dish choice combines red grapes, celery, crisp pecan halves, and stir-fried turkey breast in a creamy herb dressing. Serve with iced tea and warm Parkerhouse rolls.

2 or 3 large bunches watercress (about 1 lb. *total*)

½ cup pecan halves

1 tablespoon olive oil

2 turkey breast tenderloins (about 1 lb. *total*), cut into ½-inch pieces

¾ cup mayonnaise

¾ cup sour cream

3 tablespoons minced fresh tarragon

½ teaspoon salt

⅛ teaspoon pepper

2 cups seedless red grapes

½ cup chopped celery

Tarragon sprigs (optional)

1. Remove large leaves and tender sprigs from watercress; discard coarse stems. Rinse watercress and drain well. Divide among 6 shallow individual bowls and set aside.

2. Toast pecans in a wide nonstick frying pan over medium heat until golden (about 4 minutes), shaking pan often. Remove from pan and set aside.

3. Heat oil in pan over medium-high heat. Add turkey and cook, stirring often, until no longer pink in thickest part; cut to test (3 to 5 minutes). Remove from pan with a slotted spoon; set aside.

4. In a large bowl, stir together mayonnaise, sour cream, minced tarragon, salt, and pepper. Stir in grapes, celery, pecans, and turkey. Mound turkey mixture equally atop watercress in bowls. Garnish with tarragon sprigs, if desired.

MAKES 6 SERVINGS.

PER SERVING: 472 calories, 37 g total fat, 8 g saturated fat, 76 mg cholesterol, 430 mg sodium, 15 g carbohydrates, 3 g fiber, 23 g protein, 151 mg calcium, 2 mg iron

Turkey & White Bean Salad

30 MINUTES

Lean turkey breast tenderloin is a great choice for meals in a hurry—it's boneless, skinless, and quick to cook. Here, the meat is gently steeped to doneness while you assemble a sage-seasoned white bean salad to serve alongside.

- 2 turkey breast tenderloins (about 1 lb. *total*)
- ½ cup cider vinegar
- ¼ cup fat-free reduced-sodium chicken broth
- 2 tablespoons olive oil
- 1 teaspoon crumbled dried sage
- 1 teaspoon sugar
- 2 cans (about 15 oz. *each*) cannellini (white kidney beans), rinsed and drained
- 1¼ pounds firm-ripe pear-shaped (Roma-type) tomatoes
- 6 to 8 large red leaf lettuce leaves, rinsed and crisped
- 4 slices bacon, crisply cooked, drained, and crumbled

1. Rinse turkey and pat dry. In a 4- to 5-quart pan, bring about 2 quarts water to a boil over high heat. Add turkey, cover, and immediately remove pan from heat; let stand, undisturbed, until you are ready to check for doneness (about 20 minutes). To check, quickly cut a small slit in center of thickest part of turkey; if meat is no longer pink, remove from water. If it is still pink, immediately return to hot water, cover, and let stand until no longer pink, checking every 5 minutes. Immerse turkey in ice water until cool, then drain and pat dry. Cut turkey diagonally into ½-inch-thick slices.

2. While turkey is steeping, combine vinegar, broth, oil, sage, and sugar in a small bowl; whisk to blend. In a large bowl, combine beans and a third of the dressing; mix gently. Thinly slice tomatoes and set aside.

3. To serve, arrange lettuce leaves on a platter. Spoon bean salad over lettuce. Decoratively arrange turkey and tomatoes alongside beans. Drizzle with remaining dressing and sprinkle with bacon.

MAKES 4 SERVINGS.

PER SERVING: 427 calories, 12 g total fat, 2 g saturated fat, 76 mg cholesterol, 648 mg sodium, 39 g carbohydrates, 10 g fiber, 40 g protein, 106 mg calcium, 6 mg iron

Warm Turkey BLT Salad

25 MINUTES

Deliciously rich, this warm salad is a good choice for a casual company meal. To save time, have the turkey thigh boned and skinned for you at the meat market. You might complete the meal with a chunky cranberry relish and a basket of toasted baguette slices.

¼ cup olive oil

3 tablespoons mayonnaise

3 tablespoons white wine vinegar

1 tablespoon Dijon mustard

1 teaspoon dried thyme

12 cups (about 10 oz.) bite-size pieces butter lettuce, rinsed and crisped

1 large firm-ripe tomato (about 8 oz.), cut into wedges

1 large red or yellow bell pepper (about 8 oz.), seeded and cut into thin, short strips

¼ cup thinly sliced green onions

4 slices bacon, cut into thin slivers

1 pound boneless, skinless turkey thigh, cut into thin strips

About ¼ cup grated Parmesan cheese

Belgian endive spears, rinsed and crisped (optional)

1. In a small bowl, whisk oil, mayonnaise, vinegar, mustard, and thyme to blend smoothly; set aside.

2. In a large bowl, arrange lettuce, tomato, bell pepper, and onions.

3. In a wide frying pan, cook bacon over medium-high heat, stirring occasionally, until crisp (4 to 5 minutes). With a slotted spoon, lift out bacon, drain, and set aside. Discard all but 1 tablespoon of the drippings from pan.

4. Increase heat to high. Add turkey and cook, stirring often, until lightly browned (3 to 4 minutes). Immediately pour turkey and pan juices over lettuce mixture; then add bacon, dressing, and ¼ cup of the cheese. Mix well. Sprinkle with additional cheese and garnish with endive spears, if desired. Serve at once.

MAKES 4 SERVINGS.

PER SERVING: 456 calories, 34 g total fat, 7 g saturated fat, 103 mg cholesterol, 460 mg sodium, 9 g carbohydrates, 2 g fiber, 29 g protein, 109 mg calcium, 3 mg iron

Warm Turkey BLT Salad

Steak Salad with Horseradish Dressing

Sesame-Plum Pork Salad

20 MINUTES

Purchased plum sauce and canned crushed pineapple make a sweet, speedy dressing for store-bought barbecued pork and delicate napa cabbage. If you prefer a spicier flavor, stir a little crushed red pepper into the pork mixture.

1 can (about 8 oz.) crushed pineapple packed in juice, drained well

½ cup prepared Chinese plum sauce

2 tablespoons sugar

1 tablespoon distilled white vinegar

1 teaspoon Oriental sesame oil

2 green onions

3 cups (about 1 lb.) shredded purchased Chinese-style barbecued pork or roasted pork

6 cups (about 9 oz.) shredded napa cabbage

½ cup lightly packed cilantro leaves

Lime wedges

1. In a large bowl, stir together pineapple, plum sauce, sugar, vinegar, and oil; set aside.

2. Cut onions into 1½-inch lengths; then cut each piece lengthwise into thin shreds. Add onions and pork to sauce mixture; mix well.

3. Arrange cabbage on a rimmed platter; sprinkle evenly with cilantro. Top with pork mixture. Offer lime wedges to season individual servings to taste.

MAKES 4 SERVINGS.

PER SERVING: 322 calories, 15 g total fat, 6 g saturated fat, 50 mg cholesterol, 1,122 mg sodium, 28 g carbohydrates, 1 g fiber, 22 g protein, 170 mg calcium, 1 mg iron

Steak Salad with Horseradish Dressing

30 MINUTES

The classic combination of beef and horseradish takes perfectly to a warm main-dish salad. For even faster preparation, use purchased roast beef instead of flank steak; you'll need about 12 ounces. Serve the salad with warm onion rolls and cold beer.

1 flank steak (about 1 lb.)

Salt

½ cup sour cream

½ cup mayonnaise

1 tablespoon prepared horseradish (or to taste)

1 tablespoon lemon juice

⅛ teaspoon pepper

½ cup crumbled blue-veined cheese

12 cups (about 10 oz.) bite-size pieces romaine lettuce, rinsed and crisped

1 large tomato (about 8 oz.), cut into wedges

1 jar (about 6¼ oz.) marinated artichoke hearts, quartered and drained well

¼ cup thinly sliced red onion

About 1 teaspoon finely shredded lemon peel

1. Place steak on a lightly oiled rack in a broiler pan; sprinkle with salt. Broil about 6 inches below heat, turning once, until well browned on both sides and done to your liking; cut in thickest part to test (10 to 14 minutes for medium-rare).

2. Meanwhile, in a small bowl, stir together sour cream, mayonnaise, horseradish, lemon juice, and pepper. Stir in cheese. Set aside.

3. In a large bowl, toss together lettuce, tomato, artichokes, and onion; divide among 4 to 6 individual plates.

4. Cut steak across the grain into thin, slanting slices. Arrange steak over salads. Drizzle salads with dressing and garnish with lemon peel.

MAKES 4 TO 6 SERVINGS.

PER SERVING: 395 calories, 32 g total fat, 11 g saturated fat, 67 mg cholesterol, 542 mg sodium, 8 g carbohydrates, 3 g fiber, 20 g protein, 134 mg calcium, 3 mg iron

Fruit Salad Surprises

Mention fruit salad, and chance are the traditional dish will come to mind first: a variety of diced fresh fruits, dressed with simple blend of fruit juices or sweetened yogurt or sour cream, and often served as a ligh dessert or a breakfast starter. But as the choices on this page show, fruit salads aren always made with fruit alone, and they aren't always sweet. Mangoes, pears, melon, apples all take well to tangy, spicy seasonings and savory partners such as smoked meats an cheeses. Such snappy salads are delicious as main dishes or as accompaniments t simple meals in any season.

Smoked Chicken & Melon Salsa Salad

15 MINUTES

- 3 medium-size cantaloupes (about 1¾ lbs. *each*)
- 12 ounces purchased smoked or rotisserie chicken, boned, skinned, and cut into small cubes (about 2 cups meat)
- 1 medium-size cucumber (about 8 oz.), peeled, seeded, and diced
- About 2 tablespoons minced fresh mint
- 3 tablespoons lime juice
- 1 tablespoon honey
- Pepper
- Mint sprigs
- Lime wedges

1. Cut 2 of the melons in half lengthwise. Scoop out and discard seeds. If any of the melon halves does not sit steadily, cut a very thin slice from its base so it will sit steadily. Set melon halves aside, cut side down, to drain.

2. Peel, seed, and dice remaining melon. Transfer to a large bowl. Add chicken, cucumber, minced mint, lime juice, and honey; mix well. Season to taste with pepper.

3. Set one melon half in each of 4 shallow individual bowls. Spoon a fourth of the chicken mixture into and on top of each melon half (you may have to pack it lightly). Garnish with mint sprigs. Offer lime wedges to season salads to taste.

MAKES 4 SERVINGS.

PER SERVING: 250 calories, 8 g total fat, 2 g saturated fat, 52 mg cholesterol, 406 mg sodium, 32 g carbohydrates, 3 g fiber, 18 g protein, 44 mg calcium, 1 mg iron

Sweet Potato & Apple Salad with Ginger Dressing

30 MINUTES

- 6 small sweet potatoes or yams (about 2 lbs. *total*), scrubbed (choose slimmer sweet potatoes for faster cooking)
- 2 tablespoons honey
- 1 teaspoon grated lemon peel
- 1 tablespoon lemon juice
- ¾ teaspoon ground ginger (or to taste)
- ½ teaspoon ground cinnamon
- 1 cup plain nonfat yogurt
- 2 large red-skinned apples (about 1 lb. *total*)
- ¾ cup thinly sliced celery
- ½ cup salted roasted peanuts or almonds
- Salt

1. Place potatoes in a 5- to 6 quart pan and add enoug water to cover. Bring to boil; then reduce heat, cove and simmer just until barel tender when pierced (20 t 25 minutes). Drain. Immers potatoes in ice water unt cool, then drain and pat dry.

2. Meanwhile, in a larg bowl, whisk honey, lemo peel, lemon juice, ginger, cir namon, and yogurt to blend Core apples and cut into ¾ inch cubes. Add apple celery, and three-fourths c the peanuts to dressing; mi well.

3. Peel potatoes and cut int ¾-inch cubes; mix gentl with apple mixture. Season t taste with salt. Sprinkle wit remaining peanuts.

MAKES 8 SERVINGS.

PER SERVING: 204 calories, 5 g total fat, 1 g saturated fat, 1 mg cholesterol, 82 mg sodium, 37 g carbohydrates, 5 g fiber, 6 g protein, 93 mg calcium, 1 mg iron

Melon, Basil & Prosciutto Salad

5 MINUTES

12 to 16 large butter lettuce leaves, rinsed and crisped

4 slices prosciutto (about 3 oz. *total*)

1 tablespoon firmly packed brown sugar

8 cups bite-size cubes of peeled, seeded honeydew melon

¼ cup finely slivered fresh basil

About 2 tablespoons balsamic vinegar

2 ounces Parmesan cheese, cut into thin shavings

Pepper

Basil sprigs

1. Arrange lettuce leaves, overlapping if necessary, on a rimmed platter.

2. Cut prosciutto into strips about 1 inch long and ¼ inch wide. Place in a large bowl, add sugar, and toss lightly to coat.

3. Add melon and slivered basil; mix well. Spoon melon mixture over lettuce leaves and drizzle with vinegar. Top with cheese and sprinkle with pepper. Garnish with basil sprigs. Serve immediately (the basil's flavor grows stronger upon standing and can overpower the delicate melon).

MAKES 4 SERVINGS.

PER SERVING: 243 calories, 7 g total fat, 3 g saturated fat, 27 mg cholesterol, 658 mg sodium, 36 g carbohydrates, 4 g fiber, 13 g protein, 199 mg calcium, 1 mg iron

Litchi Chicken Salad

10 MINUTES

1 can (about 1 lb.) litchis

½ cup plain nonfat yogurt

½ teaspoon grated lemon peel

1 tablespoon lemon juice

1 teaspoon dried thyme

3 cups bite-size pieces cooked chicken

½ cup finely chopped celery

Salt and pepper

8 large butter lettuce leaves, rinsed and crisped

¼ cup thinly sliced green onions

1. Drain litchis, reserving 2 tablespoons of the syrup; set fruit aside.

2. In a large bowl, stir together reserved 2 tablespoons litchi syrup, yogurt, lemon peel, lemon juice, and thyme. Stir in chicken and celery. Season to taste with salt and pepper.

3. Line 4 individual plates with lettuce leaves; spoon chicken salad equally onto lettuce. Top salads equally with litchis and onions.

MAKES 4 SERVINGS.

PER SERVING: 305 calories, 8 g total fat, 2 g saturated fat, 94 mg cholesterol, 166 mg sodium, 26 g carbohydrates, 1 g fiber, 33 g protein, 94 mg calcium, 3 mg iron

Mango, Pear & Avocado Salad

20 MINUTES

½ cup balsamic vinegar

3 tablespoons honey

8 ounces packaged triple-washed spinach

2 large firm-ripe pears (about 1 lb. *total*)

2 tablespoons lemon juice

1 large avocado (about 8 oz.)

2 large firm-ripe mangoes (about 2½ lbs. *total*)

3 ounces feta cheese, crumbled

Pepper

1. In a small bowl, whisk vinegar and honey to blend. In a large bowl, combine spinach and a fourth of the vinegar mixture; mix well. Arrange spinach on a platter or 4 to 6 individual plates.

2. Peel and core pears; cut into ½-inch-thick slices, combine with 1 tablespoon of the lemon juice, and set aside. Pit and peel avocado; cut into ½-inch-thick slices and combine with remaining 1 tablespoon lemon juice. Peel mangoes; cut fruit away from pits in ½-inch-thick slices.

3. Arrange pears, avocado, mangoes, and cheese over spinach. Offer pepper and remaining vinegar-honey mixture to add to taste.

MAKES 4 TO 6 SERVINGS.

PER SERVING: 303 calories, 10 g total fat, 3 g saturated fat, 15 mg cholesterol, 235 mg sodium, 56 g carbohydrates, 6 g fiber, 6 g protein, 159 mg calcium, 2 mg iron

Hunan Lamb on Cool Greens

30 MINUTES

Chile lovers will enjoy this dish of quick-cooked lamb cloaked in a spicy-hot dressing and served with plenty of crisp greens and cucumber. For even more fiery flavor, offer hot chili oil to add at the table.

- 2 tablespoons seasoned rice vinegar
- 1 tablespoon soy sauce
- 2 teaspoons Oriental sesame oil
- 1 teaspoon lemon juice
- 1 tablespoon cornstarch
- 3 tablespoons hoisin sauce
- 2 tablespoons chili paste with garlic
- 1 tablespoon sugar
- 12 cups (about 10 oz.) mixed salad greens, rinsed and crisped
- 1 medium-size cucumber (about 8 oz.), halved and thinly sliced
- ⅔ cup lightly packed cilantro leaves
- 1 tablespoon vegetable oil
- 1 large onion (about 8 oz.), halved and thinly sliced
- 1 pound lean boneless leg of lamb, trimmed of fat and cut into ¾-inch cubes

1. In a small bowl, whisk vinegar, soy sauce, sesame oil, and lemon juice to blend. Add cornstarch; stir until smoothly blended. Add hoisin sauce, chili paste, and sugar; blend well. Set aside.

2. In a large serving bowl, mix greens, cucumber, and two-thirds of the cilantro.

3. Heat vegetable oil in a wide nonstick frying pan over medium-high heat. Add onion and cook, stirring often, until soft (about 5 minutes); add water, 1 tablespoon at a time, if pan appears dry. Add lamb and cook, stirring often, until done to your liking; cut in thickest part to test (2 to 3 minutes for medium-rare).

4. Stir hoisin mixture and pour into pan. Cook, stirring, until sauce boils and thickens slightly (1 to 2 minutes). Immediately spoon lamb mixture over greens. Sprinkle with remaining cilantro.

MAKES 4 SERVINGS.

PER SERVING: 307 calories, 11 g total fat, 3 g saturated fat, 73 mg cholesterol, 939 mg sodium, 23 g carbohydrates, 2 g fiber, 25 g protein, 61 mg calcium, 2 mg iron

Hunan Lamb on Cool Greens

Tuscan Bread & Bean Salad

15 MINUTES

This salad's two main ingredients—white beans and crisp croutons—give it a texture that's creamy and crunchy at the same time. Chopped ripe tomatoes bring freshness and color to the combination.

8 to 12 large butter lettuce leaves, rinsed and crisped

½ cup balsamic vinegar

¼ cup olive oil

1 tablespoon honey

2 tablespoons chopped fresh thyme (or to taste)

2 tablespoons thinly sliced green onion

⅛ teaspoon crushed red pepper flakes

2 cans (about 15 oz. *each*) cannellini (white kidney beans), rinsed and drained

2 large tomatoes (about 1 lb. *total*), chopped and drained well

4 cups purchased plain or seasoned croutons

1. Line 4 shallow individual bowls with lettuce leaves.

2. In a large bowl, whisk vinegar, oil, honey, thyme, onion, and red pepper flakes to blend. Add beans and tomatoes; mix gently but thoroughly. Mix in croutons. Spoon bean mixture into lettuce-lined bowls.

MAKES 4 SERVINGS.

PER SERVING: 455 calories, 17 g total fat, 2 g saturated fat, 0 mg cholesterol, 665 mg sodium, 63 g carbohydrates, 12 g fiber, 13 g protein, 107 mg calcium, 6 mg iron

Minted Lentils with Goat Cheese

30 MINUTES

Dried legumes may not be a typical choice for quick meals, but lentils are an exception to the rule: they require no soaking and simmer to tenderness in just 15 to 20 minutes. Here, they're combined with goat cheese and fresh mint in an unusual salad. Try it with a platter of sliced ripe tomatoes and a basket of cracked wheat rolls.

1¾ cups lentils

3 cups vegetable broth

½ teaspoon dill seeds

1 teaspoon dried thyme

3 tablespoons red wine vinegar

2 to 3 tablespoons olive oil

Red cabbage leaves, rinsed and crisped (optional)

½ cup thinly sliced red onion

About 4 ounces goat cheese, such as Montrachet or bûcheron, coarsely crumbled

¼ cup chopped fresh mint

Mint sprigs (optional)

1. Sort through lentils, discarding any debris. Rinse and drain lentils; place in a 2- to 3-quart pan and add broth, dill seeds, and thyme. Bring to a boil over high heat. Reduce heat, cover, and simmer, stirring once or twice, just until lentils are tender to bite (15 to 20 minutes). Drain, reserving liquid. Transfer lentils to a wide, shallow bowl and let cool for 5 minutes, stirring occasionally.

2. To lentils, add 4 to 6 tablespoons of the reserved cooking liquid (just enough to moisten); then add vinegar and 1 tablespoon of the oil.

3. Line a platter or individual plates with cabbage leaves, if desired; then spoon lentil mixture onto platter. Top with onion, cheese, and chopped mint; drizzle with 1 to 2 tablespoons more oil. Garnish with mint sprigs, if desired.

MAKES 4 TO 6 SERVINGS.

PER SERVING: 392 calories, 15 g total fat, 6 g saturated fat, 18 mg cholesterol, 724 mg sodium, 43 g carbohydrates, 8 g fiber, 24 g protein, 108 mg calcium, 7 mg iron

Tofu Toss with Spicy Peanut Sauce

30 MINUTES

Good in summer or winter, this assertively seasoned salad is based on firm tofu—cut into cubes, cloaked in a peanut and hoisin sauce, and tossed with a colorful combination of cabbage, radicchio, and cilantro.

1 package (about 6 oz.) frozen Chinese pea pods, thawed and drained

1 pound firm tofu, rinsed, drained, and cut into ½-inch cubes

2 cloves garlic, minced or pressed

⅛ teaspoon ground red pepper (cayenne), or to taste

½ cup creamy peanut butter

½ cup hoisin sauce

½ cup seasoned rice vinegar

1 teaspoon Oriental sesame oil

1 large head radicchio (about 10 oz.)

6 cups (about 9 oz.) finely shredded napa cabbage

½ cup lightly packed cilantro leaves

¼ cup thinly sliced shallots or red onion

1 tablespoon vegetable oil

Lime wedges

1. Cut pea pods diagonally in half. Transfer to a large bowl and add tofu, garlic, and red pepper; mix gently.

2. In a small bowl, beat peanut butter, hoisin sauce, vinegar, and sesame oil to blend smoothly. Set aside.

3. Remove 8 to 12 large outer leaves from radicchio; rinse and drain well. Arrange leaves, overlapping if necessary, in a wide, shallow bowl. Rinse, drain, and finely shred remaining radicchio; place in a large bowl and mix with cabbage, cilantro, and shallots.

4. Heat vegetable oil in a wide nonstick frying pan over medium-high heat. Add tofu mixture and cook, stirring often, until almost all liquid has evaporated and tofu is heated through (about 5 minutes). Stir in peanut butter mixture. Cook, stirring, just until sauce is heated through (1 to 2 minutes). Pour tofu mixture over cabbage mixture; mix well. Spoon into radicchio-lined bowl. Offer lime wedges to season individual servings to taste.

MAKES 4 TO 6 SERVINGS.

PER SERVING: 451 calories, 25 g total fat, 4 g saturated fat, 0 mg cholesterol, 1,146 mg sodium, 36 g carbohydrates, 3 g fiber, 25 g protein, 315 mg calcium, 11 mg iron

Cheese Ravioli with Pears & Gorgonzola

30 MINUTES

A honey-herb vinaigrette dotted with poppy seeds dresses this unusual pasta salad, a combination of plump cheese-filled ravioli, sharp watercress, and fresh pears. If you like, use fresh figs, quartered, in place of the pears.

1 package (about 9 oz.) fresh cheese-filled ravioli or tortellini

2 or 3 large bunches watercress (about 1 lb. *total*)

⅓ cup red wine vinegar

⅓ cup olive oil

¼ cup honey

1 tablespoon poppy seeds

1 tablespoon minced shallot or red onion

¼ teaspoon dried thyme

¼ teaspoon dried oregano

8 ounces sliced mushrooms

½ cup oil-packed dried tomatoes, drained and coarsely chopped

⅔ cup crumbled Gorgonzola cheese

2 small Bosc pears (8 to 10 oz. *total*), cored and thinly sliced

Cheese Ravioli with Pears & Gorgonzola

1. In a 4- to 5-quart pan, bring about 2 quarts water to a boil over medium-high heat; stir in ravioli and cook, uncovered, until just tender to bite (4 to 6 minutes). Or cook ravioli according to package directions. Drain, rinse with cold water, and drain well again.

2. Meanwhile, remove large leaves and tender sprigs from watercress; discard coarse stems. Rinse watercress and drain well.

3. In a large bowl, whisk vinegar, oil, honey, poppy seeds, shallot, thyme, and oregano to blend. Add watercress, mushrooms, tomatoes, cheese, pears, and ravioli; mix well.

MAKES 6 SERVINGS.

PER SERVING: 533 calories, 33 g total fat, 9 g saturated fat, 50 mg cholesterol, 419 mg sodium, 52 g carbohydrates, 6 g fiber, 14 g protein, 330 mg calcium, 3 mg iron

Chapter Two
SOUPS

Green & White Spring Soup

20 MINUTES

The fresh, delicate flavors of spring inspired this soup. The green comes from asparagus slices and watercress leaves, the white from thin strands of capellini and sweet scallops. For a simple feast, serve with hot cheese biscuits (either from the bakery or homemade) and a marinated vegetable platter. For dessert, offer a medley of fresh strawberries, raspberries, and blueberries with crème fraîche.

1 large can (about 49½ oz.) fat-free reduced-sodium chicken broth

1 can (about 14½ oz.) fat-free reduced-sodium chicken broth

1 teaspoon grated lemon peel

1 teaspoon dried tarragon

¼ teaspoon white pepper

2 ounces dried capellini (angel hair pasta), broken in half

1 pound slender asparagus

12 ounces bay or sea scallops

1 bunch watercress (about 4 oz.)

3 tablespoons lemon juice

1. In a 5- to 6-quart pan, combine broth, lemon peel, tarragon, and pepper. Bring to a boil over high heat. Add pasta; return broth to a boil, then reduce heat and simmer, uncovered, for 4 minutes.

2. Meanwhile, snap off and discard tough ends of asparagus; diagonally slice spears into 1-inch pieces. Rinse scallops; if using sea scallops, cut into bite-size pieces. Remove leaves from watercress; discard stems. Rinse and drain watercress. Chiffonade-cut 12 watercress leaves (see page 50) and set aside for garnish.

3. Stir asparagus and scallops into soup. Simmer, uncovered, until scallops are just opaque in center; cut to test (about 3 minutes).

4. Remove pan from heat and stir in whole watercress leaves. Cover and let stand until watercress is wilted (about 1 minute). Stir in lemon juice and sprinkle with the chiffonade of watercress. Serve immediately, since lemon juice may cause the bright green color to darken upon standing.

MAKES 5 SERVINGS (ABOUT 10 CUPS).

PER SERVING: 147 calories, 1 g total fat, 0 g saturated fat, 22 mg cholesterol, 990 mg sodium, 14 g carbohydrates, 1 g fiber, 20 g protein, 65 mg calcium, 1 mg iron

Lunchbox Vegetable Soup

30 MINUTES

Lunchtime is soup time—and vegetable soup is on the menu. This updated version includes carrot pennies, baby corn on the cob, and pasta bow ties. Round out the lunchbox with a bran muffin, an apple, and a giant-size chocolate chip cookie.

4 large carrots (about 1 lb. *total*)

1 tablespoon butter or margarine

3 stalks celery, cut into ½-inch squares

1 large onion (about 8 oz.), chopped

1½ cups sliced mushrooms

1 can (about 15 oz.) baby corn on the cob, drained

1 large can (about 49½ oz.) fat-free reduced-sodium chicken broth

1 can (about 14½ oz.) fat-free reduced-sodium chicken broth

1½ teaspoons dried tarragon

¼ teaspoon pepper

Salt

2 cups (about 2 oz.) dried pasta bow ties

1 cup frozen tiny peas

¼ cup chopped parsley

1. Peel carrots and cut crosswise into thin rounds.

2. Melt butter in a 5- to 6-quart pan over medium-high heat. Add carrots, celery, onion, mushrooms, and corn. Cook, stirring often, until celery and onion are tender to bite (5 to 6 minutes).

3. Add broth, tarragon, pepper, and salt to taste (about ¼ teaspoon); bring to a boil. Stir in pasta; return to a boil and cook, uncovered, for 5 minutes.

4. Add peas and continue to cook, uncovered, until pasta is just tender to bite (7 to 8 more minutes). Sprinkle with parsley.

MAKES 6 SERVINGS (ABOUT 12 CUPS).

PER SERVING: 159 calories, 3 g total fat, 1 g saturated fat, 5 mg cholesterol, 846 mg sodium, 25 g carbohydrates, 7 g fiber, 9 g protein, 78 mg calcium, 2 mg iron

Mexi-Corn Cheese Soup

15 MINUTES

Using frozen corn kernels lets you make this hearty cheese soup in just 15 minutes. Use your favorite prepared salsa—one with a medium-hot to hot flavor works best. For a great Southwestern-style meal, team the soup with warm tortillas and a spicy marinated tomato salad. Offer orange sorbet for dessert.

2 tablespoons butter or margarine

1 medium-size onion (about 6 oz.), finely chopped

½ teaspoon ground cumin

1 tablespoon cornstarch

2 cans (about 14½ oz. *each*) fat-free reduced-sodium chicken broth

1 package (about 10 oz.) frozen corn kernels

1 jar (about 7 oz.) roasted red peppers, drained and chopped

¼ cup salsa

8 ounces jalapeño jack cheese

1. Melt butter in a 3- to 4-quart pan over medium-high heat. Add onion and cumin; cook, stirring often, until onion is soft (4 to 5 minutes).

2. In a cup, dissolve cornstarch in about ¼ cup of the broth. Stir broth mixture into onion mixture in pan. Blend in remaining broth, corn, roasted peppers, and salsa. Bring to a boil over high heat, stirring occasionally; then reduce heat to a simmer and cook, stirring often, until soup thickens slightly.

3. Meanwhile, shred cheese. Just before serving, sprinkle soup with cheese.

MAKES 4 SERVINGS (ABOUT 6 CUPS).

PER SERVING: 399 calories, 24 g total fat, 14 g saturated fat, 76 mg cholesterol, 1,199 mg sodium, 28 g carbohydrates, 2 g fiber, 20 g protein, 418 mg calcium, 1 mg iron

Lunchbox Vegetable Soup

Roasted Pepper Gazpacho

20 MINUTES

From Spain comes this traditional cold soup, typically made with dried bread crumbs and fresh vegetables. Our version uses fresh Italian bread; roasted red peppers add depth of flavor. To eliminate the usual chilling time, make the soup with chilled ingredients.

2 slices white Italian bread (*each* about 2 inches thick; about 3 oz. *total*)

6 large ripe pear-shaped (Roma-type) tomatoes (about 1 lb. *total*), chilled

2 medium-size cucumbers (about 1 lb. *total*), chilled

1 large red onion (about 8 oz.), chilled

1 medium-size green bell pepper (about 6 oz.), chilled

3½ cups chilled tomato juice

1 cup cold water

1 jar (about 12 oz.) roasted red peppers, chilled, drained

¼ cup red wine vinegar

2 tablespoons olive oil

2 cloves garlic, minced or pressed
   Salt

½ teaspoon black pepper

¼ cup cilantro leaves

1. Remove crusts from bread; cut bread into 1-inch pieces. Set aside.

2. Seed and dice tomatoes. Peel, seed, and dice cucumbers. Chop onion; seed and dice bell pepper. Then, in a large bowl, toss together tomatoes, cucumbers, onion, and bell pepper.

3. In a food processor or blender, combine tomato juice, water, roasted peppers, bread, vinegar, oil, garlic, salt to taste (about ½ teaspoon), and black pepper. Whirl until mixture is almost smooth. Pour purée over vegetables in bowl; stir to combine.

4. Serve immediately; or cover and refrigerate for up to 3 days. Just before serving, chiffonade-cut cilantro (see page 50) and mound in a cluster in center of soup.

MAKES 4 SERVINGS (ABOUT 8 CUPS).

PER SERVING: 250 calories, 8 g total fat, 1 g saturated fat, 0 mg cholesterol, 1,085 mg sodium, 41 g carbohydrates, 5 g fiber, 6 g protein, 79 mg calcium, 4 mg iron

Sicilian Tomato Soup

25 MINUTES

Serve this cream of tomato soup with warm rosemary-prosciutto focaccia and an arugula, fennel, and red onion salad.

2 tablespoons olive oil

12 large ripe pear-shaped (Roma-type) tomatoes (about 2 lbs. *total*), seeded and diced

24 large fresh basil leaves

¾ cup fat-free reduced-sodium chicken broth

¾ cup whipping cream

1 tablespoon Worcestershire sauce
   Salt

¼ teaspoon crushed red pepper flakes

1. Heat oil in a 3- to 4-quart pan over medium-high heat. Add tomatoes and cook, stirring often, until tomatoes mash easily with a spoon (about 15 minutes).

2. Meanwhile, rinse basil leaves; drain on paper towels. Chiffonade-cut 8 of the leaves (see page 50) and set aside for garnish.

3. Transfer tomatoes to a food processor or blender. Add broth, cream, Worcestershire sauce, salt to taste (about ¼ teaspoon), red pepper flakes, and remaining 16 basil leaves. Whirl until almost smooth. Garnish with the chiffonade of basil.

MAKES 4 SERVINGS (ABOUT 4 CUPS).

PER SERVING: 247 calories, 21 g total fat, 10 g saturated fat, 50 mg cholesterol, 321 mg sodium, 12 g carbohydrates, 3 g fiber, 4 g protein, 58 mg calcium, 1 mg iron

Cinnamon-Spice Acorn Soup

Cinnamon-Spice Acorn Soup

15 MINUTES

Anytime can be the time for this squash soup, flavored with just a hint of cinnamon and nutmeg. Serve with pumpernickel raisin rolls and a salad of endive, cherry tomatoes, and green onions. Big squares of gingerbread are great for dessert.

1 large onion (about 8 oz.), cut into chunks
2 packages (about 10 oz. *each*) frozen mashed squash, thawed
2 cans (about 14½ oz. *each*) fat-free reduced-sodium chicken broth
¼ teaspoon ground cinnamon
¼ teaspoon freshly grated or ground nutmeg
2 tablespoons butter or margarine
¼ cup sour cream and additional ground cinnamon (optional)

1. In a food processor or blender, whirl onion until puréed. Add squash, broth, the ¼ teaspoon cinnamon, and nutmeg; whirl until blended.

2. Pour squash mixture into a 3- to 4-quart pan. Bring to a simmer over medium-high heat, stirring occasionally; then continue to simmer, uncovered, until heated through (2 to 3 more minutes).

3. Add butter and stir until melted. If desired, season sour cream lightly with cinnamon and swirl on top of soup.

MAKES 4 SERVINGS (ABOUT 8 CUPS).

PER SERVING: 167 calories, 6 g total fat, 4 g saturated fat, 16 mg cholesterol, 554 mg sodium, 25 g carbohydrates, 6 g fiber, 6 g protein, 56 mg calcium, 1 mg iron

Curried Zucchini Soup

25 MINUTES

Zucchini can be found in markets all year—and this soup is a great way to use it. Serve the soup hot; then chill any leftovers to serve cold. For a go-along, offer chicken, lettuce, and tomato sandwiches on whole wheat bread. Grapes and butterscotch brownies make the perfect dessert.

3 slices bacon
7 large zucchini (about 3½ lbs. *total*)
8 green onions
1 large can (about 49½ oz.) fat-free reduced-sodium chicken broth
1 to 1¼ teaspoons curry powder
Salt
¼ teaspoon white pepper
¾ cup whipping cream

1. In a 4- to 5-quart pan, cook bacon over medium-high heat until crisp (5 to 6 minutes). Lift bacon from pan; drain, crumble, and set aside. Discard all but 1 tablespoon of the drippings from pan.

2. While bacon is cooking, coarsely chop zucchini. Chop onions and reserve 2 tablespoons for garnish.

3. To drippings in pan, add remaining onions, zucchini, broth, curry powder, salt to taste (about ¼ teaspoon), and pepper. Bring to a boil over high heat; then boil, uncovered, until zucchini mashes easily with a spoon (9 to 10 minutes).

4. In a food processor or blender, whirl zucchini mixture, half at a time, until smoothly puréed. Return to pan and stir in cream; reheat until steaming (do not boil). Serve hot or cold; garnish with bacon and reserved onions.

MAKES 4 SERVINGS (ABOUT 8 CUPS).

PER SERVING: 281 calories, 20 g total fat, 11 g saturated fat, 57 mg cholesterol, 983 mg sodium, 16 g carbohydrates, 3 g fiber, 13 g protein, 123 mg calcium, 3 mg iron

Butter Bean & Ham Chowder

30 MINUTES

Hot, hearty, and filling! Serve this chowder with French bread, a wedge of farmhouse Cheddar, and a bowl of pears and red grapes. Pour glasses of Beaujolais to sip alongside.

- 1 tablespoon butter or margarine
- 12 ounces baked ham, cut into bite-size pieces
- 12 green onions, thinly sliced
- 3 large carrots (about 12 oz. *total*), chopped
- 2 cans (about 14½ oz. *each*) fat-free reduced-sodium chicken broth
- 2 cups milk
- ½ cup water
- 2 cans (about 15 oz. *each*) butter beans or cannellini (white kidney beans), rinsed and drained
- 1 package (about 10 oz.) frozen tiny peas
- ½ teaspoon pepper
- ¼ cup coarsely chopped parsley

1. Melt butter in a 5- to 6-quart pan over medium-high heat. Add ham and onions; then cook, stirring often, until onions are soft (4 to 5 minutes).

2. Stir in carrots and cook for 2 more minutes. Add broth, milk, and water; bring to a boil.

3. Reduce heat to medium-low and add beans, peas, and pepper. Cook, uncovered, stirring occasionally, until soup is bubbly (5 to 7 minutes). Sprinkle with parsley.

MAKES 6 SERVINGS (ABOUT 12 CUPS).

PER SERVING: 351 calories, 11 g total fat, 5 g saturated fat, 50 mg cholesterol, 1,616 mg sodium, 37 g carbohydrates, 11 g fiber, 26 g protein, 199 mg calcium, 4 mg iron

Red Potato Chowder

25 MINUTES

Old-fashioned potato chowder gets a new look and a touch of color from red-skinned potatoes (slice them thinly so they'll cook fast). Serve with warm herb bread and a salad of arugula, oranges, and red onion. For dessert, pick up some carrot cake from the bakery.

- 2 large red onions (about 1 lb. *total*), finely chopped
- 4 slices bacon, diced
- 8 medium-size red thin-skinned potatoes (about 2 lbs. *total*), scrubbed
- 3 tablespoons all-purpose flour
- 2 cans (about 14½ oz. *each*) fat-free reduced-sodium chicken broth
  Salt
- ½ teaspoon pepper
- 3½ cups milk
  Freshly grated nutmeg
  Chiffonade of spinach (optional; page 50)

1. In a 5- to 6-quart pan, combine onions and bacon. Cook over medium-high heat, stirring often, until onions are soft and bacon is lightly browned (4 to 5 minutes).

2. Meanwhile, thinly slice unpeeled potatoes.

3. Stir flour into onion mixture; then add potatoes, broth, salt to taste (about ½ teaspoon), and pepper. Bring to a boil; then reduce heat and simmer, uncovered, until potatoes are tender when pierced (7 to 8 minutes).

4. Stir in milk and cook until soup is simmering and heated through (3 to 4 minutes). Sprinkle with nutmeg. Top with chiffonade of spinach, if desired.

MAKES 5 SERVINGS (ABOUT 10 CUPS).

PER SERVING: 441 calories, 19 g total fat, 8 g saturated fat, 39 mg cholesterol, 656 mg sodium, 53 g carbohydrates, 5 g fiber, 15 g protein, 232 mg calcium, 2 mg iron

Butter Bean & Ham Chowder

Creamy Potato Watercress Bisque

25 MINUTES

Grated potatoes cook up fast into a creamy bisque that's light enough to serve as a first course, yet hearty enough to make a meal when teamed with a toasted mozzarella sandwich.

> 2 **large russet potatoes (about 1 lb. *total*)**
> 2 **cans (about 14½ oz. *each*) fat-free reduced-sodium chicken broth**
> 1 **bunch watercress (about 4 oz.)**
> 4 **green onions**
> 4 **ounces baked ham**
> **Salt**
> ¼ **teaspoon white pepper**
> 1 **cup reduced-fat sour cream**

1. Peel and grate potatoes and place in a 5- to 6-quart pan; stir in broth. Bring to a boil over high heat. Then reduce heat and simmer, uncovered, until potatoes are tender to bite (8 to 10 minutes).

2. Meanwhile, remove leaves from watercress; discard stems. Rinse and drain watercress. Thinly slice onions. Cut ham into slivers and set aside.

3. To potato mixture, add watercress, onions, salt to taste (about ¼ teaspoon), and pepper. Then whirl this mixture in a food processor or blender, half at a time, until almost smooth. Return to pan; reheat until steaming. Pour into a tureen and smoothly stir in sour cream. Sprinkle with ham.

MAKES 5 SERVINGS (ABOUT 5 CUPS).

PER SERVING: 204 calories, 9 g total fat, 4 g saturated fat, 29 mg cholesterol, 776 mg sodium, 19 g carbohydrates, 2 g fiber, 13 g protein, 39 mg calcium, 1 mg iron

Chicken Corn Chowder

30 MINUTES

Canned creamed corn and frozen corn kernels give this rich chowder its double-the-corn flavor. Serve with a spinach and red apple salad and a crusty loaf of sourdough bread.

> 4 **cups milk**
> 1 **cup fat-free reduced-sodium chicken broth**
> 1½ **pounds boneless, skinless chicken breasts**
> 2 **medium-size onions (about 12 oz. *total*)**
> 2 **stalks celery**
> 4 **slices bacon**
> 2 **large russet potatoes (about 1 lb. *total*)**
> 1 **can (about 17 oz.) cream-style corn**
> 1 **package (about 10 oz.) frozen white corn kernels**
> **Salt and pepper**

1. In a medium-size pan, bring milk and broth just to a full simmer over high heat (do not let boil). Remove from heat, cover, and keep hot.

2. Meanwhile, rinse chicken, pat dry, and cut into bite-size pieces. Set aside. Chop onions and celery; set aside.

3. In a 5- to 6-quart pan, cook bacon over medium-high heat until crisp (5 to 6 minutes). Lift bacon from pan; drain, crumble, and set aside. Discard all but 2 tablespoons of the drippings from pan.

4. Add chicken, onions, and celery to drippings in pan. Cook, stirring often, just until chicken is no longer pink in center; cut to test (5 to 6 minutes). Meanwhile, peel and grate potatoes.

5. To pan, add hot milk mixture, potatoes, cream-style corn, and corn kernels. Bring just to a boil. Reduce heat and simmer, uncovered, until potatoes are tender to bite (8 to 10 minutes). Season to taste with salt and pepper. Sprinkle with bacon.

MAKES 6 SERVINGS (ABOUT 12 CUPS).

PER SERVING: 471 calories, 14 g total fat, 6 g saturated fat, 96 mg cholesterol, 801 mg sodium, 49 g carbohydrates, 5 g fiber, 38 g protein, 233 mg calcium, 2 mg iron

Soup Toppings

Many delicious soup toppings are at your fingertip in the supermarket—and perhaps even right inside your refrigerator. Matching the garnish the soup depends not only on the soup's ingredients, but also on its character—whether it hot or cold, smooth or chunky, thick or thin, creamy or brothy. Whatever the garnish yo choose, place it on the soup right before serving.

Croutons

SKILLET CROUTONS. Start with 1 loaf (about 1 lb.) **unsliced bread.** You might use pumpernickel, whole-grain, sourdough, country white, or Cheddar cheese bread. Using a serrated knife, remove crusts from loaf; then cut loaf into ½-inch-thick slices. Cut slices into 1- to 1½-inch squares, circles, or triangles. Or use small cutters to make fancy shapes.

Melt ¼ cup **butter** or margarine in a wide frying pan over medium heat. Add 1 clove **garlic,** minced or pressed; freshly ground **pepper** to taste; and 2 tablespoons minced **fresh herbs,** such as rosemary, thyme, marjoram, parsley, or cilantro. Add croutons and cook, turning once, until golden and crisp on both sides (5 to 6 minutes). Transfer to a rack to cool. Makes about 4 dozen croutons.

CHEESY CROUTONS. Start with 1 loaf (about 1 lb.) **unsliced French, Italian, rye, or pumpernickel bread.** Have the baker slice it ½ inch thick. If slices are too large to fit in a soup bowl, cut them in half at home. Remove crusts, if desired.

Brush both sides of bread slices with a **seasoned oil,** such as basil oil, roasted garlic oil, or peppered oil. Arrange bread on a baking sheet and broil 4 to 6 inches below heat, turning once, until lightly browned on both sides (about 1 minute). Sprinkle top of each slice with about 1 tablespoon shredded **cheese,** such as sharp Cheddar, Colby, Gruyère, mozzarella, jalapeño jack, Münster, provolone, or Swiss. Sprinkle with **paprika.** Return to broiler until cheese is melted (about 30 seconds); watch closely to make sure cheese does not brown. Makes 12 to 15 large croutons (about 2 dozen croutons if slices of bread are cut in half).

Chiffonades

The word "chiffonade" refers to a classic cut of leafy vegetables and herbs—fine, fluffy shreds that make a fresh, decorative topping for soups and stews. Use a sharp French (chef's) knife for preparing these chiffonades.

Commonly used vegetable choices for chiffonades include arugula, basil, red or green cabbage, Belgian endive, lettuce (butterhead, leaf, romaine), mint, spinach, and watercress.

Three methods of creating the chiffonade cut are commonly used.

For large leaves, such as those of spinach or romaine, roll individual leaves into tight cylinders. Hold each cylinder tightly at one end; then slice it very thinly crosswise to make fluffy shreds of greens.

For tight heads of greens, such as red or green cabbage or Belgian endive, core head and cut it in half. Lay halves cut side down and cut lengthwise into fine, parallel shreds.

For smaller leaves, such as those of basil, mint, or arugula, stack several leaves on top of each other. Cut lengthwise into fine shreds.

Flavored Sour Cream or Yogurt

Sour cream or plain yogurt is a simple and appealing topping, especially for puréed vegetable soups and cold soups. Try flavoring the sour cream or yogurt with different seasonings, such as freshly ground black pepper; curry powder; chopped fresh dill; chopped chives; minced cilantro; grated lemon peel.

Flavored Butters

A dollop of whipped flavored butter adds richness and zest to soups. Soften unsalted butter to room temperature. Whisk or beat until light and creamy, then stir in the seasoning of your choice. You might try whole-grain mustar grated lemon, lime, or oran peel; ground cinnamon or n meg (for pumpkin or squa soup); minced cooked shrim (for seafood soups); or fine chopped fresh herbs such parsley, dill, rosemary, thyme.

Parmesan Puffs

Crisp, flaky puffs made fro frozen puff pastry sheets a delicious, foolproof, and we worth the few minutes th take to make. They're gre toppings for all sorts of sou and stews.

Start with 1 **frozen puff pa try sheet** (from a 17¼-o package), thawed. Unfold on cutting board into a 9-inc square. Using a sharp knife, c pastry sheet into nine 3-inc squares. Cut each square diag onally in half 2 times, makir 4 triangles. You will hav 36 triangles. Place on an u greased baking sheet.

Sprinkle tops of triangles ge erously with grated **Parmesa cheese;** dust with **paprik** Bake on middle rack of a 40(oven until golden, puffy, an crisp (10 to 12 minutes). B sure puffs are crisp before yo take them from the oven, they will lose height as the cool. Makes 3 dozen puffs.

TYPE OF SOUP		TOPPINGS	
CLEAR BROTHS & CONSOMMÉS	• Blanched julienne of fresh vegetables (green onions, carrots, leeks, beets, turnips, parsnips)	• Grated lemon or orange peel • Sieved hard-cooked eggs	• Diced ripe tomatoes and cucumbers
PURÉED VEGETABLE SOUPS AND CHUNKY VEGETABLE SOUPS	• Swirl of flavored sour cream • Spoonful of whipped cream • Whipped butter flavored with curry powder • Grated lemon, lime, or orange peel	• Herb-seasoned croutons • Nest of cooked capellini (angel hair pasta) • Toasted slivered almonds • Toasted chopped peanuts, pecans, or walnuts	• Diced fresh vegetables that soup is made from • Thinly sliced unpeeled red apples • Crisp apple slices (slowly baked in oven)
BAKED ONION SOUP	• Large whole wheat crouton, toasted and topped with melted Swiss and sprinkled with dried thyme	• Julienne strips of ham and red onion • Chiffonade of spinach and endive	
CHOWDERS	• Chiffonade of spinach and green onion tops • Julienne strips of carrots, celery, and chives • Herb-seasoned croutons	• Crumbled crisp bacon • Shreds of meat used in soup or a complementary meat such as ham, turkey, pastrami, salami	• Small cooked shrimp (for seafood chowders) • Shredded peeled potatoes, fried crisp
PASTA SOUPS	• Fine dice of leeks, tomatoes, and green bell peppers • Bottled roasted red peppers, drained and cut into thin strips	• Grated Parmesan cheese • Whipped butter flavored with garlic and parsley • Whipped butter flavored with Dijon mustard	• Fried Chinese chow mein noodles • Prepared salsa flavored with slivered fresh basil
CREAM SOUPS	• Toasted slivered almonds or chopped peanuts • Herb-seasoned croutons	• Grated cheese (such as Swiss, Cheddar, fontina, or jalapeño jack)	• Parmesan Puffs (facing page)
COLD SOUPS	• Swirls of sour cream, yogurt, or crème fraîche • Sour cream flavored with fresh dill • Finely chopped green, yellow, and red bell peppers	• Diced tomatoes, cucumbers, and green onions • Raspberries, blueberries, and chopped mint (for dessert soups)	• Diced cantaloupe, honeydew melon, and watermelon (for fruit soups)

Shrimp Gumbo Chowder

30 MINUTES

For a dinner from the soup pot, try this chowder, reminiscent of the gumbos found in Cajun country. Start by making a browned flour mixture called a roux; then add vegetables, cooked shrimp, and a package of chicken-flavored rice mix. Serve with hot corn bread.

2 tablespoons vegetable oil

3 tablespoons all-purpose flour

1 large green bell pepper (about 8 oz.)

3 slices bacon

1 package (about 10 oz.) frozen sliced okra

2 cloves garlic, minced or pressed

1 package (about 6 oz.) chicken-flavored rice and vermicelli mix

1 large can (about 49½ oz.) fat-free reduced-sodium chicken broth

1 large can (about 28 oz.) whole tomatoes in purée

½ cup water

1 teaspoon liquid hot pepper seasoning (or to taste)

1 pound shelled, deveined cooked shrimp (31 to 40 per lb.)

1. Heat oil in a small frying pan over medium heat. Add flour and cook, stirring occasionally, until browned (4 to 5 minutes). Set aside.

2. While roux is cooking, seed and dice bell pepper; also dice bacon. Place bell pepper and bacon in a 5- to 6-quart pan; add okra and garlic. Cook over medium-high heat, stirring often, until bacon is translucent and vegetables begin to soften (4 to 5 minutes). Stir in roux and rice mix (rice and vermicelli plus seasoning packet).

3. Add broth, tomatoes and their purée, water, and hot pepper seasoning. Bring to a boil, stirring occasionally to break up tomatoes. Reduce heat, cover, and simmer until rice is tender to bite (8 to 10 minutes). Add shrimp to soup and cook until heated through.

MAKES 6 SERVINGS (ABOUT 12 CUPS).

PER SERVING: 382 calories, 14 g total fat, 4 g saturated fat, 157 mg cholesterol, 1,554 mg sodium, 38 g carbohydrates, 3 g fiber, 25 g protein, 131 mg calcium, 4 mg iron

Louisiana Crab Chowder

30 MINUTES

Pictured on page 36

Crab is popular in the Cajun cooking of Louisiana. And for good reason—it's delicious any way you cook it! Here, it goes into a thick, spicy chowder. Because fresh crab can be expensive, we've added cod to fill out the pot.

8 ounces cooked crabmeat

8 ounces cod or scrod fillets

2 tablespoons butter or margarine

2 stalks celery, thinly sliced

1 large onion (about 8 oz.), chopped

2 large russet potatoes (about 1 lb. *total*)

2 cans (about 14½ oz. *each*) fat-free reduced-sodium chicken broth

1 tablespoon Worcestershire sauce

1½ teaspoons liquid hot pepper seasoning (or to taste)

½ teaspoon salt

3 cups milk

Thin strips of green and red bell pepper

1. Pick through crab and discard any bits of shell. Rinse fish, pat dry, and cut into bite-size pieces. Set crab and fish aside.

2. Melt butter in a 5- to 6-quart pan over medium-high heat. Add celery and onion and cook, stirring often, until onion is soft (4 to 5 minutes).

3. Meanwhile, peel and grate potatoes. To pan, add potatoes, broth, Worcestershire sauce, hot pepper seasoning, and salt. Bring to a simmer; then simmer, uncovered, for 5 to 6 minutes.

4. Stir in milk, crab, and fish. Cook until potatoes are tender to bite and fish is just opaque but still moist in thickest part; cut to test (3 to 4 more minutes). Garnish with bell pepper strips.

MAKES 4 SERVINGS (ABOUT 9 CUPS).

PER SERVING: 395 calories, 14 g total fat, 8 g saturated fat, 122 mg cholesterol, 965 mg sodium, 34 g carbohydrates, 3 g fiber, 33 g protein, 316 mg calcium, 2 mg iron

Mexican Shellfish Chowder

30 MINUTES

Thick with clams, scallops, and shrimp, this chowder gets its spicy flavor from purchased salsa. Serve with warm, soft corn or flour tortillas. Iced sangria is the perfect drink.

- 1 large can (about 49½ oz.) fat-free reduced-sodium chicken broth
- 1 can (about 14½ oz.) fat-free reduced-sodium chicken broth
- ½ cup dry white wine
- 1 can (about 14½ oz.) crushed tomatoes
- ⅓ cup medium-hot salsa
- 2 cloves garlic, minced or pressed
- 1 dried bay leaf
- ⅛ teaspoon ground saffron
- 24 small hard-shell clams in shell, scrubbed
- 8 ounces sea scallops
- 12 ounces shelled, deveined cooked shrimp (31 to 40 per lb.); leave tails on, if desired
- 3 tablespoons chopped cilantro

1. In a 5- to 6-quart pan, combine broth, wine, tomatoes and their liquid, salsa, garlic, bay leaf, and saffron. Bring to a boil over medium-high heat. Boil, uncovered, for 5 minutes.

2. Add clams; cover and simmer for 5 more minutes. Meanwhile, rinse scallops and cut crosswise into ½-inch-thick slices.

3. Add scallops and shrimp to pan. Cover and simmer until clams pop open and scallops are just opaque in center; cut to test (3 to 4 minutes). Remove pan from heat. Remove and discard bay leaf; discard any unopened clams. Sprinkle soup with cilantro.

MAKES 6 SERVINGS (ABOUT 12 CUPS).

PER SERVING: 161 calories, 1 g total fat, 0 g saturated fat, 121 mg cholesterol, 1,164 mg sodium, 6 g carbohydrates, 1 g fiber, 26 g protein, 67 mg calcium, 7 mg iron

Mexican Shellfish Chowder

Spring Shrimp Soup

25 MINUTES

Springtime—and the asparagus is fresh and plentiful. Choose thin, tender spears, then use them in this delicate shrimp soup. To complete a light meal, accompany the soup with hot popovers; offer lemon sorbet and butter cookies for dessert.

1 large can (about 49½ oz.) fat-free reduced-sodium chicken broth

1 pound peeled baby-cut carrots, cut in half lengthwise

12 ounces slender asparagus

4 green onions

1 package (about 10 oz.) frozen tiny peas

1 pound small cooked shrimp

¼ cup minced parsley

Parmesan Puffs (optional; page 50)

1. In a 5- to 6-quart pan, combine broth and carrots. Bring to a boil over high heat. Boil, uncovered, until carrots are almost tender to bite (5 to 6 minutes).

2. Meanwhile, snap off and discard tough ends of asparagus; diagonally slice spears ¼ inch thick. Thinly slice onions and set aside.

3. Add asparagus and peas to broth mixture; simmer just until asparagus is tender to bite (2 to 3 minutes).

4. Add onions, shrimp, and parsley; cook until shrimp are heated through (2 to 3 minutes). Top each serving with a Parmesan Puff, if desired.

MAKES 5 SERVINGS (ABOUT 10 CUPS).

PER SERVING: 202 calories, 2 g total fat, 0 g saturated fat, 177 mg cholesterol, 982 mg sodium, 19 g carbohydrates, 7 g fiber, 28 g protein, 97 mg calcium, 5 mg iron

Chicken & Capellini Soup

25 MINUTES

This tasty, speedy rendition of old-fashioned chicken noodle soup starts with the lemon-marinated chicken breasts sold in well-stocked supermarkets. Baby carrots, tomatoes, and Swiss chard are colorful additions (use the chard's white stems as well as its green leaves). Offer breadsticks and chunks of Cheddar alongside.

1½ pounds lemon-herb marinated boneless, skinless chicken breasts

¾ cup peeled baby-cut carrots

2 tablespoons butter or margarine

2 cans (about 14½ oz. *each*) fat-free reduced-sodium chicken broth

½ cup dry white wine

2 ounces dried capellini (angel hair pasta), broken in half

8 Swiss chard leaves (about 5 oz. *total*)

2 medium-size tomatoes (about 12 oz. *total*)

⅓ cup grated Parmesan cheese

1. Cut chicken into bite-size pieces; set aside. Cut carrots in half lengthwise; set aside.

2. Melt butter in a 4- to 5-quart pan over medium-high heat. Add chicken and cook, stirring often, until no longer pink in center; cut to test (3 to 4 minutes).

3. Add carrots, broth, and wine. Bring to a boil over high heat; stir in capellini. Reduce heat and boil gently, uncovered, until carrots are tender to bite (6 to 7 minutes). Meanwhile, trim and discard tough stem bases from chard leaves; then cut chard stems and leaves into shreds. Seed and chop tomatoes.

4. Add chard and tomatoes to pan; cover and remove from heat. Let stand just until tomatoes are heated through (2 to 3 minutes). Sprinkle with cheese.

MAKES 5 SERVINGS (ABOUT 10 CUPS).

PER SERVING: 312 calories, 10 g total fat, 5 g saturated fat, 89 mg cholesterol, 1,579 mg sodium, 20 g carbohydrates, 3 g fiber, 31 g protein, 109 mg calcium, 2 mg iron

Riviera Fish Soup

25 MINUTES

Where fresh fish is plentiful, soups and stews made with the day's catch are popular. Our version uses fillets of swordfish, salmon, and sole, but you should feel free to experiment with different fish; you might substitute monkfish for the swordfish, salmon trout for the salmon, and cod for the sole. Serve with peasant bread, wedges of Havarti or Münster cheese, and fresh pears.

1 pound swordfish
8 ounces boneless, skinless salmon fillets
8 ounces sole fillets
1 tablespoon olive oil
2 stalks celery, finely chopped
1 large onion (about 8 oz.), thinly sliced
2 cloves garlic, minced or pressed
1 jar (about 26 oz.) fat-free, reduced-sodium extra-chunky pasta sauce with Italian-style vegetables

2 cups water
½ cup dry white wine
⅛ to ¼ teaspoon crushed red pepper flakes
⅓ cup grated Parmesan cheese
⅓ cup slivered fresh basil or 2 tablespoons dried basil

1. Rinse all fish and pat dry. Cut fish into bite-size pieces and set aside.

2. Heat oil in a 5- to 6-quart pan over medium-high heat. Add celery, onion, and garlic; cook, stirring often, until celery is tender to bite (4 to 5 minutes).

3. Stir in pasta sauce, water, wine, and red pepper flakes. Bring to a boil. Then reduce heat, add fish, and simmer, uncovered, until fish is just opaque but still moist in thickest part; cut to test (5 to 6 minutes).

4. Remove pan from heat. Sprinkle soup with cheese and basil.

MAKES 6 SERVINGS (ABOUT 12 CUPS).

PER SERVING: 296 calories, 10 g total fat, 3 g saturated fat, 72 mg cholesterol, 614 mg sodium, 13 g carbohydrates, 2 g fiber, 34 g protein, 148 mg calcium, 3 mg iron

Reuben Soup Pot with Dijon Toast

30 MINUTES

The makings of the Reuben sandwich go into this soup pot—sauerkraut, corned beef, Swiss cheese, and rye bread. If possible, find a market that sells its sauerkraut right from the barrel; or look for it in jars or packages at your supermarket's deli. Accompany this soup with dill pickles, fresh carrot sticks, and cucumber slices. For dessert, serve Granny Smith apples and oatmeal-raisin cookies.

    8 ounces (about 2 cups) fresh sauerkraut
    8 ounces thinly sliced corned beef
    1 large can (about 49½ oz.) fat-free
       reduced-sodium chicken broth
    1 teaspoon caraway seeds
    1 small ripe tomato (about 4 oz.)
    2 green onions
       Dijon Toast (below)
    1 cup (about 4 oz.) shredded Swiss cheese

DIJON TOAST

    4 slices rye or pumpernickel bread
       (about 4 oz. *total*)
    3 tablespoons Dijon mustard
    ¾ cup shredded Swiss cheese
       Caraway seeds

1. Rinse and drain sauerkraut in a colander. Cut corned beef into thin strips.

2. In a 5- to 6-quart pan, bring broth, sauerkraut, and the 1 teaspoon caraway seeds to a boil. Add beef and cook, uncovered, until heated through (4 to 5 minutes).

3. Meanwhile, chop tomato and thinly slice onions. Also prepare Dijon Toast.

4. To serve, remove soup from heat and stir in tomato. Ladle soup into soup plates and sprinkle with the 1 cup cheese. Top each serving with a slice of Dijon Toast and sprinkle with onions.

DIJON TOAST

1. Arrange bread on a baking sheet. Broil 4 to 6 inches below heat, turning once, until lightly browned on both sides (about 1 minute).

2. Spread mustard evenly over one side of each toast slice; sprinkle toast evenly with the ¾ cup cheese, then sprinkle with a few caraway seeds. Return to broiler until cheese is melted (about 30 seconds).

MAKES 4 SERVINGS (ABOUT 7 CUPS).

PER SERVING: 460 calories, 25 g total fat, 13 g saturated fat, 101 mg cholesterol, 2,421 mg sodium, 20 g carbohydrates, 2 g fiber, 32 g protein, 525 mg calcium, 2 mg iron

Turkey Tortellini Soup

25 MINUTES

Fresh cheese-filled spinach tortellini from the refrigerated section of your supermarket are the secret to this fast main-dish soup. Serve with hot garlic bread; offer grapes and biscotti for dessert.

1 large can (about 49½ oz.) fat-free reduced-sodium chicken broth

2 cans (about 14½ oz. *each*) fat-free reduced-sodium chicken broth

1 package (about 9 oz.) fresh cheese-filled spinach tortellini

1½ pounds cooked turkey breast

1 large red bell pepper (about 8 oz.)

4 cups packaged triple-washed spinach

8 ounces sliced mushrooms

2 teaspoons dried tarragon

½ teaspoon black pepper

Grated Parmesan cheese

1. In a 5- to 6-quart pan, bring broth to a boil over high heat. Stir in tortellini; reduce heat and boil gently, uncovered, until just tender to bite (5 to 6 minutes).

2. Meanwhile, cut turkey into bite-size pieces; also seed and coarsely chop bell pepper. Remove and discard any coarse stems from spinach.

3. Add turkey, bell pepper, mushrooms, tarragon, and black pepper to pan; return to a boil. Reduce heat and add spinach; cover and simmer until spinach is wilted (3 to 4 minutes). Sprinkle with cheese.

MAKES 6 SERVINGS (ABOUT 12 CUPS).

PER SERVING: 327 calories, 4 g total fat, 2 g saturated fat, 121 mg cholesterol, 1,002 mg sodium, 24 g carbohydrates, 3 g fiber, 46 g protein, 131 mg calcium, 4 mg iron

Chinese Chicken Stir-fry Soup

30 MINUTES

Start with stir-fried chicken and vegetables—then turn them into a marvelous main-dish soup by adding chicken broth and purchased cooked shrimp. Round out the meal with juicy oranges or tangerines and fortune cookies.

1½ pounds boneless, skinless chicken breasts

8 green onions

2 tablespoons cornstarch

2 tablespoons reduced-sodium soy sauce

¼ teaspoon crushed red pepper flakes

1 medium-size head bok choy (about 1¾ lbs.)

1 large red bell pepper (about 8 oz.)

1 large can (about 49½ oz.) fat-free reduced-sodium chicken broth

1 tablespoon vegetable oil

8 ounces sliced mushrooms

12 ounces shelled, deveined cooked shrimp (31 to 40 per lb.)

Fried Chinese chow mein noodles (optional)

1. Rinse chicken, pat dry, and cut into bite-size pieces. Diagonally slice onions into ½-inch lengths. On a large, shallow platter, toss together chicken, onions, cornstarch, soy sauce, and red pepper flakes. Cover and refrigerate for 5 minutes.

2. While chicken marinates, cut bok choy crosswise into ¼-inch-wide strips. Seed bell pepper and cut into thin strips.

3. In a 3-quart pan, bring broth to a simmer over medium-high heat. Meanwhile, heat oil in a 5- to 6-quart pan over high heat. Add chicken mixture, mushrooms, bok choy, and bell pepper to hot oil. Cook, stirring often, just until chicken is no longer pink in center; cut to test (5 to 6 minutes).

4. Add hot broth and shrimp to pan and cook, uncovered, until shrimp are heated through (3 to 4 minutes). Mound fried noodles in center of soup, if desired.

MAKES 5 SERVINGS (ABOUT 10 CUPS).

PER SERVING: 326 calories, 6 g total fat, 1 g saturated fat, 212 mg cholesterol, 1,262 mg sodium, 14 g carbohydrates, 3 g fiber, 54 g protein, 235 mg calcium, 6 mg iron

Mediterranean Minestrone

30 MINUTES

This hearty soup features spicy sausage and the plump little dumplings called gnocchi. We call for frozen potato gnocchi here, but the dough can also be based on polenta, ricotta cheese, or semolina. For a country-style accompaniment, offer focaccia topped with rosemary and mozzarella.

- 4 ounces mild Italian sausage
- 1 medium-size onion (about 6 oz.), coarsely chopped
- 2 cloves garlic, minced or pressed
- 1½ teaspoons dried thyme
- ¼ teaspoon pepper
- 1 large can (about 49½ oz.) fat-free reduced-sodium chicken broth
- ¾ cup water
- 2 large carrots (about 8 oz. *total*), coarsely chopped
- 2 stalks celery, coarsely chopped
- 1 teaspoon grated lemon peel
- 1 package (about 9 oz.) frozen potato gnocchi
- 2 cups broccoli flowerets
- 1 medium-size tomato (about 6 oz.), cut into ¼-inch cubes
- ¼ cup grated Parmesan cheese
- Skillet Croutons flavored with garlic and parsley (optional; page 50)

1. Remove casings from sausage and crumble meat into a 5- to 6-quart pan. Add onion, garlic, thyme, and pepper. Cook over medium-high heat, stirring occasionally, until sausage is browned (4 to 5 minutes).

2. Add broth, water, carrots, celery, and lemon peel. Bring to a boil over high heat.

3. Add gnocchi and broccoli. Cook, uncovered, until gnocchi and vegetables are tender to bite (about 8 minutes). Top with tomato and sprinkle with cheese. Sprinkle with croutons, if desired.

MAKES 6 SERVINGS (ABOUT 12 CUPS).

PER SERVING: 218 calories, 8 g total fat, 3 g saturated fat, 18 mg cholesterol, 917 mg sodium, 26 g carbohydrates, 4 g fiber, 12 g protein, 129 mg calcium, 2 mg iron

Balkan Prosciutto Soup

30 MINUTES

Choose your favorite tiny pasta shapes for this creamy yet surprisingly light soup, fresh with spinach. Serve it with warm pocket bread halves stuffed with sliced tomatoes and strips of roast chicken. Offer lemon ice for dessert.

- 1 tablespoon butter or margarine
- 2 large shallots, chopped
- 1 large can (about 49½ oz.) fat-free reduced-sodium chicken broth
- ½ teaspoon pepper
- ¼ teaspoon ground nutmeg
- 1 cup (about 5½ oz.) dried pastina (tiny pasta for soup)
- 4 cups packaged triple-washed spinach
- 2 ounces prosciutto, cut into thin strips
- 1 cup sour cream

1. Melt butter in a 4- to 5-quart pan over medium-high heat. Add shallots and cook, stirring often, until soft (about 5 minutes).

2. Stir in broth, pepper, and nutmeg. Bring to a boil; then add pastina. Reduce heat and simmer, uncovered, until pastina is just tender to bite (8 to 9 minutes).

3. Meanwhile, remove and discard any coarse stems from spinach. Stir spinach and prosciutto into soup; cook until prosciutto is heated through and spinach is wilted (4 to 5 minutes).

4. Remove from heat and smoothly blend in sour cream.

MAKES 4 SERVINGS (ABOUT 8 CUPS).

PER SERVING: 367 calories, 18 g total fat, 10 g saturated fat, 45 mg cholesterol, 1,204 mg sodium, 35 g carbohydrates, 2 g fiber, 17 g protein, 129 mg calcium, 3 mg iron

Chili Beef Soup

30 MINUTES
RANGE TOP;

20 TO 25 MINUTES
MICROWAVE

Pleasantly spicy but not too fiery, this sturdy soup is thick with ground beef and red kidney beans. It's especially good dressed up with your choice of toppings—shredded Cheddar, diced tomato and avocado, sour cream, and more. Offer warm cornbread or corn muffins alongside.

1½ **pounds extra-lean ground beef**

1 **pound onions, chopped**

1 **large green bell pepper (about 8 oz.), seeded and chopped**

1 **clove garlic, minced or pressed**

1 **large can (about 28 oz.) crushed tomatoes in purée**

1 **can (about 15 oz.) red kidney beans, rinsed and drained**

1 **cup water**

2 **tablespoons chopped cilantro**

1 **teaspoon chili powder**

Salt

½ **teaspoon black pepper**

Toppings (optional): shredded Cheddar cheese, sliced green onions, sliced ripe olives, chopped tomatoes, avocado cubes, sour cream or yogurt, and/or crushed tortilla chips

1. Crumble beef into a 3-quart pan; add onions, bell pepper, and garlic. Cook over medium-high heat, stirring often, until beef is browned (4 to 5 minutes).

2. Add tomatoes and their purée, beans, water, cilantro, chili powder, salt to taste (about ½ teaspoon), and black pepper. Bring to a boil. Reduce heat, cover, and simmer until flavors are blended (about 10 minutes). Serve with toppings, if desired.

MAKES 4 SERVINGS (ABOUT 6 CUPS).

PER SERVING: 587 calories, 30 g total fat, 12 g saturated fat, 117 mg cholesterol, 575 mg sodium, 38 g carbohydrates, 8 g fiber, 41 g protein, 137 mg calcium, 6 mg iron

MICROWAVE CHILI BEEF SOUP

Crumble beef into a 3-quart microwave-safe casserole; add onions, bell pepper, and garlic. Cover and microwave on HIGH (100%) for 4 to 5 minutes or until meat loses its pink color, stirring 2 or 3 times. Add remaining ingredients except toppings; cover and microwave on HIGH (100%) for 7 to 8 minutes or until bubbly and heated through, stirring 2 or 3 times. Serve with toppings, if desired.

Ham & Black Bean Soup

25 MINUTES

Black beans, also known as turtle beans, are a staple in South American cooking. Here, they're combined with onions and plenty of ham in a hearty main-dish soup that borders on a stew. Serve with crusty bread and a round of baby Swiss.

1 **tablespoon vegetable oil**

1 **pound baked ham, cut into bite-size pieces**

1 **large onion (about 8 oz.), cut into thin slivers**

1 **large green bell pepper (about 8 oz.), seeded and chopped**

2 **cans (about 15 oz. *each*) black beans**

2 **cans (about 14½ oz. *each*) beef broth**

⅔ **cup water**

¼ **cup cider vinegar**

2 **large carrots (about 8 oz. *total*), shredded**

⅓ **cup firmly packed light brown sugar**

1 **tablespoon dry mustard**

1 **teaspoon grated lemon peel**

½ **teaspoon liquid hot pepper seasoning**

⅓ **cup coarsely chopped parsley**

Ham & Black Bean Soup

1. Heat oil in a 5- to 6-quart pan over medium-high heat. Add ham, onion, and bell pepper; cook, stirring often, until vegetables are tender to bite (4 to 5 minutes).

2. Meanwhile, pour one can of the beans and their liquid into a food processor or blender; whirl until puréed. Pour purée into pan; stir in broth, water, and vinegar. Reserve ¼ cup of the carrots for garnish, if desired; to pan, add remaining carrots, sugar, mustard, lemon peel, and hot pepper seasoning. Bring to a boil; then reduce

heat and simmer, uncovered, until flavors are blended (4 to 5 minutes).

3. Reduce heat to medium-low and add remaining can of beans and their liquid. Cook, stirring occasionally, until soup is bubbly and heated through (5 to 7 minutes). Sprinkle with parsley and, if desired, reserved carrots.

MAKES 6 SERVINGS (ABOUT 12 CUPS).

PER SERVING: 367 calories, 11 g total fat, 3 g saturated fat, 45 mg cholesterol, 2,082 mg sodium, 41 g carbohydrates, 10 g fiber, 27 g protein, 88 mg calcium, 5 mg iron

Chapter Three

MEATS

Black Bean Fillet

30 MINUTES

A delightful choice for a casual company meal, this succulent roast is delicious served with rice pilaf and braised bok choy. The narrow end of beef tenderloin is often labeled "fillet tail"; you may have to buy two pieces to equal the weight called for.

About 1¾ pounds narrow end beef tenderloin, trimmed of fat

¼ cup salted, fermented black beans, sorted of debris and rinsed

2 cloves garlic, peeled

2 tablespoons Oriental sesame oil

2 teaspoons minced fresh ginger

1. Fold narrow end of beef under to make meat evenly thick. Tie snugly every 1½ inches with cotton string.

2. In a blender or food processor, whirl beans, garlic, oil, and ginger until smooth. Rub this mixture over all sides of beef.

3. Place beef on a rack in a 9- by 13-inch baking pan. Roast in a 450° oven until a meat thermometer inserted in thickest part registers 125°F for rare (about 20 minutes). Cut off and discard strings; then thinly slice beef across the grain.

MAKES 6 SERVINGS.

PER SERVING: 272 calories, 16 g total fat, 5 g saturated fat, 82 mg cholesterol, 351 mg sodium, 1 g carbohydrates, 0 g fiber, 28 g protein, 17 mg calcium, 4 mg iron

Malaysian Satay

25 TO **30** MINUTES

An aromatic marinade flavors chunks of lean beef to skewer and quick-cook on the grill. Serve the meat on or off the skewers, with hot rice and thinly sliced cucumbers and red onions. (If you use bamboo skewers, soak them in warm water before threading the meat.)

2 cloves garlic, peeled

1 large onion (about 8 oz.), quartered

2 tablespoons ground cumin

2 tablespoons ground coriander

1 tablespoon sugar

1 teaspoon ground turmeric

1 stalk fresh lemon grass, trimmed and coarsely chopped

2 tablespoons vegetable oil

2 pounds lean boneless beef sirloin, trimmed of fat

Salt

1. In a blender or food processor, combine garlic, onion, cumin, coriander, sugar, turmeric, lemon grass, and oil. Whirl until smooth; then transfer to a large bowl.

2. Cut beef into 1-inch cubes; add to marinade and mix to coat well. Then thread beef on five 14-inch-long metal or bamboo skewers.

3. Place skewers on a lightly oiled grill 4 to 6 inches above a solid bed of very hot coals (you can hold your hand at grill level for only 1 to 2 seconds) or over very high heat on a gas grill. Close lid on gas grill. Cook, turning as needed to brown evenly, until beef is done to your liking; cut to test (5 to 7 minutes for medium). Serve beef on or off skewers; season to taste with salt.

MAKES 8 SERVINGS.

PER SERVING: 222 calories, 10 g total fat, 3 g saturated fat, 76 mg cholesterol, 60 mg sodium, 5 g carbohydrates, 1 g fiber, 27 g protein, 35 mg calcium, 4 mg iron

Malaysian Satay

Butterflying Meats

Butterflying a large piece of me[at] offers several advantages. First and most important, it saves you time: the thinner the mea[t,] the faster it cooks. Second, since butterflied meat isn't evenly thick all over, a single cookir[g] time will give you both rare and more well-done portions, letting you satisfy everyone's prefe[r-] ences. Finally, a butterflied cut of meat makes a lovely presentation and looks larger than [it] does as a roast, though the weight is of course the same.

Leg of lamb is the most widely available butterflied meat, but your butcher should be ab[le] to butterfly any of the other cuts called for below. Just be sure to specify the weight of th[e] meat and the range of thickness it should have after butterflying.

Butterflied Leg of Lamb with Herbs & Feta

25 MINUTES

- 1 **boneless butterflied leg of lamb (4 to 4½ lbs.), trimmed of fat**
- 2 **cloves garlic, thinly sliced**
- 1 **tablespoon minced fresh rosemary or crumbled dried rosemary**
- 5 **tablespoons minced fresh basil**
- ½ **cup crumbled feta cheese**
   Salt and pepper

1. Lay lamb flat, boned side up. Cut slits about ½ inch deep all over lamb. Fit garlic slices into slits. Rub rosemary and 1 tablespoon of the basil over both sides of lamb.

2. Thread 2 long (at least 18-inch) metal skewers parallel to each other lengthwise through lamb. Then place lamb on a lightly oiled grill 4 to 6 inches above a solid bed of very hot coals (you can hold your hand at grill level for only 1 to 2 seconds) or over very high heat on a gas grill. Close lid on gas grill. Cook, turning as needed to brown evenly, until a meat thermometer inserted in thickest part of lamb (not touching skewer) registers 140°F for medium-rare (about 17 minutes). Or cut meat to test. Thinner parts will be more done.

3. Transfer lamb to a carving board; sprinkle with cheese and remaining ¼ cup basil. Remove skewers and slice lamb. Season to taste with salt and pepper.

MAKES ABOUT 16 SERVINGS.

PER SERVING: 185 calories, 8 g total fat, 3 g saturated fat, 84 mg cholesterol, 109 mg sodium, 0 g carbohydrates, 0 g fiber, 26 g protein, 33 mg calcium, 2 mg iron

Butterflied Beef Rib-eye with Tapenade

25 MINUTES

- 1 **boneless beef rib-eye (prime rib) roast (2½ to 3¾ lbs.), trimmed of fat**
- 1 **jar (6 to 8 oz.) tapenade**
- 1 **teaspoon grated lemon peel**

1. Make a lengthwise cut down center of beef, cutting to within 1 inch of bottom surface; then press beef open to make a butterfly shape. Make a similar lengthwise cut through each of the 2 thick sections. Pull cuts open; press beef to make it 1½ to 2 inches thick. Thread 2 long (at least 18-inch) metal skewers parallel to each other lengthwise through beef.

2. Combine tapenade and lemon peel. Rub 2 to 3 tablespoons of the tapenade mixture all over beef. S[et] remaining tapenade mixtu[re] aside.

3. Place beef on a grill 4 to[6] inches above a solid bed [of] very hot coals (you can ho[ld] your hand at grill level f[or] only 1 to 2 seconds) or ov[er] very high heat on a gas gri[ll.] Close lid on gas grill. Coo[k,] turning as needed to brow[n] evenly, until meat in thicke[st] part is done rare; cut to te[st] (16 to 20 minutes). Thinn[er] parts will be more done.

4. Transfer beef to a carvin[g] board. Remove skewers an[d] slice meat. Offer remainin[g] tapenade mixture to add [to] taste.

MAKES 10 TO 14 SERVINGS.

PER SERVING: 248 calories, 16 g total fat, 4 g saturated fat, 68 mg cholesterol, 493 mg sodiun[m,] 0 g carbohydrates, 0 g fiber, 23 g protein, 10 mg calcium, 2 mg iro[n]

Butterflied Beef Cross-rib with Cilantro-Jalapeño Cream

MINUTES

tured on page 64

- 1 boneless beef cross-rib roast (2½ to 3 lbs.), trimmed of fat
- ¼ cup orange juice
- 5 tablespoons lime juice
- ¾ teaspoon ground cumin
- ¾ cup minced cilantro
- ½ cup nonfat or reduced-fat sour cream
- 1 fresh jalapeño chile, seeded and minced

Cilantro sprigs

Salt and pepper

. Make a lengthwise cut own center of beef, cutting within 1 inch of bottom urface; then press beef open make a butterfly shape. ake a similar lengthwise t through each of the 2 ick sections. Pull cuts open; ess beef to make it 1¼ to ½ inches thick. (If neces-ry, cut beef lengthwise gain and pull these cuts pen.)

. In a deep bowl, mix orange ice, 4 tablespoons of the me juice, cumin, and ¼ cup of the minced cilantro; add beef and turn to coat.

3. In a small bowl, mix remaining 1 tablespoon lime juice, remaining ½ cup cilantro, sour cream, and chile. Cover and refrigerate.

4. Lift beef from marinade; discard marinade. Lay beef flat and thread 3 long (at least 18-inch) metal skewers parallel to each other lengthwise through it. Place beef on a lightly oiled grill 4 to 6 inches above a solid bed of very hot coals (you can hold your hand at grill level for only 1 to 2 seconds) or over very high heat on a gas grill. Close lid on gas grill. Cook, turning as needed to brown evenly, until meat in thickest part is done rare; cut to test (about 15 minutes). Thinner parts will be more done.

5. Transfer beef to a carving board; garnish with cilantro sprigs. Remove skewers; slice meat. Offer the sour cream–chile sauce, salt, and pepper to add to taste.

MAKES 10 TO 12 SERVINGS.

PER SERVING: 307 calories, 23 g total fat, 9 g saturated fat, 71 mg cholesterol, 64 mg sodium, 3 g carbohydrates, 0 g fiber, 20 g protein, 27 mg calcium, 2 mg iron

Butterflied Pork Loin with Apricot-Sesame Glaze

25 MINUTES

- ⅓ cup apricot jam
- 2 tablespoons seasoned rice vinegar
- 1 tablespoon Oriental sesame oil
- 1 boneless center-cut pork loin roast (2½ to 3 lbs.), trimmed of fat
- 6 to 8 green onions, ends trimmed
- 2 teaspoons sesame seeds

Salt

1. In a small bowl, stir together jam, vinegar, and oil; set aside.

2. Make a lengthwise cut down center of pork, cutting to within 1 inch of bottom surface; then press pork open to make a butterfly shape. Make a similar lengthwise cut through each of the 2 thick sections. Pull cuts open; press pork to make it 1¼ to 1½ inches thick. (If necessary, cut pork lengthwise again and pull these cuts open.)

3. Thread 2 long (at least 18-inch) metal skewers parallel to each other lengthwise through pork. Then place pork on a lightly oiled grill above a solid bed of very hot coals (you can hold your hand at grill level for only 1 to 2 seconds) or over very high heat on a gas grill. Brush pork with half the jam mixture. Close lid on gas grill. Cook, turning as needed to brown evenly, until meat in thickest part is no longer pink; cut to test (about 18 minutes). Near end of cooking time, grill onions, turning once, until lightly browned; remove onions from grill as they are done. Just before pork is done, brush it with remaining jam mixture and sprinkle evenly with sesame seeds.

4. Transfer pork to a carving board. Remove skewers and slice meat thinly. Accompany with grilled green onions; season to taste with salt.

MAKES 10 TO 12 SERVINGS.

PER SERVING: 221 calories, 10 g total fat, 3 g saturated fat, 67 mg cholesterol, 114 mg sodium, 8 g carbohydrates, 0 g fiber, 25 g protein, 29 mg calcium, 1 mg iron

Simple Sukiyaki

20 MINUTES

A rich-tasting blend of consommé, sherry, and soy sauce flavors this combination of lean beef and fresh vegetables. Serve over hot, fluffy rice for a satisfying meal. Look for prewashed packaged spinach in your produce section; it's a real time-saver, sparing you the job of rinsing the greens.

½ cup condensed consommé

¼ cup dry sherry

¼ cup reduced-sodium soy sauce

1 tablespoon sugar

4 ounces packaged triple-washed baby spinach

½ teaspoon vegetable oil

8 ounces lean boneless beef rib-eye or sirloin, trimmed of fat and thinly sliced

1 tablespoon minced fresh ginger

1 medium-size onion (about 6 oz.), thinly sliced

1 cup sliced mushrooms

4 green onions, cut into 1-inch lengths

Hot cooked rice

1. In a small bowl, stir together consommé, sherry, soy sauce, and sugar. Set aside. Remove and discard any coarse stems from spinach; set spinach aside.

2. Heat oil in a wide nonstick frying pan over high heat. Add beef and ginger; cook, stirring, until beef is browned (2 to 3 minutes). With a slotted spoon, transfer beef and ginger to a bowl.

3. Add sliced onion and mushrooms to pan; cook, stirring, until onion is soft and mushrooms are tinged with brown (about 3 minutes). Add green onions and spinach; stir until spinach is wilted (about 1 minute). Add consommé mixture, then return beef to pan; bring to a boil, stirring. Serve over rice.

MAKES 2 SERVINGS.

PER SERVING: 353 calories, 11 g total fat, 4 g saturated fat, 67 mg cholesterol, 1,650 mg sodium, 25 g carbohydrates, 4 g fiber, 31 g protein, 119 mg calcium, 6 mg iron

Citrus Beef Stir-fry

25 MINUTES

Orange peel and orange juice give this stir-fry its irresistible fresh taste. It's low in fat, too; using a nonstick pan eliminates the need for oil to cook the beef, and the vegetables simmer right in the sauce. Serve over rice or Asian-style noodles.

2 large oranges (about 1 lb. *total*)

3 tablespoons dry sherry

3 tablespoons soy sauce

1 tablespoon cornstarch

1 pound lean boneless beef such as top sirloin, trimmed of fat and cut across the grain into ¼-inch-thick slices

2 tablespoons minced fresh ginger

1½ cups bean sprouts

1½ cups fresh Chinese pea pods, ends and strings removed

1. Grate peel (colored part only) from 1 orange. Squeeze juice from both oranges. Measure juice; if you have less than ¾ cup, add enough water to equal this amount. In a small bowl, stir together orange peel, orange juice, sherry, soy sauce, and cornstarch. Set aside.

2. Heat a wok or wide nonstick frying pan over high heat. When pan is hot, add beef and ginger. Cook, stirring, until beef is browned (2 to 3 minutes). With a slotted spoon, transfer beef to a bowl.

3. Pour orange juice mixture into pan and bring to a simmer. Add bean sprouts and pea pods; cook, stirring, until pea pods turn a brighter green (about 1 minute). Mix in beef and serve.

MAKES 4 SERVINGS.

PER SERVING: 243 calories, 5 g total fat, 2 g saturated fat, 69 mg cholesterol, 844 mg sodium, 17 g carbohydrates, 2 g fiber, 28 g protein, 51 mg calcium, 5 mg iron

Thai Pocket Bread Sandwiches

30 MINUTES

Tired of the same old hamburgers? Ground beef and vegetables with Thai seasonings make a sandwich filling that's great at lunch or dinner.

1 **pound lean ground beef**

2 **medium-size red bell peppers (about 12 oz.** *total***)**

2 **tablespoons minced fresh ginger**

2 **cloves garlic, minced or pressed**

½ **teaspoon crushed red pepper flakes**

½ **cup chopped cilantro**

3 **tablespoons peanut butter**

2 **tablespoons soy sauce**

2 **tablespoons lime juice**

1 **teaspoon Oriental sesame oil**

4 **pocket breads (***each* **6 to 7 inches in diameter)**

1 **large tomato (about 8 oz.), sliced**

8 **butter lettuce leaves, rinsed and crisped**

1. Crumble beef into a wide frying pan. Cook over high heat, stirring often, until browned and crumbly (5 to 7 minutes). Spoon off and discard fat.

2. While beef is browning, seed and thinly slice bell peppers. Add peppers to pan along with ginger, garlic, and red pepper flakes; cook, stirring often, until peppers are soft (3 to 5 minutes).

3. In a small bowl, smoothly mix cilantro, peanut butter, soy sauce, lime juice, and oil; add to beef mixture and stir to blend well. Remove pan from heat.

4. Cut pocket breads in half crosswise; fill equally with tomato slices, lettuce, and beef mixture.

MAKES 4 SERVINGS.

PER SERVING: 516 calories, 24 g total fat, 7 g saturated fat, 69 mg cholesterol, 965 mg sodium, 45 g carbohydrates, 4 g fiber, 31 g protein, 81 mg calcium, 4 mg iron

Fajita Sandwiches

30 MINUTES

Though fajitas are traditionally served in flour tortillas, they make excellent sandwiches, too. For extra color, you can use red, yellow, or orange bell peppers in place of the green ones.

½ **cup lime juice**

2 **tablespoons chili powder**

2 **teaspoons ground cumin**

1 **teaspoon dried oregano**

½ **teaspoon ground cinnamon**

About 1 pound skirt steak, trimmed of fat

¼ **cup salsa**

¼ **cup nonfat or reduced-fat sour cream**

1 **large onion (about 8 oz.), cut into ½-inch-thick slices**

2 **large green bell peppers (about 1 lb. *total*), seeded and cut into quarters**

4 **soft sandwich rolls (*each* about 6 inches long), split**

1. In a large bowl, stir together lime juice, chili powder, cumin, oregano, and cinnamon. Cut steak into 4 pieces; add to lime juice mixture and turn to coat evenly.

2. In a small bowl, stir together salsa and sour cream; cover and refrigerate.

3. Place onion and bell peppers on a lightly oiled grill 4 to 6 inches above a solid bed of hot coals (you can hold your hand at grill level for only 2 to 3 seconds) or over high heat on a gas grill. Close lid on gas grill. Cook, turning vegetables to brown evenly, until vegetables have dark grill marks and are slightly limp (6 to 8 minutes for onion, 10 to 15 minutes for bell peppers). As vegetables are done, remove them from grill and keep warm, covered with foil.

4. As soon as you have removed enough vegetables from grill to make room for steak, lift steak from marinade and place it on grill; discard marinade. Cook, turning once, until meat is browned on both sides and done to your liking; cut to test (7 to 9 minutes for medium-rare). Remove from grill. Place rolls on grill and cook, turning once, until crisp and golden on both sides (1 to 2 minutes).

5. When peppers are cool enough to handle, rub off any loose bits of skin. Separate onion slices into rings. Cut steak across the grain into ½-inch-wide strips.

6. To assemble sandwiches, fill rolls with steak, onion, bell peppers, and salsa mixture.

MAKES 4 SERVINGS.

PER SERVING: 436 calories, 13 g total fat, 5 g saturated fat, 58 mg cholesterol, 628 mg sodium, 48 g carbohydrates, 5 g fiber, 30 g protein, 110 mg calcium, 5 mg iron

Borrego Beef Chili

30 MINUTES

This chili's rich flavor belies its brief cooking time. Spoon it over shredded iceberg lettuce, if you like; or serve it with corn chips or tortilla chips.

1½ **pounds lean ground beef**

1 **large can (about 7 oz.) diced green chiles**

1 **large onion (about 8 oz.), chopped**

2 **cloves garlic, minced or pressed**

3 **tablespoons red wine vinegar**

3 **to 4 tablespoons chili powder**

1 **teaspoon dried oregano**

1 **teaspoon ground cumin**

1 **large can (about 28 oz.) crushed tomatoes**

1 **can (about 15 oz.) pinto beans, rinsed and drained**

Salt

1 **cup (about 4 oz.) shredded jack or Cheddar cheese (or jack-Cheddar blend)**

1. Crumble beef into a 4- to 5-quart pan; add chiles, onion, garlic, and vinegar. Cook over high heat, stirring occasionally, until beef is browned and onion is soft (about 8 minutes). Spoon off and discard fat.

2. To beef mixture, add chili powder, oregano, and cumin; cook, stirring, for 1 minute.

3. Stir in tomatoes and their liquid; then stir in beans. Bring to a boil; then reduce heat, cover, and simmer for 15 minutes, stirring occasionally. Season to taste with salt. Offer cheese to sprinkle over individual servings.

MAKES 4 TO 6 SERVINGS.

PER SERVING: 485 calories, 27 g total fat, 11 g saturated fat, 106 mg cholesterol, 900 mg sodium, 26 g carbohydrates, 7 g fiber, 36 g protein, 275 mg calcium, 6 mg iron

Borrego Beef Chili

Reuben Quesadillas

15 MINUTES

Most people think of a Reuben as a classic deli sandwich, but its ingredients work surprisingly well as a filling for quesadillas. Instead of traditional sauerkraut, team the corned beef and Swiss cheese with packaged fresh coleslaw mix—a combination of shredded cabbage and carrots—from the supermarket produce section. Serve the quesadillas with soup or a salad for a quick, satisfying meal.

½ cup salsa

½ cup sour cream

2 cups (about 8 oz.) shredded Swiss cheese

4 large flour tortillas (*each* about 10 inches in diameter)

3 cups packaged coleslaw mix

8 ounces thinly sliced corned beef

1. In a small bowl, stir together salsa and sour cream.

2. Sprinkle ¼ cup of the cheese over half of one tortilla. Then place ¾ cup of the coleslaw mix on cheese. Drizzle about 3 tablespoons of the salsa mixture over coleslaw. Lay a quarter of the corned beef over coleslaw; top with ¼ cup more cheese. Fold tortilla over to cover filling. Repeat to make 3 more quesadillas.

3. Place quesadillas slightly apart on a large baking sheet. Broil 4 to 6 inches below heat until crisp and lightly browned (1 to 2 minutes; watch closely). Using a wide spatula, carefully turn each quesadilla over. Broil until crisp and lightly browned on other side (1 to 2 more minutes).

4. Cut quesadillas into wedges. Transfer to plates and serve with remaining salsa mixture.

MAKES 4 SERVINGS.

PER SERVING: 640 calories, 37 g total fat, 18 g saturated fat, 120 mg cholesterol, 1,414 mg sodium, 43 g carbohydrates, 2 g fiber, 34 g protein, 709 mg calcium, 4 mg iron

Pounded Veal with Lemon & Thyme

25 MINUTES

Like all thin pieces of meat, these well-seasoned veal slices cook quickly, so watch them carefully to avoid overcooking. You might complete the menu with mustard-glazed new potatoes and grilled vegetables.

3 tablespoons minced fresh thyme or 1½ tablespoons dried thyme

2 teaspoons grated lemon peel

½ cup minced parsley

2 tablespoons olive oil or vegetable oil

1 pound boneless veal slices (from rib, loin, or leg), trimmed of fat

Lemon wedges

Salt and pepper

1. In a small bowl, mix thyme, lemon peel, parsley, and oil. Rub about 2 teaspoons of the thyme mixture on each side of each veal slice.

2. Place each veal slice between 2 sheets of plastic wrap. With a heavy, flat-sided mallet, pound meat firmly but gently all over to a thickness of ⅛ to ¼ inch.

3. Place veal on a lightly oiled grill 4 to 6 inches above a solid bed of hot coals (you can hold your hand at grill level for only 2 to 3 seconds) or over high heat on a gas grill. Close lid on gas grill. Cook, turning once, until veal is browned on both sides and no longer pink in center; cut to test (4 to 5 minutes).

4. Offer lemon wedges, salt, and pepper to season veal to taste.

MAKES 4 SERVINGS.

PER SERVING: 203 calories, 11 g total fat, 2 g saturated fat, 94 mg cholesterol, 112 mg sodium, 2 g carbohydrates, 0 g fiber, 23 g protein, 57 mg calcium, 3 mg iron

Veal Scaloppine with Mustard Cream Sauce

25 MINUTES

Elegant enough for a dinner party yet hearty enough for a weeknight meal, this dish features mild, tender veal slices topped with a classic mustard cream sauce.

1 pound boneless veal slices (from rib, loin, or leg), trimmed of fat

About 1 tablespoon butter or margarine

About 1 tablespoon vegetable oil

⅔ cup dry vermouth

½ cup whipping cream

2 tablespoons Dijon mustard

Dash of ground nutmeg

Salt and pepper

2 tablespoons chopped parsley

1. Place each veal slice between 2 sheets of plastic wrap. With a heavy, flat-sided mallet, pound meat firmly but gently all over to a thickness of ⅛ to ¼ inch.

2. Melt 1 tablespoon of the butter in 1 tablespoon of the oil in a wide nonstick frying pan over medium-high heat. When butter sizzles, add as many veal slices as will fit without crowding (you may need to cook veal in batches). Cook, turning once, until veal is lightly browned on both sides and no longer pink in center; cut to test (2 to 4 minutes). As veal is cooked, remove from pan and keep warm on a platter. Add more butter and oil to pan as needed.

3. When all veal has been cooked, discard any fat from pan. Pour vermouth into pan, stirring to scrape browned bits free. Bring to a boil over high heat; then boil, uncovered, until reduced by about half (2 to 3 minutes). Stir in cream, mustard, and nutmeg. Return sauce to a boil; boil, stirring, until slightly thickened. Season to taste with salt and pepper.

4. Stir any meat juices that have collected on platter into sauce; then pour sauce over veal. Sprinkle with parsley.

MAKES 4 SERVINGS.

PER SERVING: 294 calories, 20 g total fat, 9 g saturated fat, 135 mg cholesterol, 332 mg sodium, 3 g carbohydrates, 0 g fiber, 23 g protein, 43 mg calcium, 1 mg iron

Thai-spiced Loin Chops with Hot-Sweet Mustard

10 MINUTES

Even a dab of Thai curry paste packs a punch—so serve these juicy chops with cooling accompaniments, such as a chilled Asian noodle salad or a platter of sliced cucumbers and ripe tomatoes.

About 1¼ teaspoons Thai red curry paste

4 boneless center-cut pork loin chops (about 1¼ lbs. *total*), *each* about ½ inch thick, trimmed of fat

Cilantro sprigs

½ cup prepared hot-sweet mustard

1. Spread about ⅛ teaspoon of the curry paste on each side of each chop.

2. Place chops on a lightly oiled grill 4 to 6 inches above a solid bed of hot coals (you can hold your hand at grill level for only 2 to 3 seconds) or over high heat on a gas grill. Close lid on gas grill. Cook, turning once, until pork is still moist and looks faintly pink to white in center; cut to test (5 to 7 minutes).

3. Garnish chops with cilantro sprigs. Offer mustard to add to taste.

MAKES 4 SERVINGS.

PER SERVING: 267 calories, 8 g total fat, 2 g saturated fat, 90 mg cholesterol, 140 mg sodium, 12 g carbohydrates, 0 g fiber, 31 g protein, 33 mg calcium, 1 mg iron

Pork with Orange-Cranberry Sauce

20 TO 25 MINUTES

This quick weekday dinner should tempt even the most jaded appetites. Pound the pork chops thin so they'll cook fast, then top them with a tangy sauce of dried cranberries, orange juice, and Dijon mustard. Serve steamed asparagus spears alongside, if you like.

- 4 **boneless center-cut pork loin chops (about 1¼ lbs. *total*), trimmed of fat**
- ¾ **cup beef broth**
- ¼ **cup dried cranberries**
- 2 **tablespoons frozen orange juice concentrate, thawed**
- 1 **tablespoon Dijon mustard**
- 1 **teaspoon cornstarch**
- 2 **teaspoons butter or margarine**
- 2 **teaspoons olive oil**

  Orange slices and thyme sprigs (optional)

1. Place each chop between 2 pieces of plastic wrap. With a heavy, flat-sided mallet, pound meat firmly but gently all over to a thickness of ¼ to ⅓ inch.

2. In a small bowl, stir together broth, cranberries, orange juice concentrate, mustard, and cornstarch. Set aside.

3. Melt butter in oil in a wide nonstick frying pan over medium-high heat. When butter sizzles, add as many pork pieces to pan as will fit without crowding (you may need to cook pork in batches). Cook, turning once, until pork is well browned on both sides and no longer pink in center; cut to test (4 to 5 minutes). Transfer to a platter and keep warm.

4. Add broth mixture to pan, increase heat to high, and bring to a boil, stirring. Then continue to boil and stir until slightly thickened (about 1 minute). Pour over pork. Garnish with orange slices and thyme sprigs, if desired.

MAKES 4 SERVINGS.

PER SERVING: 262 calories, 9 g total fat, 4 g saturated fat, 95 mg cholesterol, 357 mg sodium, 10 g carbohydrates, 1 g fiber, 32 g protein, 33 mg calcium, 1 mg iron

Pork with Orange-Cranberry Sauce

Pounded Pork & Chili Chops

25 MINUTES

These thin pieces of pork, seasoned with chili, cumin, and garlic, grill in about 5 minutes—so have the rest of the meal at the ready before you start to cook. We suggest serving the meat with sliced ripe avocados and juicy orange wedges; to complete a warm-weather supper, you might add hot corn muffins, marinated cucumbers, and tall glasses of iced tea.

- 1 tablespoon chili powder
- ½ teaspoon ground cumin
- 2 cloves garlic, pressed or minced
- ½ cup minced onion
- 2 tablespoons vegetable oil
- 4 boneless center-cut pork loin chops (about 1¼ lbs. *total*), trimmed of fat
- 2 medium-size ripe avocados (about 12 oz. *total*), pitted, peeled, and sliced

  Cilantro sprigs

  Orange wedges

1. In a small bowl, mix chili powder, cumin, garlic, onion, and oil. Spread about 1 table-spoon of the chili mixture on each side of each chop. Place each chop between 2 sheets of plastic wrap. With a heavy, flat-sided mallet, pound meat firmly but gently all over to a thickness of about ¼ inch.

2. Place pork on a lightly oiled grill 4 to 6 inches above a solid bed of hot coals (you can hold your hand at grill level for only 2 to 3 seconds) or over high heat on a gas grill. Close lid on gas grill. Cook, turning once, until pork is well browned on both sides and no longer pink in center; cut to test (5 to 6 minutes).

3. Serve pork with avocados; garnish with cilantro sprigs and orange wedges. Squeeze orange juice over meat and avocado to taste.

MAKES 4 SERVINGS.

PER SERVING: 467 calories, 31 g total fat, 6 g saturated fat, 87 mg cholesterol, 94 mg sodium, 14 g carbohydrates, 4 g fiber, 35 g protein, 71 mg calcium, 2 mg iron

Pork with Garlic & Green Onions

20 MINUTES

Stir-fried and sauced with garlic and rice wine, this combination of slivered green onions and matchstick-size strips of pork tastes delicious over rice. Or try it as a savory filling for mandarin pancakes or flour tortillas.

- 8 ounces boneless pork (such as loin, shoulder, or butt), trimmed of fat
- 1 tablespoon cornstarch
- 1 tablespoon rice wine or dry sherry
- 6 green onions
- 1 teaspoon vegetable oil
- 1 tablespoon minced garlic
- 2 teaspoons soy sauce

1. Cut pork into matchstick strips. In a large bowl, mix pork, cornstarch, and wine.

2. Cut onions crosswise into 1-inch pieces; then cut each onion piece lengthwise into thin slivers.

3. Heat a wide nonstick frying pan over high heat. Add oil and swirl to coat pan bottom. Add pork mixture and cook, stirring, until meat is lightly browned (2 to 3 minutes). Add onions and garlic; cook, stirring, until onions are slightly softer and garlic is tinged with brown (1 to 2 minutes). Stir in soy sauce.

MAKES 2 SERVINGS.

PER SERVING: 232 calories, 9 g total fat, 3 g saturated fat, 67 mg cholesterol, 412 mg sodium, 9 g carbohydrates, 1 g fiber, 26 g protein, 62 mg calcium, 2 mg iron

Smoked Pork Chops with Polenta

30 MINUTES

Chop a little parsley and grate a little cheese—and you've done just about all the preparation this recipe demands. The smoked pork chops, polenta, and creamed corn are all precooked; just reheat them and they're ready to serve.

2 packages (about 1 lb. *each*) prepared polenta

1 small can (about 8½ oz.) cream-style corn

4 to 6 smoked pork chops (about 1¼ lbs. *total*)

About 2 tablespoons grated Parmesan cheese

2 tablespoons chopped parsley

1. With your hands, press polenta into a shallow 2½- to 3-quart baking dish, making an even layer over bottom of dish. Spread corn evenly over polenta. Place pork chops on top of corn.

2. Bake in a 400° oven until pork chops are hot in center; cut to test (about 25 minutes). Sprinkle with cheese and parsley.

MAKES 4 SERVINGS.

PER SERVING: 378 calories, 11 g total fat, 3 g saturated fat, 58 mg cholesterol, 2,237 mg sodium, 46 g carbohydrates, 5 g fiber, 24 g protein, 39 mg calcium, 3 mg iron

Pan-browned Ham with Braised Fennel

25 MINUTES

This dish has just two main ingredients—ham and fresh fennel—but they make a striking presentation when cut to the same thickness, then pan-browned. The feathery green fennel leaves are a vibrant garnish.

2 heads fennel (*each* about 4 inches in diameter)

½ cup dry white wine or fat-free reduced-sodium chicken broth

1 pound thinly sliced cooked ham

Pepper

1. Rinse fennel. Cut off coarse stalks, reserving green leaves. Trim and discard base and any discolored or bruised parts from each fennel head. Slice fennel paper-thin, using a mandoline or a food processor. Chop reserved fennel leaves and set aside.

2. In a wide frying pan, combine sliced fennel and wine. Cook over high heat, stirring, until all but 1 to 2 tablespoons of the liquid have evaporated (about 5 minutes). Transfer fennel to a platter and keep warm.

3. Add as many ham slices to pan as will fit without crowding (you may need to cook ham in batches). Cook, stirring, until lightly browned (2 to 3 minutes). Arrange ham next to fennel.

4. Sprinkle chopped fennel leaves over ham and fennel. Season to taste with pepper.

MAKES 4 SERVINGS.

PER SERVING: 248 calories, 10 g total fat, 4 g saturated fat, 67 mg cholesterol, 1,857 mg sodium, 5 g carbohydrates, 2 g fiber, 28 g protein, 87 mg calcium, 3 mg iron

Sausages with Grapes

30 MINUTES

Though it could hardly be simpler, this two-ingredient combination has extraordinary flavors. To create an interesting play of textures, you cook some of the grapes, then stir in the rest uncooked at the last. Serve a crisp green salad alongside.

> 4 mild Italian sausages (about 1 lb. *total*)
>
> 3 cups seedless green grapes

1. Prick sausages with a fork and place in a wide frying pan. Add 1 cup water. Bring to a boil over high heat; then reduce heat, cover, and simmer for 10 minutes.

2. Drain water and fat from pan. Add 2 cups of the grapes to pan; cover and simmer until grapes are soft (about 7 minutes). Uncover, increase heat to high, and continue to cook, turning sausages and stirring grapes occasion-ally. As liquid cooks away, reduce heat to medium; stir often until sausages are well browned and grapes are lightly browned (about 10 minutes). Stir in remaining 1 cup grapes.

3. Transfer sausages to a platter and spoon grapes over them.

MAKES 4 SERVINGS.

PER SERVING: 338 calories, 22 g total fat, 8 g saturated fat, 65 mg cholesterol, 767 mg sodium, 19 g carbohydrates, 2 g fiber, 17 g protein, 31 mg calcium, 1 mg iron

Butterflied Sausages with Barley-Mushroom Pilaf

25 MINUTES

Butterflying is a quick way to cook all meats—even raw sausages. Here, Italian sausages are served atop an herbed barley pilaf; you start the pilaf cooking, then cut and broil the sausages. (Use precooked sausages if you prefer; butterfly them as directed below, then broil just until well browned and heated through.)

> 1 tablespoon butter or margarine
>
> 1 large onion (about 8 oz.), chopped
>
> 1½ cups sliced mushrooms
>
> 1 cup quick-cooking barley
>
> 2 cups beef broth
>
> ¼ teaspoon dried thyme
>
> ¼ teaspoon dried marjoram
>
> 4 raw Italian sausages (¾ to 1 lb. *total*)
>
> Chopped parsley

1. Melt butter in a wide nonstick frying pan over high heat. Add onion and mushrooms; cook, stirring often, until tinged with brown (about 3 minutes). Stir in barley, broth, thyme, and marjoram. Bring to a boil; then reduce heat, cover, and simmer until barley is tender to bite (10 to 12 minutes). Remove from heat and let stand, covered, until all liquid has been absorbed.

2. Meanwhile, make a half lengthwise cut in each sausage, cutting to within about ¼ inch of bottom surface. Gently press sausages open; then place, cut side up, in a foil-lined broiler pan.

3. Broil sausages 4 to 6 inches below heat, turning once, until evenly browned on both sides and cooked through; cut to test (8 to 10 minutes).

4. Spoon barley-mushroom pilaf into a wide bowl. Top with sausages and sprinkle with parsley.

MAKES 4 SERVINGS.

PER SERVING: 429 calories, 23 g total fat, 9 g saturated fat, 65 mg cholesterol, 1,115 mg sodium, 35 g carbohydrates, 5 g fiber, 21 g protein, 41 mg calcium, 3 mg iron

Broiled Lamb Chops with Cherry Sauce

25 MINUTES

Little lamb rib chops topped with a rich-tasting sauce of dark sweet cherries, currant jelly, and balsamic vinegar are a great choice for a company meal at short notice. Complete the menu with a spinach salad and a combination of white and wild rice. We suggest making the sauce with canned cherries, but use frozen (thawed and drained) or fresh fruit if you like.

- 2 tablespoons orange juice
- 1 teaspoon cornstarch
- ⅓ cup currant jelly
- ¼ cup balsamic vinegar
- ½ teaspoon dried tarragon
- ¾ cup canned pitted dark sweet cherries, drained
- 8 lamb rib chops (about 1¾ lbs. *total*), trimmed of fat, bones Frenched

1. In a small bowl, stir together orange juice and cornstarch. Set aside.

2. In a 1½- to 2-quart pan, combine jelly, vinegar, and tarragon. Stir over high heat until steaming. Stir in orange juice mixture and bring to a simmer; mixture will thicken slightly. Stir in cherries; then remove from heat and keep warm.

3. Arrange lamb chops on a rack in a broiler pan. Broil 4 to 6 inches below heat, turning once, until lightly browned on both sides and done to your liking; cut to test (10 to 12 minutes for medium-rare).

4. Transfer lamb chops to a platter and top with cherry sauce.

MAKES 4 SERVINGS.

PER SERVING: 245 calories, 9 g total fat, 3 g saturated fat, 58 mg cholesterol, 64 mg sodium, 24 g carbohydrates, 1 g fiber, 18 g protein, 19 mg calcium, 2 mg iron

Broiled Lamb Chops with Cherry Sauce

Hoisin-Honey Lamb with Couscous

20 MINUTES

For an entrée that combines Asian and Mediterranean flavors, choose this dish. Tender strips of lamb are coated with a spicy-sweet sauce of hoisin, honey, and ginger, then served over fluffy couscous flecked with shredded carrots.

- 2 **cups fat-free reduced-sodium chicken broth**
- 1 **cup shredded carrots**
- 1 **cup couscous**
- 1 **pound lean boneless leg of lamb (a chunk or steaks), trimmed of fat**
- 6 **tablespoons hoisin sauce**
- 2 **tablespoons honey**
- 2 **to 3 teaspoons minced fresh ginger**
- ½ **teaspoon vegetable oil**
- 12 **green onions, cut into ½-inch lengths**
- ¼ **cup cilantro leaves**

1. In a 1½- to 2-quart pan, bring broth to a boil over high heat. Stir in carrots and couscous. Cover tightly, remove from heat, and let stand until almost all liquid has been absorbed (about 5 minutes).

2. Meanwhile, cut lamb across the grain into bite-size strips about ¼ inch thick. Place in a large bowl and stir in hoisin sauce, honey, and ginger.

3. Heat a wok or wide nonstick frying pan over high heat. Add oil, then onions. Cook, stirring, just until onions are tinged with brown (1 to 2 minutes). Transfer onions to a bowl.

4. Pour lamb mixture into pan; cook, stirring, until lamb is no longer pink (about 2 minutes; scrape off a little sauce to check). Return onions to pan and stir to heat through.

5. Spoon couscous mixture into a serving bowl and top with lamb mixture. Sprinkle with cilantro.

MAKES 4 SERVINGS.

PER SERVING: 445 calories, 6 g total fat, 2 g saturated fat, 73 mg cholesterol, 845 mg sodium, 61 g carbohydrates, 3 g fiber, 31 g protein, 59 mg calcium, 3 mg iron

Hoisin-Honey Lamb with Couscous

Red Pepper Mustard Rack of Lamb

30 MINUTES

Bottled roasted peppers, finely chopped and seasoned with honey, tangy balsamic vinegar, and plenty of mustard, make a vivid sauce for rack of lamb. Round out an elegant meal with French rolls and a vinaigrette-dressed salad of mixed tender greens. (When you buy the lamb, make sure the butcher removes the chine bones.)

1 cup drained bottled roasted red peppers (about one 7- to 8-oz. jar)

2 tablespoons balsamic vinegar

3 tablespoons honey

1½ tablespoons dry mustard

½ cup Dijon mustard

1 teaspoon minced fresh rosemary or crumbled dried rosemary

4 racks of lamb (13 to 16 oz. *each*), trimmed of fat, bones Frenched

1. In a blender or food processor, combine roasted peppers, vinegar, honey, dry mustard, Dijon mustard, and rosemary. Whirl just until peppers are finely chopped; do not purée.

2. Coat lamb all over with a third of the roasted pepper sauce. Set remaining sauce aside.

3. Place lamb racks, bone side down, in a foil-lined 11- by 17-inch roasting pan. Roast in a 475° oven for 15 minutes. Turn racks over and return to oven. Reduce oven temperature to 350°; continue to roast until a meat thermometer inserted in thickest part registers 140°F for medium-rare (about 10 more minutes). Or cut to test.

4. Cut racks in half or into individual chops; allow a half-rack or 3 or 4 chops for each serving. Offer reserved roasted pepper sauce to spoon over individual servings.

MAKES 6 TO 8 SERVINGS.

PER SERVING: 249 calories, 11 g total fat, 4 g saturated fat, 72 mg cholesterol, 520 mg sodium, 9 g carbohydrates, 0 g fiber, 22 g protein, 23 mg calcium, 2 mg iron

Lamb Curry

25 MINUTES

Here's a curry that's easy to put together at short notice: it's made with ingredients you probably already have on hand. Adjust the amount of cayenne to suit your taste; the more you use, the hotter the flavor will be. Serve the dish over fluffy rice.

- 1 pound lean ground lamb
- 1 large onion (about 8 oz.), chopped
- 2 teaspoons cornstarch
- 1 can (about 14½ oz.) beef broth
- 2 cloves garlic, minced or pressed
- 1 tablespoon curry powder
- ½ teaspoon ground ginger
- ½ teaspoon ground cumin
- 1 large carrot (about 4 oz.), thinly sliced
- 1 large apple (about 8 oz.), peeled, cored, and chopped
- 1 large green bell pepper (about 8 oz.), seeded and chopped

  Salt and ground red pepper (cayenne)

  Chutney

  Plain yogurt

1. Crumble lamb into a wide nonstick frying pan; add onion. Cook over high heat, stirring often, until lamb and onion are browned (about 6 minutes). Meanwhile, in a small bowl, stir together cornstarch and 2 tablespoons of the broth; set aside.

2. Spoon off and discard any fat from pan. Reduce heat to medium-low. Add garlic, curry powder, ginger, cumin, carrot, apple, bell pepper, and remaining broth. Bring to a simmer; then simmer, uncovered, until all vegetables are tender to bite (about 12 minutes).

3. Stir in cornstarch mixture; simmer, stirring often, until sauce is thickened. Season to taste with salt and red pepper. Offer chutney and yogurt to add to taste.

MAKES 4 SERVINGS.

PER SERVING: 318 calories, 16 g total fat, 7 g saturated fat, 76 mg cholesterol, 436 mg sodium, 21 g carbohydrates, 4 g fiber, 22 g protein, 55 mg calcium, 3 mg iron

Barbecued Lamb with Blackberry Sauce

20 MINUTES

If you like, you can reserve the tart-sweet marinade from these lamb chunks to serve as a sauce; just be sure to boil it briefly before serving. If time allows, add vegetables (such as onion wedges and bell pepper squares) to the skewers to cook along with the meat.

- ½ cup seedless blackberry jam
- ⅓ cup balsamic or red wine vinegar
- 1 tablespoon Dijon mustard
- 1 tablespoon minced fresh rosemary or crumbled dried rosemary
- 1½ pounds lean boneless lamb (leg or loin), trimmed of fat and cut into 1-inch cubes

  Salt

1. In a large bowl, stir together jam, vinegar, mustard, and rosemary. Pour a third of the jam mixture into a small container and set aside.

2. Add lamb cubes to remaining jam mixture in bowl; stir to coat well. Then thread lamb equally on four to six 12- to 14-inch metal skewers; discard marinade.

3. Place skewers on a lightly oiled grill 4 to 6 inches above a solid bed of medium-hot coals (you can hold your hand at grill level for 3 to 4 seconds) or over medium-high heat on a gas grill. Close lid on gas grill. Cook, turning as needed to brown evenly and basting with reserved jam mixture, until lamb is done to your liking; cut to test (about 7 minutes for medium-rare).

4. To serve, push lamb from skewers onto plates. Season to taste with salt.

MAKES 4 SERVINGS.

PER SERVING: 316 calories, 10 g total fat, 4 g saturated fat, 114 mg cholesterol, 159 mg sodium, 18 g carbohydrates, 0 g fiber, 36 g protein, 18 mg calcium, 3 mg iron

Lamb Curry

Lamb Pilaf

30 MINUTES

Rice pilaf mix is the base for this satisfying dish. While the pilaf cooks, prepare a simple yogurt-dressed cucumber salad as a cool, refreshing accompaniment.

1 **pound lean ground lamb**

1 **large onion (about 8 oz.), chopped**

1 **package (6 to 8 oz.) rice pilaf mix with Middle Eastern seasonings**

1 **European cucumber (about 1 lb.)**

1 **cup plain nonfat yogurt**

½ **cup chopped parsley**

2 **tablespoons thinly sliced green onion**

2 **tablespoons chopped fresh mint**

1 **tablespoon lemon juice**

Salt

Mint sprigs (optional)

1. Crumble lamb into a wide nonstick frying pan or 5- to 6-quart pan; add chopped onion. Cook over high heat, stirring often, until lamb is browned and onion is soft (about 6 minutes).

2. Spoon off and discard any fat from pan. Return pan to heat; add ¼ cup water and stir to scrape browned bits free. Then add pilaf mix (including seasoning packet) and amount of water specified in package directions for making entire mix. Bring to a boil; reduce heat, cover, and simmer until rice is tender to bite and liquid has been absorbed (about 15 minutes).

3. Meanwhile, coarsely chop cucumber. In a bowl, stir together yogurt, parsley, green onion, chopped mint, and lemon juice; add cucumber and mix gently. Season to taste with salt. Garnish with mint sprigs, if desired.

4. Transfer pilaf to a platter; serve with cucumber salad.

MAKES 6 SERVINGS.

PER SERVING: 293 calories, 11 g total fat, 4 g saturated fat, 51 mg cholesterol, 493 mg sodium, 30 g carbohydrates, 2 g fiber, 19 g protein, 142 mg calcium, 2 mg iron

Lamb Pilaf

Chapter Four

POULTRY

Panko-crusted Chicken with Dijon Sauce

30 MINUTES

The coarse dry bread crumbs known to the Japanese as *panko* give these baked chicken breasts an especially crunchy coating. You'll find panko in Japanese markets and in the Asian food section of your supermarket.

- ¼ cup Dijon mustard
- 1 tablespoon balsamic vinegar
- 1 clove garlic, minced or pressed
- ¾ cup panko (Japanese-style bread crumbs)
- 1 tablespoon grated Parmesan cheese
- 1 tablespoon minced parsley
- 4 boneless, skinless chicken breast halves (4 to 5 oz. *each*)
- 2 tablespoons butter or margarine, melted
- ¼ cup mayonnaise
- 1 teaspoon mustard seeds

1. In a medium-size, shallow bowl, blend 2 tablespoons of the mustard with vinegar and garlic. In another shallow bowl, stir together panko, cheese, and parsley.

2. Rinse chicken and pat dry. Turn each piece in mustard mixture to coat completely; then roll in panko mixture, pressing firmly to coat chicken well on all sides. Arrange chicken in a single layer in a lightly oiled 9- by 13-inch baking pan; drizzle evenly with butter. Bake in a 500° oven until coating is golden and meat in thickest part is no longer pink; cut to test (about 15 minutes).

3. Meanwhile, prepare sauce: in a small bowl, stir together mayonnaise, remaining 2 tablespoons mustard, and mustard seeds.

4. Serve chicken pieces whole or cut crosswise into thick slices. Accompany with sauce.

MAKES 4 SERVINGS.

PER SERVING: 369 calories, 20 g total fat, 6 g saturated fat, 99 mg cholesterol, 636 mg sodium, 9 g carbohydrates, 0 g fiber, 32 g protein, 43 mg calcium, 1 mg iron

Chicken-Pesto Pockets with Red Pepper–Chardonnay Sauce

30 MINUTES

Topped with a vivid sauce of roasted peppers and chardonnay, these pesto- and cheese-stuffed chicken breasts make a colorful entrée that's ideally suited to impromptu entertaining. To complete the meal, offer a green salad with balsamic-mustard vinaigrette and pour glasses of the remaining chardonnay (you need just ⅓ cup for the sauce).

- 4 boneless, skinless chicken breast halves (about 5 oz. *each*)
- ¼ cup prepared pesto
- 2 ounces fontina cheese, cut into 4 equal strips
- Black pepper
- 1 tablespoon olive oil
- 2 tablespoons minced shallots
- 1 jar (about 7 oz.) roasted red peppers, drained and finely chopped
- ⅔ cup fat-free reduced-sodium chicken broth
- ⅓ cup chardonnay or other dry white wine
- 2 tablespoons whipping cream
- Basil or parsley sprigs

1. Rinse chicken and pat dry. With a sharp knife, cut a horizontal slit in each piece, cutting almost through to other side. Spread 1 tablespoon of the pesto in each pocket; then stuff each with a piece of cheese. Fasten each chicken piece closed with a wooden pick. Sprinkle chicken all over with black pepper.

2. Heat oil in a wide nonstick frying pan over medium-high heat. Add chicken and cook, turning occasionally, until browned on all sides (about 8 minutes). Then transfer chicken to a 9-inch-square baking pan; cover and keep warm in a 300° oven.

3. To frying pan, add shallots; cook, stirring often, until lightly browned (about 2 minutes).

Add roasted peppers, broth, wine, and cream. Bring to a boil over high heat; then boil, uncovered, stirring to scrape browned bits free, until reduced to about 1 cup (6 to 8 minutes). Working quickly, transfer hot roasted pepper mixture to a food processor or blender; whirl until smoothly puréed. Stir any juices that have accumulated from chicken into sauce.

4. To serve, cut each chicken piece crosswise into thick slices. Spoon sauce equally onto 4 individual plates; arrange one sliced piece of chicken atop sauce on each plate. Garnish with basil sprigs.

MAKES 4 SERVINGS.

PER SERVING: 377 calories, 19 g total fat, 6 g saturated fat, 109 mg cholesterol, 518 mg sodium, 6 g carbohydrates, 0 g fiber, 39 g protein, 140 mg calcium, 2 mg iron

Chicken-Pesto Pockets with Red Pepper–Chardonnay Sauce

Crusty Mexican Chicken

25 MINUTES

Crushed tortilla chips and a sprinkle of jack cheese make a crisp crust for moist chicken breasts infused with honey and lime. Serve with a warm tomato salsa, which takes just minutes to prepare.

4 **boneless, skinless chicken breast halves (about 5 oz. *each*)**

1 **tablespoon lime juice**

1 **tablespoon honey**

⅔ **cup (about 2 oz.) finely crushed tortilla chips**

1 **can (about 14½ oz.) stewed tomatoes with onions and mild chiles**

¼ **cup cilantro leaves**

1 **large clove garlic, peeled**

½ **teaspoon dried oregano**

½ **cup shredded jack cheese**

Cilantro sprigs

Lime wedges

1. Rinse chicken and pat dry. In a shallow bowl, stir together lime juice and honey. Place tortilla chips in a bag. Turn each chicken piece in honey mixture to coat; then drop into chips and shake to coat. Arrange chicken in a single layer in a 9- by 13-inch baking dish. Bake in a 475° oven until meat in thickest part is no longer pink; cut to test (about 15 minutes).

2. Meanwhile, in a blender or food processor, combine tomatoes and their liquid, cilantro leaves, garlic, and oregano; whirl until smooth. Pour into a 2- to 3-quart pan and bring to a boil over high heat. Boil, partly covered to prevent spattering, until reduced to 1¼ cups (4 to 5 minutes). Reduce heat and keep warm.

3. Sprinkle chicken with cheese and continue to bake just until cheese is melted (1 to 2 more minutes).

4. To serve, spoon tomato sauce equally onto 4 individual plates; place a chicken piece atop sauce on each plate. Garnish with cilantro sprigs. Offer lime wedges to season chicken to taste.

MAKES 4 SERVINGS.

PER SERVING: 328 calories, 10 g total fat, 4 g saturated fat, 97 mg cholesterol, 569 mg sodium, 21 g carbohydrates, 3 g fiber, 38 g protein, 166 mg calcium, 2 mg iron

Chicken Chili Verde Tacos

20 TO 25 MINUTES

Here's a speedy departure from the traditional slow-simmered chili verde: you combine stir-fried chicken with shredded cabbage, cilantro, and green chile salsa, then wrap the combination in warm flour tortillas. Serve with refried beans and fresh pineapple wedges.

- 3 cups shredded green or red cabbage (or use a combination)
- 1 cup lightly packed cilantro leaves
- 1 cup green chile salsa
- 1 pound boneless, skinless chicken breasts
- 1 teaspoon vegetable oil
- 1 large onion (about 8 oz.), slivered lengthwise
- 3 cloves garlic, minced or pressed
- 1 teaspoon ground cumin
- ½ teaspoon dried oregano
- 8 flour tortillas (*each* 7 to 9 inches in diameter)
- ½ cup shredded jack cheese

1. In a serving bowl, combine cabbage, cilantro, and salsa; set aside.

2. Rinse chicken, pat dry, and cut crosswise into ½-inch-wide strips; set aside. Heat oil in a wide nonstick frying pan over medium-high heat. Add onion and garlic; cook, stirring often, for 2 minutes. Increase heat to high and add chicken. Cook, stirring often, until chicken is no longer pink in center; cut to test (4 to 6 minutes). Add cumin and oregano; stir for 15 more seconds. Spoon chicken mixture into a serving dish and keep warm.

3. Wrap tortillas in a cloth towel and microwave on HIGH (100%) for about 1½ minutes or until heated through.

4. To assemble tacos, spoon cabbage mixture, chicken mixture, and cheese into tortillas; fold to enclose and eat out of hand.

MAKES 4 SERVINGS.

PER SERVING: 476 calories, 12 g total fat, 4 g saturated fat, 81 mg cholesterol, 858 mg sodium, 52 g carbohydrates, 5 g fiber, 37 g protein, 259 mg calcium, 4 mg iron

Grilled Chicken Skewers with Portabella Mushrooms

25 MINUTES

Balsamic vinegar and olive oil flavored with roasted garlic give grilled chicken and portabella mushrooms a rich, mellow flavor. Serve with a spinach salad and Italian bread.

- 1 pound boneless, skinless chicken breasts
- 4 slices pancetta (about 3 oz. *total*), cut into quarters
- 1 large red onion (about 8 oz.), cut into 8 equal wedges
- 6 baby portabella mushrooms or 6 large (2½- to 3-inch-diameter) regular mushrooms (about 6 oz. *total*)
- ½ cup balsamic vinegar
- 1 tablespoon roasted garlic olive oil or regular olive oil
- Salt and pepper

1. Rinse chicken, pat dry, and cut into 1½-inch chunks. Thread chicken, pancetta, and onion alternately on four 12- to 14-inch metal skewers, dividing equally. Thread mushrooms on another 12- to 14-inch metal skewer. In a small bowl, stir together vinegar and oil. Brush foods generously with vinegar mixture.

2. Place skewers on a grill 4 to 6 inches above a solid bed of medium-hot coals (you can hold your hand at grill level for 3 to 4 seconds) or over medium-high heat on a gas grill. Close lid on gas grill. Cook for 6 minutes, then turn and baste with remaining vinegar mixture; close lid on gas grill again. Continue to cook until mushrooms and onion are browned and chicken is no longer pink in thickest part; cut to test (6 to 8 more minutes).

3. To serve, transfer skewers to a platter. Season to taste with salt and pepper.

MAKES 4 SERVINGS.

PER SERVING: 224 calories, 7 g total fat, 2 g saturated fat, 74 mg cholesterol, 276 mg sodium, 8 g carbohydrates, 1 g fiber, 31 g protein, 27 mg calcium, 2 mg iron

Chicken & Watermelon with Orange-Herb Mignonette Sauce

25 MINUTES

Orange marmalade makes a simple glaze for skewered broiled chicken. Pair the hot chicken with crisp, cool watermelon; then dip both meat and fruit in a snappy citrus-herb sauce. (If you use bamboo skewers, soak them in warm water before threading the chicken.)

- ¼ cup orange marmalade
- ½ teaspoon ground coriander
- 1 pound boneless, skinless chicken breasts
- ½ teaspoon shredded orange peel
- ½ cup orange juice
- 1½ teaspoons *each* minced fresh dill and minced fresh mint (or ½ teaspoon *each* dried dill weed and dried mint)
- 1½ teaspoons minced cilantro
- 2 teaspoons white wine vinegar
- ⅛ to ¼ teaspoon crushed red pepper flakes
- 4 cups 1-inch chunks of seedless watermelon

1. In a small bowl, stir together marmalade and coriander; set aside.

2. Rinse chicken, pat dry, and cut into 1½-inch chunks. Thread chicken equally on four 12- to 14-inch metal or bamboo skewers.

Arrange skewers in a foil-lined shallow 10- by 15-inch baking pan; brush with half the marmalade mixture. Broil about 6 inches below heat for 6 minutes. Turn, brush with remaining marmalade mixture, and continue to broil until meat in thickest part is no longer pink; cut to test (about 6 more minutes).

3. While chicken is broiling, combine orange peel, orange juice, dill, mint, cilantro, vinegar, and red pepper flakes in a small serving bowl. Stir to blend well.

4. To serve, transfer skewers to a platter; mound watermelon chunks alongside. Offer sauce for dipping.

MAKES 4 SERVINGS.

PER SERVING: 241 calories, 2 g total fat, 0 g saturated fat, 66 mg cholesterol, 89 mg sodium, 28 g carbohydrates, 1 g fiber, 27 g protein, 40 mg calcium, 1 mg iron

Chicken Thighs with Apricots & Olives

30 MINUTES

Pictured on page 92

Chunks of boneless chicken thigh bake to succulence in a savory, slightly sweet sauce of dried apricots, olives, and capers. Offer fluffy couscous or rice to absorb the flavorful sauce.

- 1¼ pounds boneless, skinless chicken thighs
- ⅓ cup calamata or Niçoise olives
- ⅓ cup dried apricots, cut in half
- ⅓ cup dry vermouth
- 2 tablespoons drained capers
- ¼ teaspoon grated orange peel
- 2 tablespoons orange juice
- 1 tablespoon white wine vinegar
- 2 teaspoons dried basil
- 2 teaspoons olive oil
- 2 cloves garlic, minced or pressed
- 3 tablespoons firmly packed brown sugar
  Italian parsley sprigs
  Orange slices (optional)

1. Rinse chicken, pat dry, and cut into 1-inch pieces. Place in a 9- by 13-inch baking dish

and add olives, apricots, vermouth, capers, orange peel, orange juice, vinegar, basil, oil, and garlic. Stir to mix well; then spread out evenly.

2. Bake, uncovered, in a 500° oven for 15 minutes. Turn oven to broil. Sprinkle chicken mixture evenly with sugar. Then broil about 6 inches below heat until top begins to brown and chicken chunks are no longer pink in thickest part; cut to test (about 5 more minutes). Garnish with parsley sprigs and, if desired, orange slices. If desired, let chicken stand for about 5 minutes before serving to let juices thicken slightly.

MAKES 4 SERVINGS.

PER SERVING: 301 calories, 11 g total fat, 2 g saturated fat, 118 mg cholesterol, 520 mg sodium, 21 g carbohydrates, 1 g fiber, 29 g protein, 49 mg calcium, 3 mg iron

Tuscan Baked Chicken & Vegetables

30 MINUTES

Chicken and vegetables baked in a fennel-seasoned tomato sauce taste delicious over hot ribbons of spinach fettuccine. Sprinkle generously with freshly grated Parmesan cheese; offer a young, fruity zinfandel or Chianti for sipping alongside.

4 **skinless chicken breast halves (about 2 lbs.** *total***)**

8 **ounces sliced mushrooms**

3 **medium-size zucchini (about 1 lb.** *total***), thinly sliced**

2 **tablespoons olive oil**

½ **teaspoon pepper**

1 **teaspoon fennel seeds**

1 **teaspoon dried basil**

1 **can (about 14½ oz.) diced tomatoes with basil and oregano**

¼ **cup dry red wine**

8 **ounces dried spinach fettuccine**

   Chopped parsley

   Grated Parmesan cheese

1. Rinse chicken and pat dry. Arrange chicken (bone side down), mushrooms, and zucchini in a 12- by 15-inch broiler pan. Drizzle with oil.

2. In a bowl, stir together pepper, fennel seeds, basil, tomatoes and their liquid, and wine. Pour evenly over chicken and vegetables; cover tightly with foil. Bake in a 500° oven for 10 minutes. Uncover and continue to bake until meat in thickest part is no longer pink; cut to test (about 12 more minutes).

3. While chicken is baking, bring about 2 quarts water to a boil in a 4- to 5-quart pan over high heat; stir in pasta and cook, uncovered, until just tender to bite (8 to 10 minutes). Or cook pasta according to package directions. Drain well.

4. To serve, spoon chicken, vegetables, and pasta onto individual plates; spoon pan juices over all. Sprinkle with parsley. Offer cheese to add to taste.

MAKES 4 SERVINGS.

PER SERVING: 494 calories, 12 g total fat, 2 g saturated fat, 139 mg cholesterol, 331 mg sodium, 50 g carbohydrates, 6 g fiber, 46 g protein, 101 mg calcium, 6 mg iron

Mediterranean Microwave Chicken Couscous

30 MINUTES

Colorful vegetables, nutty-tasting garbanzo beans, and tender chicken thighs in a tomato-based sauce add up to a full-meal microwave casserole. Serve over raisin-dotted couscous lightly spiced with cinnamon.

1 cup fat-free reduced-sodium chicken broth

¼ cup tomato paste

2 teaspoons ground cumin

¼ teaspoon ground red pepper (cayenne)

2 cloves garlic, minced or pressed

1 pound boneless, skinless chicken thighs

2 medium-size zucchini (10 to 11 oz. *total*), thinly sliced

1 *each* medium-size red and yellow bell pepper (about 12 oz. *total*), seeded and cut into 1-inch chunks

1 can (about 15 oz.) garbanzo beans, rinsed and drained

⅔ cup couscous

½ teaspoon ground cinnamon

¼ cup raisins

1½ cups boiling water

1. In a 2- to 4-cup microwave-safe container, combine broth, tomato paste, cumin, ground red pepper, and garlic. Cover and microwave on HIGH (100%) for 2 to 4 minutes or until mixture boils.

2. Meanwhile, rinse chicken, pat dry, and cut into ¾-inch pieces. Evenly arrange chicken around perimeter of a shallow 4-quart microwave-safe dish; place zucchini in center. Top evenly with bell peppers and beans. Pour hot broth mixture over all. Cover tightly and microwave on HIGH (100%) for 10 minutes. Stir, then cover again and microwave on HIGH (100%) for 10 more minutes or until chicken is no longer pink in thickest part; cut to test.

3. Meanwhile, in a 1-quart serving dish, combine couscous, cinnamon, and raisins; pour in boiling water and stir to blend. Immediately cover tightly and let stand until almost all liquid has been absorbed (about 5 minutes).

4. To serve, fluff couscous with a fork. Spoon onto individual plates and top with chicken, vegetables, and sauce.

MAKES 4 SERVINGS.

PER SERVING: 426 calories, 7 g total fat, 1 g saturated fat, 94 mg cholesterol, 500 mg sodium, 57 g carbohydrates, 8 g fiber, 34 g protein, 90 mg calcium, 5 mg iron

Five-spice Drummettes

30 MINUTES

Coated in a deep amber soy-sherry glaze, these tiny chicken drummettes are wonderful as appetizers—but they make a great main dish, too. Serve with hot, fluffy rice and stir-fried snow peas seasoned with fresh ginger.

> 4 **pounds chicken drummettes (about 40 pieces)**
> ¼ **cup soy sauce**
> ¼ **cup dry sherry**
> ¼ **cup honey**
> 2 **tablespoons Oriental sesame oil**
> 1½ **teaspoons Chinese five-spice (or ¼ teaspoon** *each* **ground cloves, ground anise, ground cinnamon, and ground ginger)**
> 1 **clove garlic, minced or pressed**

1. Rinse chicken and pat dry. In a large bowl, stir together soy sauce, sherry, honey, oil, five-spice, and garlic; add chicken and stir to coat evenly.

2. Lift chicken pieces from glaze (reserve any remaining glaze) and arrange in a single layer in 2 shallow 10- by 15-inch baking pans. Bake, uncovered, in a 500° oven until chicken is dark brown and meat near bone is no longer pink; cut to test (about 25 minutes). Halfway through baking time, switch positions of pans and brush chicken with reserved glaze. If necessary, add 1 tablespoon water to each pan near end of bakig time to prevent scorching.

MAKES 4 SERVINGS.

PER SERVING: 605 calories, 31 g total fat, 8 g saturated fat, 195 mg cholesterol, 1,225 mg sodium, 21 g carbohydrates, 0 g fiber, 59 g protein, 33 mg calcium, 3 mg iron

Chicken Chutney Burgers

20 MINUTES

Chutney lends character to these low-in-fat chicken burgers. To round out a light dinner, serve with a spinach salad and sweet cantaloupe wedges.

> ⅔ **cup Major Grey's chutney, large pieces chopped**
> 1½ **tablespoons lemon juice**
> 1 **tablespoon Dijon mustard**
> 12 **ounces ground chicken**
> ¼ **cup thinly sliced green onions**
> ½ **teaspoon ground cumin**
> 4 **hamburger buns, split and toasted**
> **Mayonnaise (optional)**
> 4 **thin slices red onion, separated into rings**
> 20 **packaged triple-washed baby spinach leaves (***each* **about 4 inches long)**

1. In a large bowl, stir together chutney, lemon juice, and mustard. Spoon two-thirds of the mixture into a small bowl and set aside.

2. To chutney mixture remaining in large bowl, add chicken, green onions, and cumin; mix lightly. Shape into 4 equal patties, each about 4 inches wide.

3. Place patties on a rack in a 12- by 15-inch broiler pan. Broil about 3 inches below heat, turning as needed, until well browned on both sides and no longer pink in center; cut to test (6 to 7 minutes).

4. Spread cut sides of buns with reserved chutney mixture and, if desired, with mayonnaise. Fill buns with red onion rings, chicken patties, and spinach leaves.

MAKES 4 SERVINGS.

PER SERVING: 430 calories, 10 g total fat, 2 g saturated fat, 71 mg cholesterol, 865 mg sodium, 62 g carbohydrates, 1 g fiber, 19 g protein, 101 mg calcium, 4 mg iron

Pan-grilled Poultry Sausages & Polenta with Dry Jack

25 MINUTES

Fresh chicken and turkey sausages with a variety of interesting seasonings are now available in many markets; you might want to try several different sorts in this recipe. Look for ready-to-eat polenta rolls in your grocer's refrigerated section. Top the polenta with thin shavings of rich-tasting dry jack cheese (make the shavings by pulling a vegetable peeler across the chunk of cheese). To complete the meal, you might serve wilted Swiss chard.

- 2 **tablespoons olive oil**
- 4 to 6 **fresh poultry sausages (about 4 oz. *each*)**
- 1 **pound prepared polenta roll (either plain or with sun-dried tomatoes), cut crosswise into 8 to 12 equal slices**
- ½ **cup thinly shaved dry jack cheese**

1. Heat 2 teaspoons of the oil in a wide non-stick frying pan over medium-high heat. Add sausages and cook, turning occasionally, until browned on all sides (about 10 minutes). Add ¼ cup water to pan; cover and continue to cook until sausages feel firm when pressed (3 to 5 more minutes). Transfer to a platter; cover and keep warm.

2. Discard any water from pan; then add remaining 4 teaspoons oil. Add polenta rounds to pan; cook, turning as needed, until well browned on both sides (about 6 minutes). Transfer to platter alongside sausages. Scatter cheese over polenta.

MAKES 4 SERVINGS.

PER SERVING: 406 calories, 24 g total fat, 9 g saturated fat, 100 mg cholesterol, 1,147 mg sodium, 16 g carbohydrates, 2 g fiber, 29 g protein, 126 mg calcium, 3 mg iron

Pan-grilled Poultry Sausages & Polenta with Dry Jack

Game Hens

Yes, you can have Rock Cornish game hens ready to serve in just under 30 minutes! The secret to speed is to choose the right technique: cut the hens half, then cook them at a very high temperature, whether by roasting, broiling, or grilling. All five of the following recipes require only a few minutes of no-fuss preparation to create superbly seasoned, succulent birds.

Grilled Game Hens with Cilantro Baste

30 MINUTES

- 2 **Rock Cornish game hens (1 to 1¼ lbs. each)**
- 1 **cup firmly packed cilantro leaves**
- 4 **cloves garlic, peeled**
- 1 **teaspoon dry mustard**
- 2 **tablespoons soy sauce**
- 3 **tablespoons honey**
- ¼ **cup marsala or apple juice**
  Cilantro sprigs

1. Reserve game hen necks and giblets for other uses. With poultry shears or a sharp knife, split each hen in half, cutting along backbone and breastbone. Rinse hens and pat dry.

2. Place hens, skin side down, on a greased grill 4 to 6 inches above a solid bed of medium-hot coals (you can hold your hand at grill level for 3 to 4 seconds) or over medium-high heat on a gas grill. Close lid on gas grill. Cook until hens are browned on bottom surface (about 15 minutes).

3. Meanwhile, in a food processor or blender, combine cilantro leaves, garlic, mustard, soy sauce, honey, and marsala; whirl until cilantro is finely chopped.

4. Turn hens skin side up. Continue to cook, basting occasionally with cilantro mixture, until meat near thighbone is no longer pink; cut to test (about 10 more minutes). Transfer to a platter; garnish with cilantro sprigs.

MAKES 4 SERVINGS.

PER SERVING: 354 calories, 16 g total fat, 4 g saturated fat, 99 mg cholesterol, 613 mg sodium, 17 g carbohydrates, 1 g fiber, 32 g protein, 43 mg calcium, 2 mg iron

Game Hens with Herb & Mustard Crust

30 MINUTES

- 2 **Rock Cornish game hens (1 to 1¼ lbs. each)**
- ⅓ **cup coarse-grained Dijon mustard**
- ¼ **cup dry white wine**
- 1 **tablespoon each chopped fresh rosemary and chopped fresh sage (or 1 teaspoon each crumbled dried rosemary and dried sage)**
- 2 **cloves garlic, minced or pressed**
  Rosemary and sage sprigs

1. Reserve game hen necks and giblets for other uses. With poultry shears or a sharp knife, split each hen in half, cutting along backbone and breastbone. Rinse hens and pat dry.

2. Place hens, skin side up, in a shallow 10- by 15-inch baking pan. Bake in lower third of a 500° oven for 10 minutes. Meanwhile, in a small bowl, stir together mustard, wine, chopped rosemary, chopped sage, and garlic.

3. Coat hens with mustard mixture and continue to bake until meat near thighbone is no longer pink; cut to test (about 15 more minutes).

4. Transfer hens to a platter. Garnish with rosemary and sage sprigs.

MAKES 4 SERVINGS.

PER SERVING: 302 calories, 15 g total fat, 4 g saturated fat, 99 mg cholesterol, 568 mg sodium, 1 g carbohydrates, 0 g fiber, 31 g protein, 27 mg calcium, 2 mg iron

me Hens with ngerine-Hoisin Glaze

MINUTES

- 2 **Rock Cornish game hens (1 to 1¼ lbs. *each*)**
- 2 **teaspoons grated tangerine or orange peel**
- 1 **cup fresh tangerine juice (or ¼ cup frozen tangerine juice concentrate, thawed and mixed with ¾ cup water)**
- 1 **tablespoon cornstarch**
- 2 **tablespoons hoisin sauce**
- ¼ **teaspoon crushed red pepper flakes**

Reserve game hen necks nd giblets for other uses. ith poultry shears or a arp knife, split each hen in lf, cutting along backbone nd breastbone. Rinse hens d pat dry.

2. Place hens, skin side up, in a shallow 10- by 15-inch baking pan. Bake in lower third of a 500° oven for 5 minutes. Meanwhile, in a small bowl, stir together tangerine peel, tangerine juice, cornstarch, hoisin sauce, and red pepper flakes.

3. Pour tangerine mixture over hens. Continue to bake, basting twice, until meat near thighbone is no longer pink; cut to test (about 20 more minutes).

4. Transfer hens to a platter. Skim fat from sauce; pour sauce into a small serving bowl. Offer sauce to spoon over hens.

MAKES 4 SERVINGS.

PER SERVING: 321 calories, 15 g total fat, 4 g saturated fat, 99 mg cholesterol, 211 mg sodium, 12 g carbohydrates, 0 g fiber, 31 g protein, 29 mg calcium, 2 mg iron

Roasted Honey-Wine Game Hens with New Potatoes

30 MINUTES

Pictured on Page 2

- 2 **Rock Cornish game hens (1 to 1¼ lbs. *each*)**
- 12 **small red thin-skinned potatoes (*each* about 2 inches in diameter), scrubbed and cut into quarters**
- ¼ **cup dry white wine or apple juice**
- 2 **tablespoons Dijon mustard**
- 2 **tablespoons honey**
- 1 **tablespoon chopped fresh thyme or 1 teaspoon dried thyme**
  Thyme sprigs
  Salt and pepper

1. Reserve game hen necks and giblets for other uses. With poultry shears or a sharp knife, split each hen in half, cutting along backbone and breastbone. Rinse hens and pat dry.

2. Place hens, skin side up, in a shallow 10- by 15-inch baking pan; scatter potatoes, cut side down, around hens. Bake in lower third of a 500° oven for 10 minutes. Meanwhile, in a small bowl, stir together wine, mustard, honey, and chopped thyme.

3. Baste hens liberally with mustard mixture. Continue to bake, basting liberally about every 5 minutes, until potatoes are tender when pierced and meat near thighbone is no longer pink; cut to test (about 15 more minutes).

4. To serve, place one hen half and a fourth of the potatoes on each of 4 individual plates; garnish with thyme sprigs. Season to taste with salt and pepper.

MAKES 4 SERVINGS.

PER SERVING: 457 calories, 16 g total fat, 4 g saturated fat, 99 mg cholesterol, 287 mg sodium, 40 g carbohydrates, 3 g fiber, 34 g protein, 26 mg calcium, 3 mg iron

roiled Lemon-Plum Game Hens

O MINUTES

- 2 **Rock Cornish game hens (1 to 1¼ lbs. *each*)**
- ½ **cup prepared Chinese plum sauce**
- 2 **tablespoons seasoned rice vinegar**
- ½ **teaspoons grated lemon peel**
- ¼ **teaspoon ground ginger**
  Lemon slices

1. Reserve game hen necks and giblets for other uses. With poultry shears or a sharp knife, split each hen in half, cutting along backbone and breastbone. Rinse hens and pat dry.

2. Place hens, skin side down, on a lightly oiled rack in a foil-lined 12- by 15-inch broiler pan. Broil 6 inches below heat until well browned (about 12 minutes). Meanwhile, in a small bowl, stir together plum sauce, vinegar, lemon peel, and ginger.

3. Turn hens skin side up and brush generously with plum glaze. Continue to broil until meat near thighbone is no longer pink; cut to test (about 10 more minutes). Brush with remaining glaze; broil just until glaze begins to brown (about 2 minutes).

4. Transfer hens to a platter and garnish with lemon slices.

MAKES 4 SERVINGS.

PER SERVING: 315 calories, 15 g total fat, 4 g saturated fat, 99 mg cholesterol, 396 mg sodium, 12 g carbohydrates, 0 g fiber, 31 g protein, 103 mg calcium, 2 mg iron

Roasted Chicken, Tomato & Spinach Pizzas

25 MINUTES

Ever-popular pizza appears in a new guise here—as a cool chicken salad on a hot, cheesy crust. The recipe takes advantage of easy-to-find shortcut ingredients. A rotisserie chicken from your deli is a quick source of moist, succulent meat, and frozen bread dough lets you make the pizza crust fast.

2 cups bite-size pieces rotisserie chicken

12 ounces firm-ripe pear-shaped (Roma-type) tomatoes, diced

3 cups firmly packed packaged triple-washed spinach, cut into slivers

⅓ cup prepared pesto

2 tablespoons seasoned rice vinegar
Salt

1 loaf (about 1 lb.) frozen white bread dough, thawed

1 tablespoon yellow cornmeal or polenta

1 to 2 cups (4 to 8 oz.) shredded mozzarella cheese

1. In a large bowl, combine chicken, tomatoes, spinach, pesto, and vinegar. Toss to mix; season to taste with salt. Set aside.

2. Divide bread dough into 4 equal pieces. On a lightly floured board, roll each piece out to a 7- to 8-inch round. Place dough rounds on 2 oiled, cornmeal-dusted 12- by 15-inch baking sheets. Bake in a 500° oven until dough looks dry and is covered with large brown spots (6 to 8 minutes); switch positions of baking sheets halfway through baking time.

3. Sprinkle crusts equally with cheese and continue to bake until cheese is melted (about 2 more minutes). Place one crust on each of 4 individual plates; top equally with chicken mixture.

MAKES 4 SERVINGS.

PER SERVING: 702 calories, 30 g total fat, 10 g saturated fat, 104 mg cholesterol, 1,089 mg sodium, 66 g carbohydrates, 4 g fiber, 41 g protein, 350 mg calcium, 5 mg iron

Roasted Chicken, Tomato & Spinach Pizzas

Turkey Cutlets with Olives & Dried Tomatoes

20 MINUTES

Salty oil-cured olives and dried tomatoes make a robust, colorful topping for oven-fried turkey cutlets. Sautéed zucchini sprinkled generously with freshly grated Parmesan cheese is a perfect partner for the crisp-crusted cutlets.

1 **cup seasoned stuffing mix (coarse-crumb style)**

1 **egg**

2 **tablespoons water**

1¼ **pounds turkey breast cutlets or slices (*each* about ⅜ inch thick)**

2 **tablespoons butter or margarine, melted**

¼ **cup oil-packed dried tomatoes**

¼ **cup chopped oil-cured black ripe olives**

Lemon wedges

1. Put stuffing mix in a heavy-duty plastic bag; seal bag, then use a rolling pin to crush stuffing into evenly coarse crumbs. Pour crumbs into a shallow pan. In another shallow pan, beat egg with water.

2. Rinse turkey and pat dry. Turn each turkey slice in egg mixture to coat; drain briefly. Then turn in crumbs, pressing firmly to coat well all over.

3. Place turkey in a single layer in a lightly oiled shallow 10- by 15-inch baking pan. Drizzle evenly with butter. Bake in a 500° oven until coating is golden brown and meat is no longer pink in thickest part; cut to test (about 10 minutes). Transfer to a platter.

4. While turkey is baking, drain tomatoes, reserving 1 tablespoon of the oil. Chop tomatoes and place in a small nonstick frying pan along with olives and reserved tomato oil. Cook over medium-low heat, stirring occasionally, for about 5 minutes to allow flavors to blend.

5. To serve, top turkey cutlets with olive-tomato mixture. Offer lemon wedges to season individual servings to taste.

MAKES 4 SERVINGS.

PER SERVING: 435 calories, 24 g total fat, 6 g saturated fat, 157 mg cholesterol, 647 mg sodium, 16 g carbohydrates, 2 g fiber, 39 g protein, 49 mg calcium, 3 mg iron

Chicken, Corn & Chile Polenta with Bacon

5 TO 30 MINUTES

Hearty with shredded chicken, corn, and chiles, this microwave-cooked polenta casserole is a meal in itself. Top with crumbled bacon; offer salsa on the side. A salad of greens and shredded red cabbage is a bright, crisp companion.

2 slices bacon

1 medium-size onion (about 6 oz.), chopped

1 package (about 10 oz.) frozen corn kernels, thawed

1 can (about 4 oz.) diced green chiles

¼ cup minced cilantro

3 to 3½ cups fat-free reduced-sodium chicken broth

1½ cups polenta or yellow cornmeal

2 cups shredded cooked chicken

½ cup shredded sharp Cheddar cheese

Salsa

1. Place bacon in a shallow 2- to 2½-quart microwave-safe casserole. Microwave on HIGH (100%), uncovered, for 2 to 3 minutes or until bacon is crisp and browned. Remove bacon from casserole and drain on paper towels.

2. To bacon drippings in casserole, add onion, corn, and chiles. Stir to mix. Microwave on HIGH (100%), uncovered, for 3 minutes. Stir in cilantro, 3 cups of the broth, and polenta. Microwave on HIGH (100%), uncovered, for 12 to 15 minutes or until liquid has been absorbed and mixture is thick but still creamy; stir every 5 minutes. If mixture gets too thick to stir, mix in remaining ½ cup broth. About 2 minutes before polenta is done, stir in chicken; then top with cheese (do not stir cheese into polenta).

3. Crumble bacon over polenta. Offer salsa to add to taste.

MAKES 4 SERVINGS.

PER SERVING: 527 calories, 16 g total fat, 6 g saturated fat, 83 mg cholesterol, 843 mg sodium, 61 g carbohydrates, 5 g fiber, 34 g protein, 130 mg calcium, 4 mg iron

Turkey Saltimbocca

5 MINUTES

Tasting every bit as good as its classic counterpart, this Italian-inspired dish calls for turkey cutlets instead of the traditional veal—for a fraction of the price. Serve with buttered orzo, a salad of arugula and radicchio tossed with balsamic vinaigrette, and a crisp Pinot Grigio.

6 turkey breast cutlets or slices (about 1 lb. *total*), *each* about ¼ inch thick

Pepper

6 thin slices prosciutto (about 1½ oz. *total*)

2 ounces Parmesan cheese, cut into 6 equal strips

1 tablespoon olive oil

⅔ cup fat-free reduced-sodium chicken broth

⅓ cup dry white wine

½ teaspoon dried sage

1 tablespoon Dijon mustard

1. Rinse turkey and pat dry. Place each piece between 2 sheets of plastic wrap. With a heavy, flat-sided mallet, pound meat firmly but gently to a thickness of about ⅛ inch. Lightly sprinkle each slice with pepper; then lay a piece of prosciutto on each slice and top with a strip of cheese. Roll up turkey to enclose filling; secure each roll with a wooden pick, if necessary.

2. Heat oil in a wide nonstick frying pan over medium-high heat. Add turkey rolls and cook, turning occasionally, until browned on all sides (about 10 minutes). Add broth, wine, sage, and mustard to pan. Cover and cook for 2 minutes.

3. Lift turkey rolls from pan and transfer to a platter; keep warm. Bring sauce to a boil over high heat; then boil, uncovered, until large, shiny bubbles form (about 3 minutes). Pour over turkey.

MAKES 4 SERVINGS.

PER SERVING: 265 calories, 10 g total fat, 4 g saturated fat, 90 mg cholesterol, 701 mg sodium, 1 g carbohydrates, 0 g fiber, 37 g protein, 210 mg calcium, 2 mg iron

Turkey & Pancetta Club with Marinated Tomatoes

15 MINUTES

Thin turkey cutlets are topped with Italian pancetta and slipped under the broiler—then served on sourdough toast with mustard, mayonnaise, and a colorful two-tone tomato salad.

1 *each* small red and yellow tomato (6 to 8 oz. *total*), sliced ¼ inch thick

1 tablespoon balsamic or red wine vinegar

2 teaspoons olive oil

2 tablespoons minced shallots

⅛ teaspoon pepper

4 turkey breast cutlets or slices (about 12 oz. *total*), *each* about ⅜ inch thick

4 thin slices pancetta (about 1½ oz. *total*)

8 slices sourdough bread, toasted

Leaf lettuce leaves, rinsed and crisped

Mayonnaise and Dijon mustard

1. Place tomatoes in a shallow bowl. In a small bowl, stir together vinegar, oil, shallots, and pepper; pour over tomatoes. Set aside.

2. Rinse turkey, pat dry, and place on a rack in a 12- by 15-inch broiler pan; top each turkey slice with a slice of pancetta. Broil 6 inches below heat until pancetta is browned and turkey is no longer pink in thickest part; cut to test (about 5 minutes).

3. To assemble each sandwich, place a pancetta-topped turkey slice on a slice of toast; top with a fourth of the tomatoes and their dressing, then add lettuce, mayonnaise, and mustard to taste. Cover with another slice of toast.

MAKES 4 SERVINGS.

PER SERVING: 320 calories, 8 g total fat, 2 g saturated fat, 59 mg cholesterol, 503 mg sodium, 32 g carbohydrates, 2 g fiber, 28 g protein, 55 mg calcium, 3 mg iron

Turkey, Potatoes & Asparagus with Lemon-Thyme Aïoli

25 TO 30 MINUTES

Colorful and fresh, this complete meal is perfect for family or guests. Lemon and thyme season both the turkey tenderloins and the garlicky aïoli you serve alongside.

2 tablespoons olive oil

2 tablespoons lemon juice

2 teaspoons minced fresh thyme or 1 teaspoon dried thyme

2 turkey breast tenderloins (about 1 lb. *total*), cut in half crosswise

10 small red thin-skinned potatoes (*each* about 2 inches in diameter), scrubbed and cut into ¼-inch-thick slices

1 teaspoon dried rosemary

1 pound asparagus

½ cup mayonnaise

½ teaspoon grated lemon peel

2 cloves garlic, minced or pressed

1. In a shallow dish, stir together 1 tablespoon of the oil, 1 tablespoon of the lemon juice, and half the fresh or dried thyme.

2. Turn turkey in lemon-thyme mixture to coat (reserve remaining mixture). Arrange turkey in a 9- by 13-inch baking pan. Bake in upper third of a 500° oven until meat in thickest part is no longer pink; cut to test (18 to 20 min-

utes). Halfway through cooking time, baste with remaining lemon-thyme mixture.

3. Meanwhile, place potatoes in an oiled shallow 10- by 15-inch baking pan; brush with remaining 1 tablespoon oil and sprinkle with rosemary. Bake on next-to-lowest rack of a 500° oven until soft when pierced (20 minutes).

4. Once turkey and potatoes are in the oven, bring 1 inch of water to a boil in a wide frying pan over high heat. Snap off and discard tough ends of asparagus; add asparagus to water and cook, uncovered, until just tender when pierced (3 to 5 minutes). Drain, immerse in ice water until cool, and drain. Set aside.

5. In a small bowl, mix mayonnaise, lemon peel, garlic, remaining 1 tablespoon lemon juice, and remaining fresh or dried thyme. Arrange turkey and potatoes on a platter alongside asparagus; offer aïoli to spoon over foods.

MAKES 4 SERVINGS.

PER SERVING: 533 calories, 31 g total fat, 5 g saturated fat, 87 mg cholesterol, 227 mg sodium, 31 g carbohydrates, 3 g fiber, 34 g protein, 50 mg calcium, 4 mg iron

Stir-fried Turkey Fajitas

25 MINUTES

Sizzling strips of marinated turkey, green bell pepper, and red onion fill warmed flour tortillas in this light, lean entrée. For a rich finishing touch, embellish the fajitas with guacamole (purchased or homemade) and sour cream.

¼ cup lime juice

1 tablespoon balsamic or red wine vinegar

1 clove garlic, minced or pressed

½ teaspoon ground coriander

½ teaspoon ground cumin

½ teaspoon honey

1 pound turkey breast strips; or 1 pound turkey breast tenderloins, cut into ½- by 2-inch strips

1 tablespoon olive oil

1 large green bell pepper (about 8 oz.), seeded and cut into thin strips

1 very large red onion (about 12 oz.), thinly sliced

4 to 6 flour tortillas (*each* 7 to 9 inches in diameter)

Lime wedges

Guacamole

Sour cream

1. In a large bowl, stir together lime juice, vinegar, garlic, coriander, cumin, and honey. Add turkey and stir to coat. Set aside.

2. Heat 2 teaspoons of the oil in a wide nonstick frying pan or wok over medium-high heat. Add bell pepper and onion; cook, stirring often, until vegetables are lightly browned (5 to 7 minutes). Remove vegetables from pan with a slotted spoon and keep warm.

3. Heat remaining 1 teaspoon oil in pan over medium-high heat. Lift turkey from marinade and drain briefly (reserve marinade). Add turkey to pan and cook, stirring often, until no longer pink in center; cut to test (2 to 3 minutes). Add marinade and bring to a boil; then return vegetables to pan and mix gently. Spoon mixture onto a platter.

4. Just before turkey is done, wrap tortillas in a cloth towel and microwave on HIGH (100%) for about 1½ minutes or until heated through. To serve, offer tortillas and lime wedges alongside turkey mixture. Fill tortillas with turkey mixture; add a squeeze of lime, guacamole, and sour cream. Fold to enclose and eat out of hand.

MAKES 4 TO 6 SERVINGS.

PER SERVING: 283 calories, 6 g total fat, 1 g saturated fat, 56 mg cholesterol, 222 mg sodium, 30 g carbohydrates, 3 g fiber, 27 g protein, 81 mg calcium, 3 mg iron

Roasted Thai Turkey Nuggets

20 TO 25 MINUTES

The peppery rub that coats these tender chunks of turkey breast delivers quite a punch—but the spicy-sweet relish manages to tame the heat just enough. To cut down on preparation time, look for whole peeled cloves of garlic in the produce section of your supermarket.

1 pound turkey breast tenderloins

3 tablespoons minced cilantro

2 teaspoons coarsely ground pepper

8 cloves garlic, minced or pressed

¼ teaspoon ground ginger

⅓ cup canned tomato sauce

1 tablespoon firmly packed brown sugar

1 tablespoon cider vinegar or distilled white vinegar

½ cup raisins

1. Rinse turkey and pat dry. Cut each tenderloin in half lengthwise, trimming away the white tendon; cut each half crosswise into 10 equal pieces. In a small bowl, combine cilantro, pepper, and 6 cloves of the garlic; rub all over turkey pieces. Place pieces well apart in a lightly oiled shallow 10- by 15-inch baking pan. Bake in a 500° oven until meat is lightly browned on outside and no longer pink in thickest part; cut to test (10 to 12 minutes).

2. Meanwhile, in a food processor or blender, whirl remaining 2 cloves garlic, ginger, tomato sauce, sugar, vinegar, and raisins until raisins are chopped. Serve sauce with turkey.

MAKES 4 SERVINGS.

PER SERVING: 222 calories, 2 g total fat, 0 g saturated fat, 70 mg cholesterol, 183 mg sodium, 22 g carbohydrates, 2 g fiber, 29 g protein, 43 mg calcium, 2 mg iron

Grilled Turkey-Pesto Burgers with Dried Tomato Mayonnaise

25 MINUTES

Many of the small bakeries producing artisan-style breads now supply grocery stores with a wonderful array of Italian country loaves. One such bread is ciabatta, a flat, crusty loaf with a chewy interior; it's perfect with these flavorful grilled turkey burgers.

1 pound lean ground turkey

1 large egg white

1 medium-size onion (about 6 oz.), finely chopped

¾ cup soft bread crumbs

¼ cup prepared pesto

¼ cup mayonnaise

2 tablespoons drained, minced oil-packed dried tomatoes

1 loaf (12 to 16 oz.) ciabatta, francese, or pane pugliese bread, cut crosswise into 4 equal pieces and split

4 thin slices provolone cheese (about ½ oz. *each*), optional

Leaf lettuce leaves, rinsed and crisped

1. In a large bowl, combine turkey, egg white, onion, bread crumbs, and pesto. Mix lightly. Shape into 4 equal patties, each about 4 inches wide.

2. Arrange patties on a greased grill 4 to 6 inches above a solid bed of hot coals (you can hold your hand at grill level for only 2 to 3 seconds) or over high heat on a gas grill. Close lid on gas grill. Cook, turning once, until patties are no longer pink in center; cut to test (about 10 minutes).

3. Meanwhile, in a small bowl, stir together mayonnaise and tomatoes; set aside. When turkey patties are almost done, toast bread, cut sides down, on grill for 1 to 2 minutes. If desired, top each patty with a piece of cheese at this time.

4. To serve, spread cut sides of bread with mayonnaise mixture. Then assemble 4 sandwiches, filling each with a turkey patty and a few lettuce leaves.

MAKES 4 SERVINGS.

PER SERVING: 722 calories, 37 g total fat, 7 g saturated fat, 68 mg cholesterol, 921 mg sodium, 63 g carbohydrates, 4 g fiber, 33 g protein, 155 mg calcium, 5 mg iron

Turkey Paella

Turkey Paella

25 MINUTES

Saffron-tinted rice laden with chunks of turkey sausage, tomatoes, and artichokes makes a hearty one-dish meal for family or guests. Serve this lively entrée with a crisp green salad and a mellow Spanish red wine.

1 pound turkey Italian sausage

1 tablespoon olive oil (if needed)

1 large onion (about 10 oz.), chopped

2 cloves garlic, minced or pressed

1 can (about 14½ oz.) fat-free reduced-sodium chicken broth

1 can (about 14½ oz.) diced tomatoes with onions and mild chiles

⅛ to ¼ teaspoon saffron threads

1 package (about 9 oz.) frozen artichoke hearts, thawed and drained

¼ cup minced parsley

1 cup quick-cooking white rice

Lemon wedges

1. Remove casings from sausage and crumble meat into a wide nonstick frying pan. Cook over medium-high heat until sausage is browned (7 to 9 minutes), stirring sausage to break it into small chunks. Remove sausage from pan with a slotted spoon; set aside. Discard all but 1 tablespoon of the drippings from pan. (If there are no drippings, add the oil instead.)

2. To pan, add onion and garlic. Cook, stirring often, until onion is lightly browned (about 5 minutes). If pan appears dry, stir in water, 1 tablespoon at a time. Stir in broth, tomatoes and their liquid, saffron, artichokes, and parsley; then return sausage to pan. Bring to a boil; then reduce heat and simmer for 5 minutes. Add rice; cover and simmer until liquid has been absorbed and rice is tender to bite (about 5 more minutes). Garnish with lemon wedges.

MAKES 4 TO 6 SERVINGS.

PER SERVING: 302 calories, 12 g total fat, 4 g saturated fat, 57 mg cholesterol, 1,112 mg sodium, 28 g carbohydrates, 6 g fiber, 21 g protein, 60 mg calcium, 3 mg iron

Turkey Sausage & Mushroom Tortilla Pizzas

25 MINUTES

While the sausage topping cooks, you can brush the tortillas with oil and prepare the vegetables. To save time, take advantage of prepared ingredients: use ready-sliced mushrooms and packaged shredded cheese. Serve these great-tasting pizzas with icy cold beer.

- 12 **ounces turkey Italian sausage**
- 1 **teaspoon olive oil (if needed)**
- 1 **clove garlic, minced or pressed**
- ½ **cup canned tomato sauce**
- ¼ **teaspoon dried basil**
- ¼ **teaspoon dried oregano**
- 4 **flour tortillas (***each* **7 to 9 inches in diameter)**
- **Olive oil**
- ½ **large green bell pepper, seeded and cut into thin strips**
- 1½ **cups sliced mushrooms**
- 1 **small onion (about 4 oz.), chopped**
- 1 **can (about 2¼ oz.) sliced ripe olives, drained**
- 1 **cup (about 4 oz.) shredded jack cheese**
- ¼ **cup grated Parmesan cheese**

1. Remove casings from sausage and crumble meat into a wide nonstick frying pan. Cook over medium-high heat until sausage is browned (7 to 9 minutes), stirring sausage to break it into small chunks. Spoon off and discard all but 1 teaspoon of the drippings from pan. (If there are no drippings, add the 1 teaspoon oil instead.) Add garlic, tomato sauce, basil, and oregano; bring to a boil. Then reduce heat and simmer, uncovered, stirring often, until almost all liquid has evaporated (about 5 minutes).

2. Meanwhile, lightly brush both sides of each tortilla with oil (make sure to oil edges). Arrange tortillas well apart on two 12- by 15-inch baking sheets.

3. Distribute sausage mixture equally over tortillas; then sprinkle evenly with bell pepper, mushrooms, onion, and olives. Sprinkle with jack and Parmesan cheeses.

4. Bake in a 475° oven until tortillas are crisp and golden brown and cheese is melted (6 to 8 minutes); switch positions of baking sheets halfway through baking time.

MAKES 4 SERVINGS.

PER SERVING: 468 calories, 26 g total fat, 11 g saturated fat, 87 mg cholesterol, 1,282 mg sodium, 30 g carbohydrates, 4 g fiber, 29 g protein, 386 mg calcium, 4 mg iron

Minced Turkey in Lettuce

25 MINUTES

This lean, soy- and ginger-seasoned stir-fry of ground turkey and Asian vegetables goes together very quickly, especially if you use a food processor to mince the vegetables. Spoon the spicy mixture into lettuce cups and season with a little hoisin sauce, if desired.

2 teaspoons cornstarch

1 tablespoon dry sherry

2 tablespoons soy sauce

2 tablespoons water

½ teaspoon sugar

3 medium-size shiitake or large regular mushrooms (*each* about 2 inches in diameter), stems trimmed

1 can (about 8 oz.) sliced bamboo shoots, drained

1 can (about 8 oz.) water chestnuts, drained

6 green onions, cut into 2-inch lengths

1½ teaspoons Oriental sesame oil

1½ teaspoons vegetable oil

2 cloves garlic, minced or pressed

1½ teaspoons grated fresh ginger

¼ teaspoon crushed red pepper flakes

1 pound lean ground turkey

½ cup frozen tiny peas, thawed

12 large butter lettuce leaves, rinsed and crisped

Hoisin sauce (optional)

1. In a small bowl, stir together cornstarch, sherry, soy sauce, water, and sugar; set aside.

2. In a food processor, combine mushrooms, bamboo shoots, water chestnuts, and onions; whirl until minced. Or mince ingredients with a sharp knife. Set aside.

3. Heat sesame oil and vegetable oil in a wide nonstick frying pan over medium-high heat. Add garlic, ginger, and red pepper flakes; stir once. Crumble in turkey and cook, stirring often, until no longer pink (3 to 5 minutes). Remove turkey mixture from pan and set aside.

4. Add minced vegetable mixture to pan; cook, stirring often, for 3 minutes. Return turkey mixture to pan along with peas. Stir in soy mixture; cook, stirring, until sauce is thickened (about 1 more minute).

5. To serve, lightly coat center of a lettuce leaf with hoisin sauce, if desired; spoon some of the turkey mixture on top, then roll up and eat out of hand.

MAKES 6 SERVINGS.

PER SERVING: 177 calories, 8 g total fat, 2 g saturated fat, 55 mg cholesterol, 443 mg sodium, 10 g carbohydrates, 3 g fiber, 16 g protein, 29 mg calcium, 2 mg iron

Turkey & Stuffing Croquettes

20 MINUTES

After Thanksgiving—or at any other time when you have a lot of leftover turkey on hand—take advantage of the cooked meat to prepare these crusty pan-browned croquettes. Serve with cranberry sauce and buttered green beans.

3 cups finely chopped cooked turkey

1 cup seasoned stuffing mix (coarse-crumb style)

1 medium-size onion (about 6 oz.), finely chopped

1 cup finely chopped celery

2 large egg whites

2 tablespoons minced parsley

¼ cup grated Parmesan cheese

¼ teaspoon pepper

¾ cup fat-free reduced-sodium chicken broth

1 tablespoon olive oil

Prepared cranberry sauce or relish

1. In a large bowl, combine turkey, stuffing mix, onion, celery, egg whites, parsley, cheese, pepper, and broth. Mix until very well blended. Shape mixture into 8 equal-size logs, each about 3½ inches long, packing turkey mixture firmly together.

2. Heat oil in a wide nonstick frying pan over medium-high heat. Add turkey croquettes and cook, turning croquettes gently to keep them from breaking apart, until well browned on all sides (8 to 10 minutes).

3. To serve, transfer croquettes to a platter. Offer cranberry sauce to add to taste.

MAKES 4 SERVINGS.

PER SERVING: 319 calories, 10 g total fat, 3 g saturated fat, 85 mg cholesterol, 532 mg sodium, 16 g carbohydrates, 2 g fiber, 38 g protein, 133 mg calcium, 3 mg iron

Turkey & Stuffing Croquettes

Turkey-Avocado Tostadas with Blue Cheese

15 TO 20 MINUTES

A blue cheese vinaigrette seasons chunks of cooked turkey in this mouthwatering variation on the popular Mexican dish. Top crisp-baked tortillas with hot refried beans and packaged prewashed salad mix; then add the turkey mixture, diced tomatoes, and cool slices of avocado.

2 cups bite-size pieces cooked turkey

3 tablespoons balsamic or red wine vinegar

1½ tablespoons olive oil

⅓ cup crumbled blue-veined cheese

¼ cup thinly sliced green onions

⅛ teaspoon pepper

4 flour tortillas (*each* 7 to 9 inches in diameter)

1 can (about 14½ oz.) fat-free refried beans

4 cups packaged salad mix (including iceberg lettuce, red cabbage, and carrots)

1 cup diced tomatoes

2 medium-size firm-ripe avocados (about 12 oz. *total*), pitted, peeled, and sliced

1. In a bowl, combine turkey, vinegar, 1 tablespoon of the oil, cheese, onions, and pepper. Set aside.

2. Lightly brush both sides of each tortilla with remaining 1½ teaspoons oil (make sure to oil edges). Arrange tortillas well apart on two 12-by 15-inch baking sheets. Bake in a 475° oven until crisp and golden brown (about 5 minutes; switch positions of baking sheets halfway throught baking time).

3. Meanwhile, place beans in a microwave-safe bowl; cover lightly and microwave on HIGH (100%) for 3 minutes or until heated through, stirring once.

4. To assemble tostadas, set one hot tortilla on each individual plate. Spread tortillas equally with heated beans, then top equally with salad mix, turkey mixture, tomatoes, and avocado slices.

MAKES 4 SERVINGS.

PER SERVING: 528 calories, 24 g total fat, 6 g saturated fat, 62 mg cholesterol, 726 mg sodium, 45 g carbohydrates, 9 g fiber, 34 g protein, 197 mg calcium, 6 mg iron

Turkey-Avocado Tostadas with Blue Cheese

Chapter Five

SEAFOOD

Broiled Trout Dijonnaise

20 MINUTES

Perfectly simple, this classic French entrée is an ideal quick supper, good for body and soul. Serve it with rice, sautéed zucchini, and crusty rolls.

- 2 tablespoons butter or margarine, melted
- 1 tablespoon dry white wine
- 1 tablespoon Dijon mustard
- ¼ teaspoon dried tarragon
- 4 whole trout (about 8 oz. *each*), gutted (and heads removed, if desired)

    Salt

    Lemon wedges

1. In a small bowl, stir together butter, wine, mustard, and tarragon. Set aside.

2. Rinse fish and pat dry. Sprinkle lightly with salt. Brush fish inside and out with butter mixture, using about half the mixture. Place fish on a rack in a broiler pan. Broil about 4 inches below heat, turning once and brushing with remaining butter mixture after turning, until just opaque but still moist in thickest part; cut to test (8 to 10 minutes). Offer lemon wedges to season fish to taste.

MAKES 4 SERVINGS.

PER SERVING: 222 calories, 13 g total fat, 5 g saturated fat, 80 mg cholesterol, 207 mg sodium, 0 g carbohydrates, 0 g fiber, 23 g protein, 51 mg calcium, 2 mg iron

Poached Tilapia with Lemon & Basil

20 MINUTES

This is a beautiful dish—elegant and bright, with clean, refreshing flavors. Serve with a tomato salad, sourdough bread, and iced tea.

- ¼ cup fat-free reduced-sodium chicken broth
- 3 tablespoons orange juice
- 2 tablespoons lemon juice
- 2 tablespoons fruity extra-virgin olive oil
- 1½ to 1¾ pounds tilapia or red snapper fillets

    About 8 large fresh basil leaves

- 1 tablespoon shredded lemon peel

1. In a wide frying pan, combine broth, orange juice, lemon juice, and oil. Cover and bring to a boil over high heat. Rinse and drain fish; arrange in pan in a single layer. Reduce heat, cover, and simmer gently for 4 minutes.

2. Lay 1 or 2 basil leaves diagonally across each fillet. Cover and continue to simmer until fish is just opaque but still moist in thickest part; cut to test (1 to 2 more minutes). Using a slotted spatula, transfer fish to individual plates; keep warm.

3. Bring cooking liquid to a boil over high heat; then boil, uncovered, until reduced to about ¼ cup (2 to 3 minutes). Spoon sauce over fish and sprinkle with lemon peel.

MAKES 4 SERVINGS.

PER SERVING: 250 calories, 11 g total fat, 1 g saturated fat, 89 mg cholesterol, 133 mg sodium, 2 g carbohydrates, 0 g fiber, 35 g protein, 106 mg calcium, 1 mg iron

Salmon Teriyaki

Salmon Teriyaki

25 MINUTES

Thick salmon steaks with teriyaki glaze are especially good with short-grain rice and fresh spinach in just about any form—steamed, sautéed, or served raw in a salad. You might pour chilled sake to sip with the meal.

   6 tablespoons soy sauce

   3 tablespoons firmly packed brown sugar

   1 teaspoon minced fresh ginger

   1 clove garlic, minced or pressed

   ½ teaspoon Oriental sesame oil

   4 salmon steaks (about 8 oz. *each*), *each* about 1 inch thick

1. In a small pan, combine soy sauce, sugar, ginger, garlic, and oil. Cook over medium-high heat, stirring occasionally, until slightly thickened (about 3 minutes). Pour through a fine wire strainer into a small bowl. Set aside.

2. Rinse fish, pat dry, and arrange on a rack in a broiler pan. Broil about 4 inches below heat for 3 minutes; brush generously with teriyaki sauce, then broil for 3 more minutes. Turn fish over and broil for 3 more minutes; again brush generously with teriyaki sauce. Then continue to broil until fish is just opaque but still moist in thickest part; cut to test (about 3 more minutes). Brush with any remaining teriyaki sauce.

MAKES 4 SERVINGS.

PER SERVING: 343 calories, 13 g total fat, 2 g saturated fat, 110 mg cholesterol, 1,635 mg sodium, 13 g carbohydrates, 0 g fiber, 41 g protein, 39 mg calcium, 2 mg iron

Salmon with Citrus-Mint Gremolata

25 MINUTES

Pictured on page 120

This salmon has a marvelously intense flavor, thanks to a vibrant orange-lemon baste and a topping of citrus peels and fresh mint. Keep the side dishes very simple; you might offer hot rice and sugar snap peas. Be sure to use a frying pan with an ovenproof handle.

   ¼ cup chopped fresh mint

   1 tablespoon grated orange peel

   1 tablespoon grated lemon peel

   ½ cup frozen orange juice concentrate, thawed

   ¼ cup lemon juice

   4 salmon fillets with skin (6 to 7 oz. *each*), *each* 1 to 1¼ inches thick

   1 tablespoon butter or margarine

   Mint sprigs (optional)

1. Mince together the ¼ cup mint, orange peel, and lemon peel; set aside. In a small bowl, stir together orange juice concentrate and lemon juice.

2. Rinse fish and pat dry. In a wide frying pan with an ovenproof handle, melt butter over medium-high heat. When butter sizzles, add fish, skin side down. Cook until skin is well browned and crisp (about 7 minutes). Gently slide a spatula under skin of each fillet to release it from pan, but leave fish in pan.

3. Brush fish with about a fourth of the orange juice mixture. Leaving fish in pan, broil it about 4 inches below heat until just opaque but still moist in thickest part; cut to test (3 to 4 minutes).

4. With a wide spatula, transfer fish to individual plates or a platter. Keep warm. Add remaining orange juice mixture to frying pan and stir to blend with pan drippings. Then return pan to broiler just until sauce is bubbly (about 4 minutes). Pour sauce over fish; sprinkle with mint mixture. Garnish with mint sprigs, if desired.

MAKES 4 SERVINGS.

PER SERVING: 351 calories, 15 g total fat, 4 g saturated fat, 109 mg cholesterol, 112 mg sodium, 16 g carbohydrates, 0 g fiber, 38 g protein, 42 mg calcium, 2 mg iron

Red Snapper with Fennel, Mint & Olives

25 MINUTES

Hot fish topped with a cool, minty blend of fresh fennel, red onion, and olives makes a winning summer supper. We call for picholine olives—wonderful green olives from France—but feel free to use any Mediterranean-style green olive. Serve this dish with couscous and a vegetable vinaigrette; offer scoops of raspberry sorbet for dessert.

1 **head fennel (about 4 inches in diameter)**

3 **tablespoons olive oil**

2 **tablespoons minced red onion**

2 **tablespoons finely chopped pitted picholine olives**

1 **tablespoon minced fresh mint**

2 **teaspoons lemon juice**

½ **teaspoon grated lemon peel**

Salt and pepper

1½ **pounds red snapper fillets (*each* about ¾ inch thick)**

1. Rinse fennel. Cut off stalks; trim and discard base and any discolored or bruised parts of fennel head. Then cut fennel into matchstick pieces. In a bowl, combine fennel, 1 tablespoon of the oil, onion, olives, mint, lemon juice, and lemon peel. Season to taste with salt and pepper.

2. Rinse fish and pat dry. Heat remaining 2 tablespoons oil in a wide frying pan over medium-high heat. Add fish, a few pieces at a time (do not crowd pan). Cover and cook, turning once, until just opaque but still moist in thickest part; cut to test (about 8 minutes).

3. With a wide spatula, transfer fish to a platter or individual plates. Top with fennel mixture.

MAKES 4 SERVINGS.

PER SERVING: 280 calories, 13 g total fat, 2 g saturated fat, 63 mg cholesterol, 288 mg sodium, 3 g carbohydrates, 1 g fiber, 36 g protein, 97 mg calcium, 1 mg iron

Red Snapper with Fennel, Mint & Olives

Sole en Papillote with Potatoes & Mint

30 MINUTES

Serve these savory packets of sole and red potatoes with warm French bread and a bowl of lightly buttered tiny peas. You'll find parchment paper in cookware shops, specialty food stores, and many supermarkets.

¼ **cup minced shallots**

3 **tablespoons unsalted butter, melted and cooled**

3 **tablespoons finely shredded fresh mint**

¾ **teaspoon grated lemon peel**

10 **ounces small red thin-skinned potatoes, scrubbed and very thinly sliced**

Salt and pepper

1½ **pounds sole fillets (*each* about ¼ inch thick)**

Vegetable oil

Mint sprigs (optional)

1. In a large bowl, mix shallots, butter, shredded mint, and lemon peel. Add potatoes and toss gently to coat well. Season to taste with salt and pepper. Rinse fish, pat dry, and cut into 4 equal pieces.

2. Cut 4 pieces of parchment paper, each about 4 times wider and 6 inches longer than each portion of fish. On each piece of parchment, coat an area the size of fish with oil, starting 1 inch from a long side (fish will be centered between top and bottom edges of parchment). Place fish on oiled areas and sprinkle with salt and pepper; top each portion of fish with a fourth of the potato mixture.

3. Fold long edge of parchment closest to fish over fish; then roll over several times to enclose fish. With seam side down, double-fold ends of packet, pressing lightly to crease and tucking ends under. Place packets, folded ends underneath, slightly apart on a baking sheet; coat lightly with oil. Bake in a 500° oven until fish is just opaque but still moist in thickest part; cut a tiny slit through parchment into fish to test (about 10 minutes).

4. Immediately transfer packets to individual plates. To serve, cut packets open with a sharp knife or scissors just enough to expose contents without letting juices run out. Garnish with mint sprigs, if desired.

MAKES 4 SERVINGS.

PER SERVING: 316 calories, 13 g total fat, 6 g saturated fat, 105 mg cholesterol, 146 mg sodium, 15 g carbohydrates, 1 g fiber, 34 g protein, 39 mg calcium, 1 mg iron

Oven-fried Fish

There's nothing like a perfectly cooked pie[ce] of fish—and oven-frying offers one of the best ways to get those perfect results. It's an esp[e]cially quick and easy method: just coat the fish with flour, seasoned crumbs, or even pl[a]s sesame seeds, arrange it in a shallow pan with oil or melted butter, and slip it in the oven. C[] recipes call for fillets or small whole fish, but steaks also take well to this technique.

Oven-fried Sea Bass with Caper-Parsley Salsa

20 MINUTES

- ½ **cup olive oil**
- 3 **green onions, sliced**
- 3 **cloves garlic, minced or pressed**
- ¾ **cup chopped parsley**
- 3 **tablespoons drained capers, chopped**
- 2 **tablespoons fat-free reduced-sodium chicken broth**
- 2 **tablespoons chopped fresh basil**
- 1 **tablespoon chopped fresh mint**
- ¼ **teaspoon grated lemon peel**
- **Salt and pepper**
- 1½ **pounds sea bass fillets (*each* about ½ inch thick)**
- **All-purpose flour**

1. Heat ¼ cup of the oil in a small frying pan over medium-low heat. Add onions and garlic; cook, stirring often, until onions are softened (about 3 minutes). Transfer to a bowl and stir in parsley, capers, broth, basil, mint, and lemon peel. Season to taste with salt and pepper. Set aside.

2. Select a shallow baking pan in which fish fillets will just fit without overlapping. Place empty pan in a 500° oven.

3. Rinse fish, pat dry, and sprinkle with salt and pepper. Coat each piece with flour; shake off excess.

4. Remove pan from oven and add remaining ¼ cup oil; swirl pan to coat with oil. Turn fish in oil to coat both sides. Return pan to oven and bake until fish is just opaque but still moist in thickest part; cut to test (4 to 6 minutes). Serve with caper-parsley salsa.

MAKES 4 SERVINGS.

PER SERVING: 441 calories, 31 g total fat, 5 g saturated fat, 70 mg cholesterol, 425 mg sodium, 8 g carbohydrates, 1 g fiber, 33 g protein, 49 mg calcium, 2 mg iron

Pistachio-crusted Fish Fillets

25 MINUTES

- ½ **cup shelled salted pistachio nuts, finely chopped**
- ⅓ **cup fine dry bread crumbs**
- ¼ **cup minced parsley**
- ½ **teaspoon pepper**
- 1 **large egg**
- 1 **pound boneless, skinless white-fleshed fish fillets, such as sole or orange roughy**
- ¼ **cup butter or margarine**
- 2 **green onions, thinly sliced**
- 1 **tablespoon drained capers**
- **Lime or lemon wedges**
- **Salt**

1. On a sheet of wax paper or foil, mix pistachios, bread crumbs, parsley, and pepper. In a shallow pan, beat egg to blend.

2. Rinse fish and pat dry. [] fillets, one at a time, in eg[g] coat; drain briefly, then t[] in pistachio mixture to c[] well, pressing fillets into m[ix]ture. Arrange fillets v[] apart in a greased shallow [] by 15-inch baking pan.

3. Melt butter in a small [] ing pan over medium he[] Add onions and capers; co[] stirring, just until onions t[] a brighter green. Hold [] onions and capers back wit[] spoon, pour butter eve[] over fish.

4. Bake in a 450° oven u[] fish is just opaque but s[] moist in thickest part; cut[] test (about 10 minutes). W[] a wide spatula, transfer f[] to individual plates; [] equally with onion mixtu[] Offer lime wedges and salt[] season fish to taste.

MAKES 4 SERVINGS.

PER SERVING: 357 calories, 22 g total fat, 9 g saturated fat, 139 mg cholesterol, 469 mg sodium, 12 g carbohydrates, 1 g fiber, 28 g protein, 83 mg calci[um] 3 mg iron

en-fried Sand Dabs
h Basil-Chili Butter

MINUTES

- tablespoons butter or margarine, at room temperature
- teaspoon chili powder
- tablespoon minced fresh basil or 1 teaspoon dried basil
- whole sand dabs (about 8 oz. *each*), gutted (and heads removed, if desired); or 1 pound sole fillets (*each* about ¼ inch thick)
- Salt and pepper
- All-purpose flour
- tablespoons vegetable oil

In a small bowl, beat cup of the butter with li powder and basil until oothly blended. Set aside.

2. Select a shallow baking pan in which fish fillets will just fit without overlapping. Place empty pan in a 500° oven.

3. Rinse fish, pat dry, and sprinkle with salt and pepper. Coat each piece with flour; shake off excess.

4. Remove pan from oven. Add oil and remaining 2 tablespoons butter; swirl pan until butter is melted. Turn fish in butter mixture to coat both sides. Return pan to oven and bake until fish is just opaque but still moist in thickest part; cut to test (about 4 minutes). Serve with basil-chili butter.

MAKES 4 SERVINGS.

PER SERVING WITH BASIL-CHILI BUTTER: 332 calories, 26 g total fat, 12 g saturated fat, 101 mg cholesterol, 274 mg sodium, 3 g carbohydrates, 0 g fiber, 22 g protein, 30 mg calcium, 1 mg iron

man Sole

MINUTES

- pounds sole fillets (*each* about ¼ inch thick)
- Salt and pepper
- All-purpose flour
- cup butter or margarine (or 2 tablespoons butter or margarine and 2 tablespoons olive oil)

Select a shallow baking n in which fish fillets will t fit without overlapping. ace empty pan in a 500° en.

2. Rinse fish, pat dry, and sprinkle with salt and pepper. Coat each piece with flour; shake off excess.

3. Remove pan from oven and add butter; swirl pan until butter is melted. Turn fish in butter to coat both sides. Then return pan to oven and bake until fish is just opaque but still moist in thickest part; cut to test (about 4 minutes).

MAKES 4 SERVINGS.

PER SERVING: 278 calories, 14 g total fat, 8 g saturated fat, 113 mg cholesterol, 255 mg sodium, 4 g carbohydrates, 0 g fiber, 33 g protein, 35 mg calcium, 1 mg iron

Oven-fried Orange Roughy with Sesame Seeds

20 MINUTES

- 1 large egg white
- ⅓ cup sesame seeds
- 4 boneless, skinless orange roughy fillets (6 to 8 oz. *each*)
- 2 tablespoons vegetable oil
- Lemon wedges
- Soy sauce

1. In a shallow pan, beat egg white until slightly frothy. Spread sesame seeds in another shallow pan.

2. Place a shallow 10- by 15-inch baking pan in a 500° oven and heat for about 5 minutes.

3. Meanwhile, rinse fish and pat dry. Dip fillets on one side only in egg white; drain briefly. Then press egg-moistened side in sesame seeds to coat generously. Place fillets, seed sides up, in a single layer on wax paper.

4. Remove pan from oven and add oil; swirl pan to coat with oil. Arrange fillets, seed sides down, in pan. Bake on lowest oven rack until seeds are lightly browned and fish is just opaque but still moist in thickest part; cut to test (about 8 minutes). With a wide spatula, carefully transfer fillets, seed sides up, to individual plates. Offer lemon wedges and soy sauce to season fish to taste.

MAKES 4 SERVINGS.

PER SERVING: 269 calories, 14 g total fat, 2 g saturated fat, 40 mg cholesterol, 140 mg sodium, 3 g carbohydrates, 1 g fiber, 32 g protein, 176 mg calcium, 2 mg iron

Tuna with Mint-Mango Chutney

30 MINUTES

Topped with a fresh tropical fruit chutney, this dish has no added fat—but it does offer plenty of zippy flavor. Serve it with a crisp green salad and tall glasses of icy limeade.

¼ **cup chopped fresh mint**

¼ **cup orange juice**

2 **tablespoons lime juice**

1 **tablespoon minced fresh ginger**

⅛ **to ¼ teaspoon minced fresh habanero chile or 1 to 2 teaspoons minced fresh serrano chile**

4 **tuna steaks (4 to 6 oz.** *each***),** *each* **about 1 inch thick**

1 **large firm-ripe mango (about 1 lb.)**

Mint sprigs

Salt and pepper

1. In a medium-size bowl, mix chopped mint, orange juice, lime juice, and ginger. Stir in chile to taste.

2. Rinse fish and pat dry. Place fish in a large bowl, spoon half the mint mixture over it, and turn to coat well. Let stand for 15 minutes, turning once.

3. Meanwhile, cut peel from mango; then slice fruit from pit and cut into ½-inch cubes. Add mango to remaining mint mixture; add more chile to taste, if desired.

4. Lift fish from mint mixture and drain briefly; discard any mint mixture left in bowl. Place fish on a lightly greased grill 4 to 6 inches above a solid bed of hot coals (you can hold your hand at grill level for only 2 to 3 seconds) or over high heat on a gas grill. Close lid on gas grill. Cook, turning once, until fish is lightly browned on outside but still red in thickest part; cut to test (6 to 8 minutes).

5. With a wide spatula, transfer fish to a platter or individual plates; top with mango mixture and garnish with mint sprigs. Season to taste with salt and pepper.

MAKES 4 SERVINGS.

PER SERVING: 193 calories, 1 g total fat, 0 g saturated fat, 57 mg cholesterol, 49 mg sodium, 15 g carbohydrates, 1 g fiber, 30 g protein, 31 mg calcium, 1 mg iron

Grilled Tuna Provençal

25 MINUTES

To add even more Provençal flavor to these herbed tuna steaks, sprinkle thyme sprigs and fennel seeds on the coals just before grilling; you might also add lavender flowers if you have some on hand. This dish is great served with a vinaigrette-dressed potato salad, roasted bell peppers, or a butter lettuce salad—or all three.

¼ cup extra-virgin olive oil

2 teaspoons fennel seeds, crushed

1 teaspoon minced fresh thyme

1 teaspoon minced fresh basil

1 teaspoon minced parsley

¼ cup lemon juice

Salt and pepper

4 tuna steaks (about 4 oz. *each*), *each* about ¾ inch thick

Thyme sprigs (optional)

Lemon wedges

1. Combine oil, fennel seeds, minced thyme, basil, and parsley in a small pan. Place over medium heat; cook until mixture is very hot (about 3 minutes). Remove from heat and let stand for 10 minutes. Stir in lemon juice. Season to taste with salt and pepper.

2. Rinse fish, pat dry, and place on a lightly greased grill 4 to 6 inches above a solid bed of hot coals (you can hold your hand at grill level for only 2 to 3 seconds) or over high heat on a gas grill. Brush with oil mixture. Close lid on gas grill. Cook, turning once and brushing with oil mixture after turning, until fish is lightly browned on outside but still red in thickest part; cut to test (6 to 8 minutes).

3. Transfer fish to a platter and brush with remaining oil mixture. Garnish with thyme sprigs, if desired; offer lemon wedges to season fish to taste.

MAKES 4 SERVINGS.

PER SERVING: 273 calories, 19 g total fat, 3 g saturated fat, 38 mg cholesterol, 41 mg sodium, 2 g carbohydrates, 0 g fiber, 24 g protein, 15 mg calcium, 1 mg iron

Baguette Bagnat Niçoise

25 MINUTES

This quick and easy version of a famous sandwich from the south of France makes a lunch or supper not to be missed. It's a great choice for picnics, since it can be wrapped tightly and chilled for up to 6 hours after you assemble it.

2 tablespoons extra-virgin olive oil

1½ tablespoons red wine vinegar

2 tablespoons chopped parsley

¼ teaspoon coarsely ground pepper

¼ teaspoon dried thyme

1 clove garlic, minced

1 baguette (about 8 oz.)

¾ cup lightly packed arugula leaves

1 can (6 to 7 oz.) water-packed or oil-packed tuna, drained

¼ cup thinly sliced red onion

½ cup thinly sliced firm-ripe tomato

2 hard-cooked large eggs, thinly sliced

4 flat anchovy fillets, drained well

Salt

1. In a small bowl, mix oil, vinegar, parsley, pepper, thyme, and garlic. Set aside. Cut baguette in half crosswise; then cut each half in half horizontally making bottom half of baguette slightly thicker than top. Pull out soft interior (reserve for other uses), leaving bread shells about ½ inch thick. Brush interior of shells with half the dressing.

2. Line each bottom section of baguette with arugula. Arrange tuna, onion, tomato, eggs, and anchovies atop arugula; drizzle with remaining dressing. Sprinkle with salt to taste.

3. Cover filling with baguette tops. Serve; or wrap airtight and refrigerate for up to 6 hours.

MAKES 2 SERVINGS.

PER SERVING: 542 calories, 23 g total fat, 4 g saturated fat, 251 mg cholesterol, 1,094 mg sodium, 43 g carbohydrates, 3 g fiber, 40 g protein, 146 mg calcium, 6 mg iron

Grilled Fresh Tuna Sandwich with Tapenade

20 MINUTES

Here's a tuna sandwich for adults! Serve with potato salad or coleslaw and a pitcher of fresh lemonade. Tapenade is available in specialty food stores and some supermarkets.

1 tablespoon fruity extra-virgin olive oil

1 tablespoon balsamic vinegar

Salt and pepper

4 tuna steaks (about 4 oz. *each*), *each* about ¾ inch thick

½ cup mayonnaise

3 to 4 tablespoons prepared tapenade

1 tablespoon minced parsley

4 seeded sandwich rolls, split

Romaine or leaf lettuce leaves, rinsed and crisped

4 to 8 slices ripe tomato

1. In a cup, stir together oil and vinegar; season to taste with salt and pepper.

2. Rinse fish, pat dry, and brush with oil mixture. Then place, oiled side down, on a lightly greased grill 4 to 6 inches above a solid bed of hot coals (you can hold your hand at grill level for only 2 to 3 seconds) or over high heat on a gas grill. Brush again with oil mixture. Close lid on gas grill. Cook, turning once and brushing with oil mixture after turning, until fish is lightly browned on outside but still red in thickest part; cut to test (6 to 8 minutes).

3. Meanwhile, in a small bowl, stir together mayonnaise, tapenade, and parsley; season to taste with salt and pepper. Spread cut sides of roll bottoms with mayonnaise mixture, using about half the mixture.

4. Cover bottom half of each roll with lettuce leaves and top with a hot tuna steak; cut fish to fit, if necessary. Top fish with tomato slices, then with remaining mayonnaise mixture; cover with roll tops.

MAKES 4 SERVINGS.

PER SERVING: 586 calories, 37 g total fat, 5 g saturated fat, 55 mg cholesterol, 850 mg sodium, 32 g carbohydrates, 1 g fiber, 30 g protein, 62 mg calcium, 3 mg iron

Swordfish Steaks with Salsa

20 MINUTES

Unlike many salsas, the tomato salsa that accompanies this swordfish is cooked—and since it's made in the same pan as the fish, it absorbs the cooking liquid for extra flavor. Serve with black beans and sliced avocados (topped with sour cream, if you like).

4 swordfish steaks (about 2 lbs. *total*), *each* about ¾ inch thick

2 tablespoons vegetable oil

1 fresh jalapeño chile, seeded and minced

2 cloves garlic, minced or pressed

5 medium-size firm-ripe pear-shaped (Roma-type) tomatoes (about 10 oz. *total*), seeded and diced

½ cup chopped cilantro

1. Rinse fish and pat dry. Heat oil in a wide frying pan over medium-high heat. Add fish and cook, turning once, until well browned on outside and just opaque but still moist in thickest part; cut to test (about 7 minutes). Transfer fish to a platter and keep warm.

2. Add chile and garlic to pan and cook, stirring, until fragrant (about 30 seconds). Add tomatoes and cilantro; stir until heated through (about 3 minutes). Spoon salsa over fish.

MAKES 4 SERVINGS.

PER SERVING: 319 calories, 15 g total fat, 3 g saturated fat, 79 mg cholesterol, 187 mg sodium, 3 g carbohydrates, 1 g fiber, 41 g protein, 16 mg calcium, 2 mg iron

South Seas Swordfish

25 MINUTES

All the flavor of the South Seas—with no shopping for hard-to-find ingredients. The fish and spinach are permeated with the flavor of coconut, but because we use coconut extract rather than coconut milk, the dish stays lean. Add hot rice and you have a complete meal.

1½ cups fat-free reduced-sodium chicken broth

2 tablespoons minced fresh ginger

½ teaspoon coconut extract

1 to 1¼ pounds swordfish (about ¾ inch thick)

2 packages (about 10 oz. *each*) triple-washed spinach

3 cups hot cooked long-grain white rice

1 tablespoon cornstarch blended with 1 tablespoon cold water

¼ cup lemon juice

Salt

1. In a wide frying pan, combine broth, ginger, and coconut extract. Bring to a boil over high heat. Rinse and drain fish; add to boiling broth. Reduce heat, cover, and simmer until fish is just opaque but still moist in thickest part; cut to test (8 to 10 minutes).

2. Meanwhile, remove and discard any coarse stems from spinach. With a slotted spatula, transfer fish to a platter; keep warm. Add spinach to pan and stir over high heat until wilted (about 5 minutes). Using a slotted spoon, transfer spinach to platter alongside fish; spoon rice next to spinach.

3. Stir cornstarch mixture, then add to pan liquid. Bring to a boil, stirring. Stir in lemon juice and season to taste with salt; then pour over fish.

MAKES 4 SERVINGS.

PER SERVING: 404 calories, 6 g total fat, 3 g saturated fat, 50 mg cholesterol, 445 mg sodium, 51 g carbohydrates, 4 g fiber, 35 g protein, 165 mg calcium, 7 mg iron

Hawaiian Fish with Thai Banana Salsa

30 MINUTES

A spicy banana salsa tops your choice of Hawaiian fish in this marvelous dish from an Oahu restaurant; you might serve it with sautéed red and yellow bell peppers. Among the fish listed below, the most widely available are tuna, mahi mahi, and swordfish. The other three choices (hebi, ono, and opah) may have to be special-ordered from your fish market. Hebi (spearfish) and opah (moonfish) are both pink-fleshed (white when cooked) and sweet in flavor; ono (wahoo) is delicate and tender, turning from pink-tan to white with cooking.

1 teaspoon Oriental sesame oil

1 large firm-ripe banana (about 8 oz.), peeled and cut in half lengthwise

½ cup golden raisins, chopped

6 tablespoons chopped cilantro

2 tablespoons minced fresh lemon grass or 1 teaspoon grated lemon peel

½ teaspoon grated orange peel

¼ teaspoon ground red pepper (cayenne)

1½ to 2 pounds fillets or steaks of tuna, mahi mahi, swordfish, hebi, ono, or opah (*each* about ¾ inch thick)

1 tablespoon olive oil

1 teaspoon vegetable oil

1. Heat sesame oil in a wide nonstick frying pan over high heat. Add banana and cook, turning as needed, until well browned on all sides (about 8 minutes). Remove banana from pan, chop coarsely, and place in a bowl. Mix in raisins, 2 tablespoons of the cilantro, lemon grass, orange peel, and red pepper. Set aside.

2. Cut off and discard any skin from fish. Rinse fish, pat dry, and cut into 6 equal portions. Rub fish all over with olive oil; then pat remaining ¼ cup cilantro over fish.

3. Place a wide nonstick frying pan over high heat. When pan is hot, add vegetable oil and oiled fish. Cook, turning once or twice (drippings may scorch and smoke), until fish is done to your liking; cut to test. For rare fish (it will still have its raw color in center), allow about 3 minutes. For fish that is evenly cooked throughout (it will be slightly translucent in center), allow 5 to 6 minutes.

4. With a wide spatula, transfer fish to individual plates; serve with banana salsa.

MAKES 6 SERVINGS.

PER SERVING: 237 calories, 5 g total fat, 1 g saturated fat, 60 mg cholesterol, 51 mg sodium, 16 g carbohydrates, 1 g fiber, 32 g protein, 31 mg calcium, 1 mg iron

Hawaiian Fish with Thai Banana Salsa

Seafood Stew with Orzo

30 MINUTES

Served over tiny orzo, this hearty dish of cod, shrimp, and mussels in a chunky vegetable sauce makes a complete meal in a bowl. Fresh fruit is a nice choice for dessert; you might offer tangerines, bunches of grapes, or ripe pears.

- 2 **tablespoons olive oil**
- 1 **small onion (about 4 oz.), thinly sliced**
- 1 **clove garlic, minced or pressed**
- ½ **teaspoon fennel seeds, crushed**
- 1 **can (about 14½ oz.) pear-shaped tomatoes**
- 1 **small crookneck squash or yellow zucchini (about 4 oz.), cut into matchstick pieces**
- 1 **small yellow bell pepper (about 5 oz.), seeded and cut into matchstick pieces**
- 3 **tablespoons minced parsley**
- 6 **ounces cod fillet**
- 8 **raw shrimp in shells (31 to 40 per lb.)**
- 8 **mussels in shell, scrubbed, beards pulled off**
- 1 **teaspoon lemon juice**
- ⅓ **cup (about 2 oz.) dried orzo**
- ½ **cup grated Parmesan cheese**

1. Heat oil in a wide nonstick frying pan over medium heat. Add onion, garlic, and fennel seeds. Cook, stirring often, until onion begins to soften (about 4 minutes). Add tomatoes (break up with a spoon) and their liquid, squash, bell pepper, and 2 tablespoons of the parsley. Increase heat to medium-high and bring mixture to a simmer; then simmer, uncovered, until slightly thickened (about 5 minutes).

2. Rinse fish, pat dry, and cut into 2 portions. Add fish to sauce. Cover and simmer gently for 3 minutes. Add shrimp, mussels, and lemon juice. Cover and simmer until mussels pop open and shrimp are just opaque in center; cut to test (5 to 7 minutes). Discard any unopened mussels.

3. While you are preparing sauce, bring about 1½ quarts of water to a boil in a 3-quart pan over high heat; stir in pasta and cook, uncovered, until just tender to bite (10 to 12 minutes). Or cook pasta according to package directions. Drain well and toss with cheese; keep warm.

4. To serve, divide pasta between 2 soup bowls or individual casseroles. Ladle seafood stew over pasta and sprinkle with remaining 1 tablespoon parsley.

MAKES 2 SERVINGS.

PER SERVING: 553 calories, 23 g total fat, 6 g saturated fat, 132 mg cholesterol, 891 mg sodium, 44 g carbohydrates, 5 g fiber, 44 g protein, 424 mg calcium, 6 mg iron

Spicy Shrimp Fajitas

Spicy Shrimp Fajitas

25 MINUTES

Top these fajitas with diced ripe avocado, a fresh homemade salsa, and spoonfuls of sour cream. Alongside, serve a crisp romaine and orange salad and tall glasses of cold beer. We suggest warming the tortillas in the oven, but if you prefer, wrap them in a cloth towel and microwave on HIGH (100%) for about 1½ minutes.

Radish & Tomato Salsa (below)

8 flour tortillas (*each 7 to 9 inches in diameter*)

2 green onions, sliced

3 tablespoons lime juice

1 teaspoon vegetable oil

1 clove garlic, minced or pressed

½ teaspoon ground cumin

½ teaspoon ground coriander

½ teaspoon chili powder

¼ teaspoon salt

¼ teaspoon ground red pepper (cayenne)

1 pound shelled, deveined raw shrimp (31 to 40 per lb.)

1 medium-size ripe avocado (about 6 oz.)

½ cup sour cream

RADISH & TOMATO SALSA

3 medium-size tomatoes (1 to 1¼ lbs. *total*), seeded and chopped

½ cup thinly sliced radishes

½ cup minced red or white onion

1 fresh jalapeño chile, seeded and minced

1 tablespoon minced cilantro

Salt and ground red pepper (cayenne)

1. Prepare Radish & Tomato Salsa; cover and set aside.

2. Lightly brush tortillas with hot water. Stack, wrap in foil, and heat in a 350° oven until warm (10 to 12 minutes).

3. Meanwhile, in a large bowl, stir together green onions, lime juice, oil, garlic, cumin, coriander, chili powder, the ¼ teaspoon salt, and the ¼ teaspoon red pepper. Add shrimp and stir to coat; then let marinate for 5 minutes, turning a few times.

4. While shrimp marinate, pit, peel, and dice avocado; place in a small bowl. Spoon sour cream into another small bowl.

5. Place a wide nonstick frying pan over medium heat. Add shrimp and their marinade. Cook, stirring often, until shrimp are just opaque in center; cut to test (3 to 4 minutes).

6. To serve, pour shrimp onto a platter. Fill tortillas with shrimp, avocado, Radish & Tomato Salsa, and sour cream; fold to enclose and eat out of hand.

MAKES 4 SERVINGS.

RADISH & TOMATO SALSA

In a bowl, mix tomatoes, radishes, red onion, chile, and cilantro. Season to taste with salt and red pepper.

PER SERVING: 541 calories, 22 g total fat, 6 g saturated fat, 185 mg cholesterol, 812 mg sodium, 54 g carbohydrates, 5 g fiber, 33 g protein, 213 mg calcium, 6 mg iron

Shrimp Puttanesca Sauce with Penne

30 MINUTES

While the zesty sauce simmers, prepare a simple arugula salad and slice a loaf of Italian bread. You might try spreading the slices with a mixture of extra-virgin olive oil, garlic, and parsley, then heating them in the oven (wrapped tightly in foil).

- 1 tablespoon olive oil
- 2 cloves garlic, minced or pressed
- 1 large can (about 28 oz.) pear-shaped tomatoes
- 2 tablespoons chopped pitted Niçoise olives
- 1 tablespoon drained capers, chopped
- 1 teaspoon minced fresh oregano
- 1 teaspoon crushed red pepper flakes
  Salt
- 1 pound dried penne
- 1 pound shelled, deveined raw shrimp (31 to 40 per lb.)
- 3 tablespoons minced parsley

1. Heat oil in a 3-quart pan over low heat; add garlic and cook, stirring, for 1 minute. Add tomatoes (break up with a spoon) and their liquid, olives, capers, oregano, and red pepper flakes. Increase heat to medium and bring mixture to a low boil; then cook, uncovered, stirring occasionally, until thickened (about 18 minutes). Season to taste with salt.

2. Meanwhile, in a 6- to 8-quart pan, bring about 4 quarts water to a boil over high heat; stir in pasta and cook, uncovered, until just tender to bite (10 to 12 minutes). Or cook pasta according to package directions. Drain well and pour into a large bowl.

3. Stir shrimp and 2 tablespoons of the parsley into simmering sauce. Cover pan and remove from heat. Let stand until shrimp are just opaque in center; cut to test (3 to 4 minutes).

4. Pour sauce over pasta; mix lightly. Sprinkle with remaining 1 tablespoon parsley.

MAKES 4 TO 6 SERVINGS.

PER SERVING: 497 calories, 7 g total fat, 1 g saturated fat, 138 mg cholesterol, 506 mg sodium, 77 g carbohydrates, 4 g fiber, 32 g protein, 115 mg calcium, 7 mg iron

Sautéed Hoisin Shrimp with Bok Choy

25 MINUTES

Served with rice, this makes a complete dinner—but you may decide you need ginger ice cream and butter cookies to make you thoroughly happy.

- 3 tablespoons hoisin sauce
- 2 tablespoons rice vinegar
- ¼ cup water
- 2 teaspoons sugar
- ½ teaspoon ground ginger
- ½ teaspoon cornstarch
- ⅛ teaspoon crushed red pepper flakes
- About 2 pounds baby bok choy
- 3 tablespoons vegetable oil
- 1 pound shelled, deveined raw shrimp (31 to 40 per lb.); leave tails on, if desired
- 1 clove garlic, minced
- 6 green onions, cut diagonally into 1-inch lengths

1. In a small bowl, stir together hoisin sauce, vinegar, 2 tablespoons of the water, sugar, ginger, cornstarch, and red pepper flakes. Set aside.

2. Discard any bruised or yellowed bok choy leaves. Rinse and drain bok choy; cut each head in half lengthwise. If bases of bok choy pieces are thicker than 1 inch, cut each piece in half lengthwise. Heat 1 tablespoon of the oil in a wide nonstick frying pan or wok over medium-high heat. Add bok choy and remaining 2 tablespoons water; cover and cook, stirring often, until bok choy stems are just tender when pierced (3 to 5 minutes). Transfer bok choy to a platter. Discard liquid from pan. Wipe pan dry with a paper towel.

3. Heat remaining 2 tablespoons oil in pan over medium-high heat. Add shrimp and garlic and cook, stirring often, for 2 minutes. Add onions and hoisin mixture. Continue to cook, stirring, until sauce is thickened and shrimp are just opaque in center; cut to test (about 3 more minutes). Spoon shrimp over bok choy.

MAKES 4 SERVINGS.

PER SERVING: 293 calories, 13 g total fat, 2 g saturated fat, 173 mg cholesterol, 556 mg sodium, 18 g carbohydrates, 3 g fiber, 27 g protein, 315 mg calcium, 5 mg iron

Sautéed Hoisin Shrimp with Bok Choy

Crab Singapore

20 MINUTES

Surprise—this dish gets its exotic, enticing flavors from ingredients you can easily find in the supermarket. Make it with cracked crab or shelled cooked crabmeat.

1 teaspoon cornstarch

¾ cup fat-free reduced-sodium chicken broth

¼ cup catsup

1 tablespoon salted, fermented black beans, sorted of debris and rinsed (or 1 tablespoon soy sauce)

2 or 3 small fresh hot red or green chiles, such as Thai, serrano, Fresno, or jalapeño, seeded and minced

1 large cooked Dungeness crab (2 to 2½ lbs.), cleaned and cracked; or 8 ounces cooked crabmeat

3 cloves garlic, peeled

1 tablespoon chopped fresh ginger

1 tablespoon vegetable oil

Cilantro sprigs (optional)

2 cups hot cooked long-grain white rice

Crab Singapore

1. In a small bowl, smoothly blend cornstarch, broth, and catsup. Stir in beans and chiles; set aside.

2. If you are using cracked crab, rinse it under cold running water to remove any loose bits of shell; then pat crab dry with paper towels. Set aside.

3. Pound garlic and ginger into a paste with a mortar and pestle (or finely mince with a knife).

4. Heat oil in a 5- to 6-quart pan or wok over high heat. Add garlic-ginger paste; stir until golden (30 seconds to 1 minute). Add broth mixture and cracked crab or cooked crabmeat; stir with a wide spatula until crab is heated through and sauce is boiling (3 to 4 minutes). Arrange crab on a platter. Garnish with cilantro springs, if desired. Serve with rice. (Or spoon rice into individual bowls and top with crab; garnish with cilantro sprigs, if desired.)

MAKES 2 SERVINGS.

PER SERVING: 511 calories, 10 g total fat, 1 g saturated fat, 123 mg cholesterol, 1,133 mg sodium, 70 g carbohydrates, 1 g fiber, 33 g protein, 173 mg calcium, 4 mg iron

Half-shell Oysters with Tangy Sauces

10 MINUTES

If you want to serve oysters on the half-shell, remember to ask the dealer to save one shell from each oyster when you buy the shucked shellfish. Oysters with these sauces are delightful for a late supper; you might serve them with a simple salad.

36 chilled shucked small to medium-size oysters
⅓ cup prepared cocktail sauce
Vinegar-Soy Sauce (below)
Mignonette Sauce (below)

VINEGAR-SOY SAUCE

2 tablespoons balsamic vinegar
¼ cup soy sauce
1 tablespoon thinly sliced green onion

MIGNONETTE SAUCE

¼ cup white wine vinegar
2 tablespoons water
2 teaspoons minced shallot
¼ to ½ teaspoon coarsely ground pepper

1. Arrange chilled oysters on a platter; or serve on ice.

2. Spoon cocktail sauce into a small bowl. Prepare Vinegar-Soy Sauce and Mignonette Sauce. Offer all 3 sauces to add to oysters to taste.

MAKES 4 SERVINGS.

VINEGAR-SOY SAUCE

In a small bowl, mix vinegar, soy sauce, and onion.

MAKES ABOUT 6 TABLESPOONS.

MIGNONETTE SAUCE

In a small bowl, mix vinegar, water, shallot, and pepper.

MAKES ABOUT 6 TABLESPOONS.

PER SERVING OF OYSTERS WITH COCKTAIL SAUCE: 111 calories, 3 g total fat, 1 g saturated fat, 70 mg cholesterol, 395 mg sodium, 11 g carbohydrates, 0 g fiber, 9 g protein, 57 mg calcium, 9 mg iron

PER TABLESPOON OF VINEGAR-SOY SAUCE: 7 calories, 0 g total fat, 0 g saturated fat, 0 mg cholesterol, 686 mg sodium, 1 g carbohydrates, 0 g fiber, 1 g protein, 3 mg calcium, 0 mg iron

PER TABLESPOON OF MIGNONETTE SAUCE: 3 calories, 0 g total fat, 0 g saturated fat, 0 mg cholesterol, 0 mg sodium, 1 g carbohydrates, 0 g fiber, 0 g protein, 1 mg calcium, 0 mg iron

Cracked Crab with Red Pepper Aïoli

10 MINUTES

Cold cracked crab turns festive when dipped in a tangy mayonnaise made with roasted red peppers. To share the aïoli, offer a crusty sourdough loaf and a romaine salad or an assortment of blanched or raw fresh vegetables.

- 1 jar (about 12 oz.) roasted red peppers, drained and patted dry
- 1 or 2 cloves garlic, peeled and halved
- 1 cup mayonnaise
- 2 or 3 cooked Dungeness crabs (1½ to 2 lbs. *each*), cleaned and cracked

1. In a blender or food processor, whirl roasted peppers and garlic until smooth. Transfer to a small bowl and stir in mayonnaise. If made ahead, cover and refrigerate for up to 1 week.

2. Rinse crab under cold running water to remove any loose bits of shell. Pat dry with paper towels. Pile crab on a platter. To eat, shell crab and dip meat into aïoli.

MAKES 4 TO 6 SERVINGS.

PER SERVING: 438 calories, 37 g total fat, 5 g saturated fat, 122 mg cholesterol, 661 mg sodium, 6 g carbohydrates, 0 g fiber, 20 g protein, 109 mg calcium, 2 mg iron

Wine-steamed Clams

25 MINUTES

Make this dish with tarragon rather than thyme, if you like—it's just as lovely. Serve either version with French bread and soft butter, glasses of crisp white wine or sparkling cider, and a salad of mixed baby greens.

- 2 tablespoons butter or margarine
- 2 small leeks (about 8 oz. *total*), white parts only, rinsed well and thinly sliced; or 1 medium-size onion (about 6 oz.), diced
- 1 clove garlic, minced or pressed
- 2 cups water
- 1 cup dry white wine
- 1 tablespoon chopped fresh thyme or 1 teaspoon dried thyme
- ½ teaspoon pepper
- 6 pounds small hard-shell clams in shell, scrubbed

  Lemon wedges

1. Melt butter in a 6- to 8-quart pan over medium-high heat; add leeks and garlic. Cook, stirring often, until leeks are soft (about 5 minutes). Add water, wine, thyme, and pepper. Cover and bring to a boil over high heat.

2. Add clams to boiling wine mixture; cover and cook until shells pop open (8 to 10 minutes). Discard any unopened clams.

3. Ladle clams and broth into bowls; offer lemon wedges to season individual servings to taste.

MAKES 4 TO 6 SERVINGS.

PER SERVING: 176 calories, 6 g total fat, 3 g saturated fat, 40 mg cholesterol, 103 mg sodium, 14 g carbohydrates, 1 g fiber, 12 g protein, 105 mg calcium, 13 mg iron

Mussels with Thai Broth

25 MINUTES

For an easy and elegant meal, serve these spicy mussels with a green salad and crusty bread; offer mango or coconut sorbet for dessert. If you can't find curry paste, make your own for this recipe by blending 1 tablespoon minced fresh ginger, 1 teaspoon curry powder, 1 teaspoon chili powder, and ¼ teaspoon ground red pepper (cayenne).

1 cup dry white wine

½ cup thinly slivered onion

1 teaspoon minced garlic

32 mussels in shell, scrubbed, beards pulled off; or 32 small hard-shell clams in shell, scrubbed

1 can (about 14 oz.) unsweetened regular or low-fat coconut milk

3 to 4 teaspoons Thai red curry paste (or to taste)

¼ cup slivered fresh basil

1. In a 5- to 6-quart pan, bring wine, onion, and garlic to a boil over high heat. Add shellfish; cover and cook over medium heat until shells pop open (5 to 7 minutes for mussels, 8 to 10 minutes for clams). Discard any unopened shellfish.

2. While shellfish are cooking, combine coconut milk and curry paste in a small bowl; stir to blend smoothly.

3. With a slotted spoon, lift shellfish from pan; divide equally among 4 soup bowls. Stir coconut milk mixture into cooking liquid in pan; stir in basil and bring to a simmer. Ladle broth over shellfish in bowls.

MAKES 4 SERVINGS.

PER SERVING: 325 calories, 25 g total fat, 19 g saturated fat, 19 mg cholesterol, 331 mg sodium, 8 g carbohydrates, 1 g fiber, 10 g protein, 62 mg calcium, 7 mg iron

Mussels with Thai Broth

Chapter Six

PASTA

◀ *Previous page: Linguine with Prosciutto & Olives (page 173)*

Capellini with Broccoli Cream Sauce

25 MINUTES

Rich and subtly flavored, this elegant entrée combines cooked fresh broccoli and delicate capellini with warm, nutmeg-spiced whipping cream and plenty of grated Parmesan.

- 1½ **pounds broccoli**
- 10 **ounces dried capellini (angel hair pasta)**
- 6 **tablespoons butter or margarine**
- ⅓ **cup water**
- 2 **cups whipping cream**
- ¼ **teaspoon ground nutmeg**

  About 2 cups (about 6 oz.) grated Parmesan cheese

1. Trim and discard tough ends of broccoli stalks; peel stalks, if desired. Reserve a few whole flowerets for garnish; finely chop remaining broccoli. Set aside.

2. In a 5- to 6-quart pan, bring about 3 quarts water to a boil over high heat; stir in pasta and cook, uncovered, until just tender to bite (about 3 minutes). Or cook pasta according to package directions. Drain well; keep warm.

3. While water is heating, melt butter in a wide frying pan over medium-high heat; add broccoli (including reserved flowerets) and the ⅓ cup water. Cover and cook until broccoli is tender when pierced (3 to 5 minutes). Remove flowerets from pan and set aside.

4. Add cream and nutmeg to broccoli remaining in pan; bring to a boil. Then add drained pasta. Cook, stirring, until mixture is heated through and cream clings to pasta. Remove from heat. Sprinkle with 1¼ cups of the cheese; mix gently, using 2 forks.

5. Pour pasta onto a platter or individual plates; top with reserved broccoli flowerets and sprinkle evenly with 3 to 4 tablespoons more cheese. Serve at once; offer remaining cheese to add to taste.

MAKES 6 SERVINGS.

PER SERVING: 641 calories, 44 g total fat, 27 g saturated fat, 139 mg cholesterol, 620 mg sodium, 42 g carbohydrates, 3 g fiber, 20 g protein, 436 mg calcium, 3 mg iron

Orecchiette with Cheddar Sauce

30 MINUTES

This dressed-up version of macaroni and cheese is made with whimsical orecchiette ("little ears"); if you like, you can also use other fancy pasta shapes or plain elbow macaroni. The creamy sauce is dotted with smoky ham and flavored with three kinds of cheese: sharp Cheddar, piquant Asiago, and mild jack.

- 1 **pound dried orecchiette**
- 1½ **cups milk**
- 1½ **cups whipping cream**
- 2 **cups (about 8 oz.) shredded extra-sharp Cheddar cheese**
- 1 **cup (about 4 oz.) shredded Asiago cheese**
- 1 **cup (about 4 oz.) shredded jack cheese**
- 4 **ounces Black Forest ham, cut into ¼-inch cubes**

  Salt, black pepper, and ground red pepper (cayenne)
- 1 **cup fine dry bread crumbs**

1. In a 6- to 8-quart pan, bring about 4 quarts water to a boil over high heat; stir in pasta and cook, uncovered, until just tender to bite (10 to 12 minutes). Or cook pasta according to package directions.

2. Meanwhile, in a medium-size pan, bring milk and cream to a simmer over medium heat. Add all 3 cheeses and ham; stir until cheese is melted and smoothly blended into sauce. Season to taste with salt, black pepper, and red pepper.

3. Drain pasta well and transfer to a 9- by 13-inch baking dish. Pour cheese sauce over pasta and stir to mix well. Spread out evenly, then sprinkle with bread crumbs. Bake in a 350° oven until top is golden brown and sauce is bubbly (about 20 minutes).

MAKES 6 SERVINGS.

PER SERVING: 903 calories, 48 g total fat, 29 g saturated fat, 161 mg cholesterol, 1,269 mg sodium, 75 g carbohydrates, 3 g fiber, 40 g protein, 744 mg calcium, 5 mg iron

Orecchiette with Cheddar Sauce

Orzo with Sun-dried Tomatoes & Feta

25 MINUTES

Serve this colorful dish for a quick hot dinner; or make it ahead and enjoy it cold as a salad, perhaps as part of a summer picnic.

1 pound dried orzo

¾ cup oil-packed dried tomatoes

2 tablespoons finely chopped fresh oregano

2 tablespoons lemon juice

¼ cup fat-free reduced-sodium chicken broth

4 ounces feta cheese, crumbled

4 ounces smoked chicken breast, shredded

1. In a 6- to 8-quart pan, bring about 4 quarts water to a boil over high heat; stir in pasta and cook, uncovered, until just tender to bite (10 to 12 minutes). Or cook pasta according to package directions.

2. Meanwhile, drain tomatoes, reserving 1 tablespoon of the oil. Cut tomatoes into thin slivers and place in a large bowl. Add oregano, lemon juice, broth, cheese, and chicken. Add the reserved 1 tablespoon tomato oil and toss to combine.

3. Drain pasta well and add to chicken mixture; toss to combine. Serve warm or cold.

MAKES 6 SERVINGS.

PER SERVING: 518 calories, 21 g total fat, 5 g saturated fat, 25 mg cholesterol, 432 mg sodium, 65 g carbohydrates, 4 g fiber, 18 g protein, 126 mg calcium, 4 mg iron

Avocado Linguine

25 MINUTES

Cambozola, a double-cream blue cheese, blends with yogurt and broth to make a rich, piquant sauce for linguine. Smooth avocado slices and crunchy sunflower seeds are served atop the pasta for contrasts in flavor and texture.

1 pound dried linguine

1 large firm-ripe avocado (about 10 oz.)

2 tablespoons lemon juice

½ cup diced cambozola cheese

½ cup plain nonfat yogurt

⅓ cup fat-free reduced-sodium chicken broth

Salt and pepper

⅓ cup salted toasted sunflower seeds

2 tablespoons minced parsley

1. In a 6- to 8-quart pan, bring about 4 quarts water to a boil over high heat; stir in pasta and cook, uncovered, until just tender to bite (8 to 10 minutes). Or cook pasta according to package directions.

2. Meanwhile, pit and peel avocado, then cut lengthwise into ½-inch-thick slices. Place slices on a plate, sprinkle with lemon juice, and set aside.

3. Drain pasta well, then return to cooking pan. Set pan over low heat. Add cheese, yogurt, and broth; mix, lifting with 2 forks, until cheese is melted and almost all liquid has been absorbed. Season to taste with salt and pepper.

4. To serve, pour pasta onto a platter. Arrange avocado slices atop pasta; sprinkle with sunflower seeds and parsley.

MAKES 4 TO 6 SERVINGS.

PER SERVING: 522 calories, 17 g total fat, 4 g saturated fat, 11 mg cholesterol, 309 mg sodium, 75 g carbohydrates, 3 g fiber, 18 g protein, 145 mg calcium, 5 mg iron

Linguine with Escarole

20 MINUTES

Here's a simply seasoned pasta dish for two—a combination of linguine, thin shreds of escarole, and handy packaged sliced mushrooms. Serve with marinated sliced tomatoes and crunchy sesame breadsticks.

8 ounces dried linguine

2 tablespoons extra-virgin olive oil

8 ounces sliced mushrooms

2 cloves garlic, minced or pressed

¼ teaspoon crushed red pepper flakes

2 teaspoons anchovy paste or minced anchovies (optional)

½ cup vegetable broth

1 pound escarole, rinsed, drained, and cut into ¼-inch-wide shreds

Grated Parmesan cheese

1. In a 4- to 5-quart pan, bring about 2 quarts water to a boil over high heat; stir in pasta and cook, uncovered, until just tender to bite (8 to 10 minutes). Or cook pasta according to package directions.

2. Meanwhile, heat oil in a wide frying pan over high heat. Add mushrooms and cook, stirring often, until lightly browned (about 8 minutes). Stir in garlic, red pepper flakes, and anchovy paste (if used). Add broth and escarole; bring to a boil, then stir until escarole is wilted (2 to 3 minutes). Remove from heat and keep warm.

3. Drain pasta well and pour into a large bowl. Add escarole mixture and toss to mix. Spoon onto individual plates; offer cheese to add to taste.

MAKES 2 SERVINGS.

PER SERVING: 618 calories, 17 g total fat, 2 g saturated fat, 0 mg cholesterol, 312 mg sodium, 100 g carbohydrates, 9 g fiber, 20 g protein, 150 mg calcium, 8 mg iron

Garden Pasta

25 MINUTES

For a quick summer supper, serve this green-and-red dish. To save time on preparation, we use frozen rather than fresh Swiss chard (you can substitute spinach, if you prefer).

3 tablespoons extra-virgin olive oil

1 pound sliced mushrooms

1 medium-size onion (about 6 oz.), chopped

3 cloves garlic, minced or pressed

1 pound dried rotelle

½ cup fat-free reduced-sodium chicken broth

1 package (about 10 oz.) frozen chopped Swiss chard, thawed and drained very well

½ cup grated Parmesan cheese

1½ pounds pear-shaped (Roma-type) tomatoes, chopped

Salt and pepper

1. Heat oil in a wide frying pan over medium-high heat. Stir in mushrooms, onion, and garlic. Cover and cook until mushrooms have released their liquid and onion is soft (about 6 minutes).

2. Meanwhile, in a 6- to 8-quart pan, bring about 4 quarts water to a boil over high heat; stir in pasta and cook, uncovered, until just tender to bite (about 10 minutes). Or cook pasta according to package directions.

3. While pasta is cooking, uncover frying pan and stir vegetables until liquid has evaporated and mushrooms are lightly browned. Add broth and chard; cook over high heat, stirring, until chard is heated through (about 1 minute). Remove from heat and keep warm.

4. Drain pasta well and pour into a serving bowl. Pour chard-mushroom mixture over pasta; sprinkle with ¼ cup of the cheese and top with tomatoes. Mix lightly; season to taste with salt and pepper. Sprinkle with remaining ¼ cup cheese.

MAKES 4 TO 6 SERVINGS.

PER SERVING: 535 calories, 14 g total fat, 3 g saturated fat, 8 mg cholesterol, 435 mg sodium, 84 g carbohydrates, 7 g fiber, 20 g protein, 212 mg calcium, 6 mg iron

Tortellini with White Beans, Tomatoes & Kale

30 MINUTES

Deep green, vitamin-rich kale pairs beautifully with tomatoes and white beans to make a colorful sauce for fresh cheese tortellini. To complete a wonderful winter meal, add warm garlic bread and a salad of fennel, oranges, and ripe olives.

2 tablespoons olive oil

3 cloves garlic, minced or pressed

5 cups chopped kale or Swiss chard

⅓ cup water

1 can (about 15 oz.) cannellini (white kidney beans) or Great Northern beans, rinsed and drained

2 cans (about 14½ oz. *each*) diced tomatoes

Salt and crushed red pepper flakes

2 packages (about 9 oz. *each*) fresh cheese-filled plain or spinach tortellini (or use 1 package of each)

Shredded Romano cheese

1. Heat oil in a wide frying pan over high heat. Add garlic and stir for 30 seconds. Add kale and the ⅓ cup water; cover and simmer until kale is wilted (about 3 minutes). Add beans, then tomatoes and their liquid; bring to a boil. Then reduce heat and simmer until flavors are blended (7 to 8 minutes). Season to taste with salt and red pepper flakes.

2. Meanwhile, bring about 3 quarts water to a boil in a 5- to 6-quart pan over high heat; stir in tortellini and cook, uncovered, until just tender to bite (4 to 6 minutes). Or cook tortellini according to package directions.

3. Drain tortellini well and pour into a large bowl. Add kale mixture; toss to mix. Spoon onto individual plates or into shallow bowls. Offer cheese to add to taste.

MAKES 4 SERVINGS.

PER SERVING: 599 calories, 17 g total fat, 5 g saturated fat, 50 mg cholesterol, 1,015 mg sodium, 91 g carbohydrates, 13 g fiber, 25 g protein, 349 mg calcium, 6 mg iron

Tortellini with White Beans, Tomatoes & Kale

Risotto

Risotto—like many pasta dishes—is a culinary masterpiece from Italy th[at] begins with a nutritious but ordinary starch (rice, in this case) and transforms it into an elega[nt] first course or entrée. Start with the basic recipe below; then dress it up by adding addition[al] ingredients, such as seafood, meat, herbs, cheese, or cooked vegetables. (For variety, we'[ve] even included a rice-less "risotto" made from diced potatoes.)

For best results, use the imported arborio rice sold in Italian markets and specialty foo[d] stores. Domestic short- or long-grain rice also makes good risotto.

In the following recipes, we specify the number of first-course servings; if you'd like to ser[ve] these dishes as main courses, increase the portion size.

Basic Risotto

30 MINUTES

- 3½ cups fat-free reduced-sodium chicken broth
- 3 tablespoons butter or margarine
- 1 medium-size onion (about 6 oz.), chopped
- 1 cup arborio or other short-grain white rice
- ¼ cup grated Parmesan cheese

1. In a 1½-quart pan, bring broth to a simmer over medium heat. Reduce heat to low.

2. Meanwhile, melt butter in a 2- to 3-quart pan over medium-high heat. Add onion and cook, stirring often, until soft (about 4 min-utes). Add rice and stir until opaque and well coated with butter (2 to 3 minutes).

3. Add ½ cup of the broth and cook, stirring, until absorbed. Continue to cook, adding remaining 3 cups broth ½ cup at a time, until rice is just tender to bite but not starchy tasting (about 20 more minutes); after each addition, stir constantly until broth is absorbed. Remove from heat and stir in cheese; let stand, uncovered, for 2 minutes. To serve, spoon into warm bowls.

MAKES 4 SERVINGS.

PER SERVING: 307 calories, 10 g total fat, 6 g saturated fat, 27 mg cholesterol, 674 mg sodium, 43 g carbohydrates, 1 g fiber, 9 g protein, 81 mg calcium, 2 mg iron

Risotto with Asparagus & Lemon

30 MINUTES

- 8 ounces asparagus
- 3½ cups fat-free reduced-sodium chicken broth
- 3 tablespoons butter or margarine
- 1 medium-size onion (about 6 oz.), chopped
- 1 cup arborio or other short-grain white rice
- 2 teaspoons grated lemon peel
- ¼ cup lemon juice
- ¼ cup grated Parmesan cheese

1. Snap off and discard tough ends of asparagus; cut spears diagonally into thirds. Meanwhile, in a wide frying pan, bring about 1 inch water to a boil over high heat. Add asparagus and cook, uncov-ered, until just tender when pierced (3 to 5 minutes). Drain well and set aside.

2. While asparagus is cook-ing, pour broth into a 1½-quart pan and bring to a simmer over medium he[at]. Reduce heat to low.

3. Meanwhile, melt butter [in] a 2- to 3-quart pan ov[er] medium-high heat. A[dd] onion and cook, stirri[ng] often, until soft (about 4 mi[n-]utes). Add rice and stir un[til] opaque and well coated wi[th] butter (2 to 3 minutes). S[tir] in lemon peel and lem[on] juice.

4. Add ½ cup of the bro[th] and cook, stirring, un[til] absorbed. Continue to coo[k,] adding remaining 3 cu[ps] broth ½ cup at a time, un[til] rice is just tender to bite b[ut] not starchy tasting (about [20] more minutes); after eac[h] addition, stir constantly un[til] broth is absorbed.

5. Remove from heat and st[ir] in asparagus and cheese; l[et] stand, uncovered, for 2 min[-]utes. To serve, spoon in[to] warm bowls.

MAKES 4 SERVINGS.

PER SERVING: 321 calories, 11 g total fat, 6 g saturated fat, 27 mg cholesterol, 678 mg sodiu[m] 46 g carbohydrates, 2 g fiber, 10[g] protein, 94 mg calcium, 3 mg iro[n]

eet Corn Risotto

MINUTES

- cups fat-free reduced-sodium chicken broth
- cups finely chopped mild sweet onions
- tablespoons butter or margarine
- cup arborio or other short-grain white rice

  About ¼ cup lime juice
- medium-size ears corn (*each* about 8 inches long)
- cup grated Parmesan cheese

  Salt and pepper
- to 2 tablespoons snipped chives

  Finely shaved Parmesan cheese

In a 1½-quart pan, bring oth to a simmer over edium heat. Reduce heat to v.

Meanwhile, in a wide fry-g pan, combine 1 cup of the ions, butter, and 2 table-oons water. Cook over edium-high heat, stirring en, until liquid has evapo-ted and onions are soft (about 5 minutes). Add rice and stir until opaque (2 to 3 minutes). Add 2 tablespoons of the lime juice and 3 cups of the broth to rice; cook, stirring often, until liquid is absorbed (about 10 minutes).

3. Meanwhile, remove husks and silk from corn. In a shallow pan, hold each ear of corn upright; with a sharp knife, cut kernels from cob. Then, using blunt edge of knife, scrape juice from cob into pan. Set corn kernels and juice aside.

4. To rice mixture, add remaining 1 cup broth, corn kernels and juice, and remaining 1 cup onions. Continue to cook, stirring often, until rice is tender to bite and mixture is creamy (6 to 7 minutes). Stir in the ¼ cup cheese. Season to taste with remaining lime juice, salt, and pepper.

5. To serve, spoon into warm bowls and sprinkle with chives and shaved cheese.

MAKES 4 SERVINGS.

PER SERVING: 366 calories, 8 g total fat, 5 g saturated fat, 19 mg cholesterol, 735 mg sodium, 62 g carbohydrates, 4 g fiber, 12 g pro-

Radicchio Risotto

30 MINUTES

- 3 to 3¼ cups fat-free reduced-sodium chicken broth
- 2 tablespoons olive oil
- 3 cups shredded radicchio leaves
- 1 tablespoon lemon juice
- 3 tablespoons butter or margarine
- 1 small onion (about 4 oz.), finely chopped
- 1 small clove garlic, minced or pressed
- 1 cup arborio or other short-grain white rice

  About ⅓ cup grated Parmesan cheese
- 4 to 6 whole radicchio leaves, rinsed and crisped

1. In a 1½-quart pan, bring broth to a simmer over medium heat. Reduce heat to low.

2. Meanwhile, heat 1 tablespoon of the oil in a 3- to 4-quart pan over high heat. Add shredded radicchio and lemon juice. Stir until radicchio is wilted (about 2 minutes). Remove from pan with a slotted spoon and set aside.

3. To pan, add remaining 1 tablespoon oil, 2 tablespoons of the butter, onion, and garlic. Reduce heat to medium and cook, stirring occasionally, until onion is golden (about 5 minutes). Add rice and stir until opaque and well coated with butter (2 to 3 minutes). Add ½ cup of the broth and cook, stirring, until absorbed. Continue to cook, adding remaining 2¾ cups broth about ½ cup at a time, until rice is just tender to bite but not starchy tasting (about 20 more minutes); after each addition, stir constantly until broth is absorbed.

4. Stir in cooked radicchio. Remove from heat and add remaining 1 tablespoon butter and ⅓ cup of the cheese; mix gently. To serve, place a whole radicchio leaf on each individual plate. Spoon risotto into radicchio leaves. Offer additional cheese to add to taste.

MAKES 4 TO 6 SERVINGS.

PER SERVING: 318 calories, 14 g total fat, 6 g saturated fat, 23 mg cholesterol, 612 mg sodium, 38 g carbohydrates, 3 g fiber, 9 g protein, 192 mg calcium, 3 mg iron

tato Risotto

MINUTES

- ¼ cup butter or margarine
- 1 small onion (about 4 oz.), finely chopped
- 1 clove garlic, minced or pressed
- ½ teaspoon fresh thyme leaves or ¼ teaspoon dried thyme
- 2 cups fat-free reduced-sodium chicken broth

- 3 cups cubed boiled thin-skinned potatoes (about 1¼ lbs.)
- ¼ cup whipping cream
- ¼ cup grated Parmesan cheese

  Salt

  Thyme sprigs

1. Melt butter in a 2- to 3-quart pan over medium-high heat. Add onion, garlic, and thyme leaves; cook, stirring often, until onion is soft (about 4 minutes). Add broth and bring to a boil over high heat. Then boil, uncovered, until mixture is reduced to 1½ cups (about 5 minutes).

2. Add potatoes and cook over medium heat, stirring often, until heated through (about 5 minutes). Remove from heat, stir in cream and cheese, and season to taste with salt. To serve, spoon into warm bowls and garnish with thyme sprigs.

MAKES 4 TO 6 SERVINGS.

PER SERVING: 234 calories, 14 g total fat, 9 g saturated fat, 42 mg cholesterol, 391 mg sodium, 21 g carbohydrates, 2 g fiber, 5 g protein, 93 mg calcium, 0 mg iron

Ravioli with Fennel & Bread Crumbs

Ravioli with Fennel & Bread Crumbs

30 MINUTES

Good raw or cooked, fennel has a sweet, clean flavor reminiscent of licorice. Here, sautéed sliced fennel in a light tomato sauce is served over ravioli and topped with crisp herbed bread crumbs. Serve with a green salad and more Italian bread (you need just two slices for the crumb topping) with olive oil for dipping.

2 slices Italian bread (*each* about 3 by 4 inches and 1 inch thick), cut into chunks

¼ cup olive oil

½ teaspoon dried rosemary

About ¼ cup grated Parmesan cheese

1 head fennel (about 4 inches in diameter)

1 medium-size onion (about 6 oz.), thinly sliced

2 cloves garlic, minced or pressed

1 can (about 14½ oz.) diced tomatoes

Salt and pepper

2 packages (about 9 oz. *each*) fresh cheese-filled ravioli

Rosemary sprigs (optional)

1. Whirl bread in a blender or food processor to form coarse crumbs. Heat 2 tablespoons of the oil in a wide frying pan over medium-high heat. Add bread crumbs and dried rosemary; cook, stirring often, until crumbs are toasted (about 3 minutes). Transfer to a bowl, stir in ¼ cup of the cheese, and set aside.

2. Rinse fennel. Cut off stalks; trim and discard base and any discolored or bruised parts of fennel head. Then thinly slice fennel. In frying pan, heat remaining 2 tablespoons oil over high heat; add fennel, onion, and garlic. Cook, stirring often, until fennel is softened (about 4 minutes). Add tomatoes and their liquid. Bring to a boil; then reduce heat, cover, and simmer for about 5 minutes. Season to taste with salt and pepper.

3. Meanwhile, bring about 3 quarts water to a boil in a 5- to 6-quart pan over high heat; stir in ravioli and cook, uncovered, until just tender to bite (4 to 6 minutes). Or cook ravioli according to package directions.

4. Drain ravioli well and pour into a large serving bowl. Add fennel mixture and toss to mix; sprinkle with crumb mixture. Spoon onto individual plates; garnish with rosemary sprigs, if desired. Offer additional cheese to add to taste.

MAKES 4 SERVINGS.

PER SERVING: 655 calories, 30 g total fat, 10 g saturated fat, 108 mg cholesterol, 938 mg sodium, 70 g carbohydrates, 6 g fiber, 26 g protein, 451 mg calcium, 4 mg iron

Spinach Ravioli with Lemon-Caper Sauce

20 MINUTES

A zesty lemon sauce, its tartness mellowed with a touch of whipping cream, cloaks green ravioli filled with spinach and cheese in a simple dish that's perfect for a late supper. Alongside, you might serve a butter lettuce salad and a loaf of crusty bread with sweet butter.

2 packages (about 9 oz. *each*) fresh spinach- and cheese-filled spinach ravioli

2 tablespoons olive oil

1 tablespoon butter or margarine

3 tablespoons minced shallots

¼ cup fat-free reduced-sodium chicken broth

¼ cup whipping cream

2 teaspoons grated lemon peel

3 tablespoons lemon juice

2 tablespoons drained capers

1. In a 5- to 6-quart pan, bring about 3 quarts water to a boil over high heat; stir in ravioli and cook, uncovered, until just tender to bite (4 to 6 minutes). Or cook ravioli according to package directions.

2. Meanwhile, in a 2- to 3-quart pan, combine oil and butter. Set over medium heat. When butter is melted, add shallots and cook, stirring often, until soft (about 2 minutes). Add broth, cream, lemon peel, and lemon juice. Cook just until sauce comes to a boil (about 3 minutes). Reduce heat and stir in capers.

3. Drain ravioli well, then stir into sauce and serve.

MAKES 4 SERVINGS.

PER SERVING: 472 calories, 21 g total fat, 9 g saturated fat, 43 mg cholesterol, 684 mg sodium, 52 g carbohydrates, 3 g fiber, 19 g protein, 335 mg calcium, 4 mg iron

Pasta alla Puttanesca

20 MINUTES

Piquant in both flavor and name (*pasta alla puttanesca* means "harlot's pasta"), this dish is easy to make on the spur of the moment from ingredients you're likely to have on hand. If you prefer a less pronounced flavor of anchovies, cook the anchovy fillets on their own in a little olive oil before adding them to the sauce.

8 ounces dried linguine or vermicelli (not coil vermicelli)

1 jar (about 26 oz.) marinara sauce

¼ teaspoon crushed red pepper flakes

½ teaspoon dried basil

½ teaspoon dried oregano

½ cup oil-cured black ripe olives, rinsed, patted dry, and pitted (if desired)

1 can (about 2 oz.) flat anchovy fillets, rinsed, patted dry, and diced

1 tablespoon drained capers

1 can (6 to 7 oz.) water-packed chunk light tuna, drained

⅓ cup chopped parsley

Parsley and rosemary sprigs (optional)

Pasta alla Puttanesca

1. In a 4- to 5-quart pan, bring about 2 quarts water to a boil over high heat; stir in pasta and cook, uncovered, until just tender to bite (8 to 10 minutes). Or cook pasta according to package directions.

2. Meanwhile, warm marinara sauce in a 3-quart pan over medium heat. Add red pepper flakes, basil, oregano, olives, anchovies, capers, tuna, and chopped parsley. Cook, stirring occasionally, until heated through.

3. Drain pasta well and pour onto a platter or individual plates; top with sauce. Garnish with parsley and rosemary sprigs, if desired.

MAKES 4 SERVINGS.

PER SERVING: 478 calories, 15 g total fat, 2 g saturated fat, 23 mg cholesterol, 2,411 mg sodium, 64 g carbohydrates, 2 g fiber, 26 g protein, 103 mg calcium, 6 mg iron

Penne with Smoked Salmon

25 MINUTES

Vodka emphasizes the flavor of a creamy, tomato-dotted sauce for silken smoked salmon and pasta tubes. Serve the dish with tender-crisp green beans and a simple salad.

12 ounces dried tube-shaped pasta, such as penne, mostaccioli, or ziti

2 tablespoons olive oil

1 small shallot, thinly sliced

4 small pear-shaped (Roma-type) tomatoes (about 6 oz. *total*), peeled, seeded, and chopped

2/3 cup whipping cream

Pinch of ground nutmeg

2 tablespoons chopped fresh dill or 1/2 teaspoon dried dill weed

1/3 cup vodka

4 to 6 ounces sliced smoked salmon or lox, cut into bite-size strips

White pepper

Dill sprigs

1. In a 5- to 6-quart pan, bring about 3 quarts water to a boil over high heat; stir in pasta and cook, uncovered, until just tender to bite (10 to 12 minutes). Or cook pasta according to package directions.

2. Meanwhile, heat oil in a wide frying pan over medium-low heat. Add shallot and cook, stirring often, until soft but not brown (about 3 minutes). Stir in tomatoes, cover, and simmer for 5 minutes. Add cream, nutmeg, chopped dill, and vodka. Increase heat to high and bring to a boil; then boil for 1 minute.

3. Drain pasta well; add to sauce and mix lightly, using 2 spoons, until pasta is well coated with sauce. Remove from heat, add salmon, and mix lightly. Season to taste with pepper. Pour onto a platter or individual plates; garnish with dill sprigs.

MAKES 4 SERVINGS.

PER SERVING: 586 calories, 22 g total fat, 9 g saturated fat, 53 mg cholesterol, 301 mg sodium, 67 g carbohydrates, 3 g fiber, 19 g protein, 52 mg calcium, 4 mg iron

Pasta with Shrimp in Tomato Cream

30 MINUTES

Sun-dried tomatoes join shrimp, fresh basil, and cream in an elegant sauce for linguine. Be sure you buy oil-packed tomatoes; the oil helps give the rosy sauce its rich, full flavor.

⅓ cup oil-packed dried tomatoes

1 clove garlic, minced or pressed

1 pound raw shrimp (31 to 40 per lb.), shelled and deveined

¼ cup thinly sliced green onions

1½ tablespoons chopped fresh basil or 1 teaspoon dried basil

¼ teaspoon white pepper

1 cup fat-free reduced-sodium chicken broth

¾ cup dry vermouth

1 cup whipping cream

10 ounces dried linguine

Basil sprigs (optional)

Grated Parmesan cheese

1. Drain tomatoes, reserving 2 tablespoons of the oil. Cut tomatoes into thin slivers and set aside.

2. Heat the reserved 2 tablespoons tomato oil in a wide frying pan over medium-high heat. Add garlic and shrimp. Cook, stirring often, until shrimp are just opaque in center; cut to test (3 to 5 minutes). Lift shrimp from pan and set aside. Add onions, chopped basil, slivered tomatoes, pepper, broth, vermouth, and cream to pan. Bring to a boil over high heat; then boil, uncovered, stirring occasionally, until reduced to about 1½ cups (about 10 minutes).

3. While you are preparing sauce, bring about 3 quarts water to a boil in a 5- to 6-quart pan over high heat; stir in pasta and cook, uncovered, until just tender to bite (8 to 10 minutes). Or cook pasta according to package directions. Drain well.

4. Return shrimp to sauce and stir just until heated through. Pour pasta onto a platter or individual plates; spoon sauce over pasta. Garnish with basil sprigs, if desired. Offer cheese to add to taste.

MAKES 4 SERVINGS.

PER SERVING: 766 calories, 38 g total fat, 14 g saturated fat, 206 mg cholesterol, 316 mg sodium, 63 g carbohydrates, 3 g fiber, 31 g protein, 123 mg calcium, 6 mg iron

Coriander-Curry Shrimp

20 MINUTES

Pineapple juice and coconut give these spicy curried shrimp a tropical accent. Serve over hearty penne, with crunchy breadsticks and a spinach salad alongside. For dessert, you might serve fresh papaya wedges with a squeeze of lime; or try Hot Papaya Sundaes (page 226).

8 ounces dried penne

1 large onion (about 8 oz.), thinly sliced

1 clove garlic, minced or pressed

1 teaspoon olive oil

1 tablespoon curry powder

1 tablespoon ground coriander

¼ teaspoon ground red pepper (cayenne)

1½ pounds raw shrimp (31 to 40 per lb.), shelled and deveined

⅔ cup unsweetened pineapple juice

¼ cup sweetened shredded coconut mixed with 2 teaspoons all-purpose flour

2 tablespoons minced parsley

Salt

Lime wedges

1. In a 4- to 5-quart pan, bring about 2 quarts water to a boil over high heat; stir in pasta and cook, uncovered, until just tender to bit (10 to 12 minutes). Or cook pasta according to package directions.

2. Meanwhile, in a wide frying pan, combine onion, garlic, oil, and 2 tablespoons water. Cook over high heat, stirring often, until liquid has evaporated and onion is soft and tinged with brown (3 to 5 minutes). Stir in curry powder, coriander, and red pepper. Add shrimp and cook, stirring often, for about 2 minutes. Add pineapple juice and coconut mixture and continue to cook, stirring, until sauce comes to a boil and shrimp are just opaque in center; cut to test (about 3 more minutes). Stir in parsley and season to taste with salt.

3. Drain pasta well and pour onto a platter or individual plates. Spoon shrimp sauce over pasta. Offer lime wedges to season individual servings to taste.

MAKES 6 SERVINGS.

PER SERVING: 297 calories, 4 g total fat, 1 g saturated fat, 140 mg cholesterol, 150 mg sodium, 39 g carbohydrates, 2 g fiber, 25 g protein, 76 mg calcium, 4 mg iron

Coriander-Curry Shrimp

Lemon Scallops with Rotelle

20 MINUTES

Gently cook tiny scallops in a light, buttery wine sauce; then catch the sauce's good flavo in the twists and turns of corkscrew-shaped pasta. Steamed broccoli flowerets taste grea alongside—and provide a nice color contrast, too.

8 ounces dried rotelle or other medium-size pasta shapes

¼ cup dry white wine

¼ teaspoon grated lemon peel

2 teaspoons lemon juice

2 green onions, thinly sliced

2 tablespoons drained capers

1 teaspoon dried rosemary

½ teaspoon dried basil

2 cloves garlic, minced or pressed

8 ounces bay scallops

¼ cup butter or margarine

Salt

Chopped parsley

1. In a 4- to 5-quart pan, bring about 2 quarts water to a boil over high heat; stir in pasta and cook, uncovered, until just tender to bite (about 10 minutes). Or cook pasta according to package directions.

2. Meanwhile, in a wide frying pan, combine wine, lemon peel, lemon juice, onions, capers, rosemary, basil, and garlic. Bring to a boil over high heat; then boil, stirring often, until liquid is reduced by half. Rinse and drain scallops. Add scallops to pan and stir until coated with lemon mixture and just opaque in center; cut to test (2 to 3 minutes). Remove pan from heat and add butter all at once, stirring constantly to incorporate it into sauce. Season to taste with salt.

3. Drain pasta well and add to sauce. Lift with 2 spoons to mix well. Pour onto a platter or individual plates and sprinkle with parsley.

MAKES 3 SERVINGS.

PER SERVING: 495 calories, 17 g total fat, 10 g saturated fat, 66 mg cholesterol, 540 mg sodium, 61 g carbohydrates, 2 g fiber, 23 g protein, 59 mg calcium, 4 mg iron

Lemon Scallops with Rotelle

Scallop Fettuccine with Orange-Tomato Sauce

25 MINUTES

For a wonderful dinner in a hurry, serve this pretty dish with packaged mesclun in vinaigrette dressing, sourdough bread, and a dessert of lemon sorbet and your favorite crisp cookies. Start the sauce going as soon as you put the pasta water on to boil.

- 1 orange
- 1 pound dried fettuccine
- 3 tablespoons butter or margarine
- 1 large onion (about 8 oz.), thinly sliced
- 1 large can (about 28 oz.) pear-shaped tomatoes
- 3 tablespoons chopped parsley
- 2 teaspoons fresh thyme leaves
- 2 teaspoons minced fresh ginger
  Salt and pepper
- 12 ounces bay scallops

1. Using a small, sharp knife or a vegetable peeler, cut peel (colored part only) from orange in long strips. Squeeze ¼ cup juice from orange. Set peel and juice aside.

2. In a 6- to 8-quart pan, bring about 4 quarts water to a boil over high heat; stir in pasta and cook, uncovered, until just tender to bite (8 to 10 minutes). Or cook pasta according to package directions.

3. Meanwhile, melt butter in a wide frying pan over medium-high heat. Add onion and cook, stirring often, until soft (about 5 minutes). Add tomatoes (break up with a spoon) and their liquid, orange peel, orange juice, 2 tablespoons of the parsley, thyme, and ginger. Cook for 2 minutes. Season to taste with salt and pepper.

4. Rinse scallops and pat dry. Add scallops to sauce and simmer, stirring often, until just opaque in center; cut to test (3 to 4 minutes). Remove and discard orange peel.

5. Drain pasta well and pour into a large bowl; top with sauce and mix lightly. Sprinkle with remaining 1 tablespoon parsley.

MAKES 4 TO 6 SERVINGS.

PER SERVING: 520 calories, 9 g total fat, 5 g saturated fat, 41 mg cholesterol, 448 mg sodium, 83 g carbohydrates, 4 g fiber, 25 g protein, 96 mg calcium, 5 mg iron

Gingered Clam Pasta

25 MINUTES

Fresh ginger lends its mild bite and distinctive aroma to this simple entrée. To add extra flavor to the capellini and Chinese pea pods, drain the liquid from the clams into the pasta cooking water.

- 1 tablespoon sesame seeds
- 2 tablespoons minced fresh ginger
- 2 teaspoons sugar
- 1 teaspoon grated lemon peel
- ¼ teaspoon crushed red pepper flakes
- ⅓ cup reduced-sodium soy sauce
- 1 tablespoon vegetable oil
- 8 ounces fresh Chinese pea pods, ends and strings removed
- 2 cans (about 6½ oz. *each*) chopped clams
- 8 to 9 ounces fresh capellini (angel hair pasta)
- ¼ cup thinly sliced green onions

1. Pour sesame seeds into a small frying pan. Stir over medium heat until pale gold (2 to 3 minutes). Pour out of pan and set aside.

2. In a small bowl, stir together ginger, sugar, lemon peel, red pepper flakes, soy sauce, and oil. Place pea pods in a colander; set colander in the sink. Drain clams, reserving liquid.

3. In a 4- to 5-quart pan, bring about 2 quarts water to a boil over high heat; stir in reserved clam liquid and pasta and cook, uncovered, until pasta is just tender to bite (1 to 2 minutes). Or cook pasta according to package directions, adding clam liquid to water.

Gingered Clam Pasta

4. Pour pasta and its cooking water into colander over pea pods and drain well. Return pasta and pea pods to pan and set over low heat. Add clams, ginger mixture, and onions. Mix well with 2 forks, then pour onto a platter or individual plates and sprinkle with sesame seeds.

MAKES 4 SERVINGS.

PER SERVING: 338 calories, 7 g total fat, 1 g saturated fat, 76 mg cholesterol, 865 mg sodium, 45 g carbohydrates, 3 g fiber, 23 g protein, 115 mg calcium, 17 mg iron

Turkey Rigatoni Marinara

30 MINUTES

Lean ground turkey makes a lower-fat substitute for beef in this hearty dish. The sauce goes together quickly from fresh vegetables, dried herbs, and your favorite purchased marinara sauce.

1 tablespoon olive oil

1 small onion (about 4 oz.), finely chopped

6 mushrooms, thinly sliced

1 tablespoon chopped parsley

1 clove garlic, minced

1 teaspoon dried basil

½ teaspoon dried rosemary

½ teaspoon dried oregano

1 pound lean ground turkey

1 jar (about 26 oz.) marinara sauce

⅓ cup dry red wine

1 dried bay leaf

8 to 12 ounces dried rigatoni

Salt and pepper

Grated Parmesan cheese (optional)

Turkey Rigatoni Marinara

1. In a wide frying pan, combine oil, onion, mushrooms, parsley, garlic, basil, rosemary, and oregano. Cook over medium-high heat, stirring often, until onion and mushrooms are soft (3 to 5 minutes).

2. Crumble turkey into pan and cook, stirring often, until lightly browned (about 5 minutes). Add marinara sauce, wine, and bay leaf; bring to a boil. Adjust heat so sauce boils gently; then cook, stirring occasionally, until sauce is thickened (about 20 minutes).

3. Meanwhile, in a 5- to 6-quart pan, bring about 3 quarts water to a boil over high heat;

stir in pasta and cook, uncovered, until just tender to bite (10 to 12 minutes).

4. Season sauce to taste with salt and pepper; remove and discard bay leaf. Drain pasta well and pour onto a platter or individual plates. Spoon sauce over pasta. Offer cheese to add to taste, if desired

MAKES 4 TO 6 SERVINGS.

PER SERVING: 492 calories, 16 g total fat, 3 g saturated fat, 66 mg cholesterol, 1,019 mg sodium, 61 g carbohydrates, 2 g fiber, 26 g protein, 69 mg calcium, 5 mg iron

Chicken Pasta Italiano

30 MINUTES

Choose the reddest, ripest tomatoes you can find for this zesty, garlicky pasta sauce. Hearty with strips of chicken and crisp bacon bits, it's delicious served over hot spaghetti for a satisfying casual supper.

    4 ounces sliced bacon, chopped

    4 cloves garlic, minced or pressed

    12 ounces boneless, skinless chicken breast,
       cut into ¼-inch-wide strips

    4 medium-size tomatoes (about 1½ lbs.
       total), seeded and chopped

    ½ cup dry sherry or fat-free reduced-sodium
       chicken broth

    1 tablespoon Italian herb seasoning (or
       ¾ teaspoon *each* dried basil, oregano,
       thyme, and marjoram)

    ⅛ teaspoon ground red pepper (cayenne)

    6 ounces dried spaghetti

    ½ cup grated Parmesan cheese

1. Cook bacon in a wide frying pan over medium heat, stirring occasionally, until crisp (4 to 5 minutes). Lift out with a slotted spoon, drain, and set aside. Discard all but 2 table-spoons of the drippings.

2. Add garlic and chicken to drippings in pan. Increase heat to high and cook, stirring, until

chicken is lightly browned (about 3 minutes). Remove chicken from pan and set aside on a plate. Add tomatoes, sherry, herb seasoning, and red pepper to pan; bring to a boil. Then boil, stirring often, until almost all liquid has evaporated (about 10 minutes).

3. Meanwhile, in a 4- to 5-quart pan, bring about 2 quarts water to a boil over high heat; stir in pasta and cook, uncovered, until just tender to bite (10 to 12 minutes). Or cook pasta according to package directions. Drain well and pour onto a platter or individual plates.

4. Add chicken and any accumulated liquid to tomato sauce; stir until heated through. Spoon sauce over pasta and sprinkle with bacon. Offer cheese to add to taste.

MAKES 3 SERVINGS.

PER SERVING: 575 calories, 19 g total fat, 7 g saturated fat, 91 mg cholesterol, 668 mg sodium, 55 g carbohydrates, 4 g fiber, 44 g protein, 226 mg calcium, 4 mg iron

Pasta Amatriciana

25 MINUTES

Savory morsels of bacon and onion add emphasis to this peppery tomato sauce. It's traditionally served over long, hollow noodles called bucatini, but you can use spaghetti or other pasta strands if you prefer. For a classic Italian feast, accompany the dish with warm garlic bread and red wine.

- 4 slices thick-cut bacon, chopped
- 1 large onion (about 8 oz.), chopped
- ½ teaspoon crushed red pepper flakes
- 1 large can (about 28 oz.) pear-shaped tomatoes
- 1 pound dried bucatini, spaghetti, or other pasta strands

   Grated Parmesan cheese

1. Cook bacon in a wide frying pan over medium-high heat, stirring often, just until fat is rendered (about 3 minutes). Add onion and cook, stirring often, until soft (about 5 more minutes). Stir in red pepper flakes. Add tomatoes (break up with a spoon) and their liquid; bring to a boil. Then reduce heat and simmer, uncovered, stirring occasionally, until sauce is slightly thickened (about 10 minutes).

2. Meanwhile, in a 6- to 8-quart pan, bring about 4 quarts water to a boil over high heat; stir in pasta and cook, uncovered, until just tender to bite (about 10 minutes). Or cook pasta according to package directions. Drain well and pour into a large bowl; add tomato sauce and toss to mix.

3. To serve, spoon pasta and sauce onto individual plates. Offer cheese to add to taste.

MAKES 4 TO 6 SERVINGS.

PER SERVING: 555 calories, 19 g total fat, 7 g saturated fat, 20 mg cholesterol, 475 mg sodium, 79 g carbohydrates, 4 g fiber, 16 g protein, 69 mg calcium, 5 mg iron

Bacon & Egg Carbonara

25 TO 30 MINUTES

To make each serving of this variation on classic spaghetti carbonara, you spoon hot cooked pasta mixed with bacon and sour cream into a warmed bowl, then top with an egg yolk. Let diners mix the ingredients together as they eat.

- 4 ounces sliced bacon, cut into 1-inch pieces
- 8 ounces dried capellini (angel hair pasta) or coil vermicelli
- ¼ cup thinly sliced green onions
- 2 cups reduced-fat sour cream
- 4 large egg yolks
- 1 cup (about 3 oz.) grated Parmesan cheese

1. Cook bacon in a wide frying pan over medium heat, stirring occasionally, until crisp (4 to 5 minutes). Spoon off and discard all but about 3 tablespoons of the drippings; keep pan with bacon warm.

2. While bacon is cooking, bring about 2 quarts water to a boil in a 4- to 5-quart pan over high heat; add pasta and cook, uncovered, until just tender to bite (about 3 minutes). Or cook pasta according to package directions. Drain pasta well; immediately add to bacon. Then add onions and sour cream and mix well.

3. Spoon pasta mixture equally into 4 wide 1½- to 2-cup soup bowls. Make a nest in center of each serving and slip in an egg yolk. Let diners mix pasta with egg; offer cheese to add to taste.

MAKES 4 SERVINGS.

PER SERVING: 670 calories, 39 g total fat, 17 g saturated fat, 281 mg cholesterol, 592 mg sodium, 52 g carbohydrates, 2 g fiber, 28 g protein, 290 mg calcium, 3 mg iron

Italian Sausage & Pasta with Basil

30 MINUTES

The combination of robust sausages and bell peppers recalls the bustle of an Italian street fair—and when you serve this entrée, you'll create that same festive atmosphere. Sausage, onion, and red bell pepper are sautéed, combined with garlic and tomatoes, and served over hot vermicelli.

- 12 **ounces dried vermicelli (not coil vermicelli) or spaghettini**
- 1 **pound mild Italian sausages**
- 1 **large onion (about 8 oz.), coarsely chopped**
- 1 **large red bell pepper (about 8 oz.), seeded and coarsely chopped**
- 2 **cloves garlic, minced or pressed**
- 1 **can (about 14½ oz.) whole tomatoes**
- 2 **to 3 tablespoons dried basil**
- ¼ **cup chopped parsley**
- ¾ **to 1 cup (2¼ to 3 oz.) grated Parmesan cheese**
- ¼ **cup olive oil**

1. In a 5- to 6-quart pan, bring about 3 quarts water to a boil over high heat; stir in pasta and cook, uncovered, until just tender to bite (about 10 minutes). Or cook pasta according to package directions.

2. Meanwhile, remove casings from sausages and crumble meat into a wide nonstick frying pan. Cook over medium-high heat, stirring often, until meat begins to brown. Add onion and bell pepper; continue to cook, stirring often, until onion is soft but not brown (about 5 minutes). Spoon off and discard excess fat. Stir in garlic; stir in tomatoes (break up with a spoon) and their liquid. Bring to a boil; then reduce heat to a simmer.

3. Drain pasta well. In a large serving bowl, combine basil, parsley, ½ cup of the cheese, and oil. Add pasta and mix lightly, using 2 forks. Top with sausage-tomato sauce. Offer remaining cheese to add to taste.

MAKES 6 SERVINGS.

PER SERVING: 610 calories, 33 g total fat, 10 g saturated fat, 60 mg cholesterol, 882 mg sodium, 53 g carbohydrates, 3 g fiber, 25 g protein, 267 mg calcium, 5 mg iron

Italian Sausage & Pasta with Basil

Linguine with Prosciutto & Olives

20 MINUTES

Pictured on page 148

An assertive combination of salty prosciutto and green olives complements mild, tender linguine. Serve with a salad of sliced oranges and romaine, if you like.

8 ounces dried linguine or spaghetti

2 ounces thinly sliced prosciutto, cut into ¼-inch-wide strips

2 tablespoons olive oil

½ cup thinly sliced green onions

1 small jar (about 3 oz.) pitted green olives, drained

1 cup cherry tomatoes, halved

Grated Parmesan cheese

1. In a 4- to 5-quart pan, bring about 2 quarts water to a boil over high heat; stir in pasta and cook, uncovered, until just tender to bite (8 to 10 minutes). Or cook pasta according to package directions.

2. Meanwhile, in a wide frying pan, combine prosciutto and oil. Stir over medium-high heat until prosciutto is lightly browned (about 3 minutes). Add onions and stir until soft (about 2 more minutes). Add olives and tomatoes; cook, shaking pan often, until olives are hot (about 2 more minutes).

3. Drain pasta well and return to cooking pan. Pour prosciutto mixture over pasta and toss to mix, using 2 spoons. Pour onto a platter or individual plates; offer cheese to add to taste.

MAKES 3 SERVINGS.

PER SERVING: 452 calories, 17 g total fat, 2 g saturated fat, 15 mg cholesterol, 1,041 mg sodium, 60 g carbohydrates, 3 g fiber, 16 g protein, 45 mg calcium, 4 mg iron

Fresh Fettuccine with Sausages & Cream

25 MINUTES

Serve this luxurious sausage-sauced pasta with crisp greens in a tart vinaigrette and a loaf of hot, crusty bread.

12 ounces hot Italian sausages

1 clove garlic, minced or pressed

2 teaspoons olive oil

½ cup thinly sliced bottled roasted red peppers

½ cup dry white wine

¼ teaspoon crushed red pepper flakes

¼ cup canned tomato sauce

2 cups *each* milk and whipping cream (or 4 cups milk mixed smoothly with 2 tablespoons all-purpose flour)

Salt and pepper

16 to 18 ounces fresh fettuccine

¼ cup minced Italian parsley

Thinly shaved Parmesan cheese

1. In a 6- to 8-quart pan, bring about 4 quarts water to a boil over high heat.

2. Meanwhile, pierce sausages in several places with a fork. Then place sausages in a wide frying pan and cook over medium-high heat, turning as needed, until lightly browned on all sides (5 to 8 minutes). Remove sausages to a plate and cut into ½-inch-thick slices.

3. Wipe frying pan clean, return to heat, and add garlic and oil; cook over medium-high heat, stirring, until garlic is lightly browned (1 to 2 minutes). Return sausages to pan; stir in roasted peppers, wine, red pepper flakes, and tomato sauce. Increase heat to high and bring to a full rolling boil, stirring several times; boil for 2 minutes. Add milk and cream (or milk-flour mixture) and stir until sauce returns to a full boil. Boil, stirring, for 1 minute. Season to taste with salt and pepper.

4. When water comes to a boil, stir in pasta and cook, uncovered, until just tender to bite (2 to 3 minutes). Or cook pasta according to package directions. Drain pasta and pour into a large bowl. Pour sauce over pasta and mix, using 2 forks, until pasta has absorbed some of the sauce. Spoon pasta and sauce into shallow individual bowls; sprinkle with parsley and offer cheese to add to taste.

MAKES 6 SERVINGS.

PER SERVING: 685 calories, 41 g total fat, 21 g saturated fat, 191 mg cholesterol, 558 mg sodium, 53 g carbohydrates, 2 g fiber, 22 g protein, 181 mg calcium, 4 mg iron

Couscous Paella

25 MINUTES

Paella is traditionally based on rice, but this creative version starts with couscous—granular semolina that cooks to tenderness in just 5 minutes. Couscous is sold both packaged and in bulk in many supermarkets and specialty food stores.

> 4 ounces chorizo sausages
> 1 large onion (about 8 oz.), chopped
> 1 bottle (about 8 oz.) clam juice
> 1¼ cups fat-free reduced-sodium chicken broth
> 2 teaspoons cumin seeds
> 1¼ cups couscous
> 1 medium-size red bell pepper (about 6 oz.), seeded and chopped
> 8 ounces small cooked shrimp
> Lime or lemon wedges

1. Remove casings from sausages and crumble meat into a wide nonstick frying pan; add onion. Cook over medium heat, stirring often, until meat is well browned (8 to 10 minutes); if pan appears dry or mixture sticks to pan bottom, add water, 1 tablespoon at a time.

2. Add clam juice, broth, and cumin seeds. Increase heat to medium-high and bring to a boil. Stir in couscous; then cover tightly, remove from heat, and let stand until all liquid has been absorbed (about 5 minutes).

3. To serve, transfer couscous mixture to a wide serving bowl. Stir in bell pepper, then top with shrimp. Offer lime wedges to season individual servings to taste.

MAKES 4 TO 6 SERVINGS.

PER SERVING: 369 calories, 10 g total fat, 3 g saturated fat, 104 mg cholesterol, 505 mg sodium, 47 g carbohydrates, 3 g fiber, 21 g protein, 60 mg calcium, 3 mg iron

Pad Thai

30 MINUTES

A favorite dish in Thailand, pad thai—mildly spiced stir-fried noodles—has achieved considerable popularity in Thai restaurants in the West. Noodles made from rice flour (not from wheat) are heated with tofu, meat, and a tart-sweet-spicy cooking sauce; at the table, diners season their servings with fresh lime.

Some supermarkets and most Asian grocery stores carry rice noodles (also called rice sticks or *maipun*) and fish sauce.

> 8 ounces dried rice noodles (preferably about ¼ inch wide, but thinner noodles will work)
> 2 pounds firm tofu
> 1 cup fat-free reduced-sodium chicken broth
> 3 tablespoons fish sauce (*nam pla* or *nuoc mam*)
> 3 tablespoons catsup
> 2 tablespoons lime juice
> 2 tablespoons sugar
> ¼ to ½ teaspoon ground red pepper (cayenne)
> 1 tablespoon vegetable oil
> 4 cloves garlic, minced or pressed
> 6 ounces lean boneless pork, trimmed of fat and thinly sliced; or 6 ounces boneless, skinless chicken breast, thinly sliced
> 1 large egg, beaten to blend
> 6 green onions, cut into 2-inch lengths
> 12 ounces bean sprouts
> 3 to 4 tablespoons finely chopped salted roasted peanuts
> ¼ cup cilantro leaves
> ½ cup finely shredded carrot
> Lime wedges

Pad Thai

1. Place noodles in a bowl and add enough hot (not boiling) water to cover. Let stand until pliable (10 to 20 minutes). Drain well.

2. While noodles are soaking, slice tofu and place on paper towels; press gently to remove water. Cut tofu into ½-inch cubes. In a small bowl, mix broth, fish sauce, catsup, lime juice, sugar, and red pepper.

3. Place a wok or wide frying pan over high heat. When pan is hot, add oil; swirl to coat pan. Add tofu; cook, stirring often, until browned (about 5 minutes). Remove from pan with a slotted spoon; set aside. Add garlic and pork; cook, stirring often, until pork is lightly browned (about 2 minutes). Push mixture to side of pan and add egg to empty area. Cook until egg begins to set, then stir to break apart. Add broth mixture, tofu, and drained noodles; cook, stirring often, until noodles are heated through (2 to 3 minutes). Add onions and bean sprouts. Stir until sprouts are barely wilted (about 30 seconds).

4. Spoon noodle mixture equally onto individual plates; top with peanuts, cilantro and carrots. Offer lime wedges to season individual servings to taste

MAKES 4 SERVINGS.

PER SERVING: 791 calories, 32 g total fat, 5 g saturated fat, 78 mg cholesterol, 940 mg sodium, 80 g carbohydrates, 3 g fiber, 55 g protein, 526 mg calcium, 26 mg iron

Chapter Seven

VEGETARIAN

◀ *Previous page: Vegetable Tabbouleh*

Vegetable Tabbouleh

25 MINUTES

This refreshing salad makes a wonderful main course for a summer meal. Accompany it with celery sticks and calamata olives; offer ripe peaches or plums for dessert. To speed preparation, use your food processor to grate the carrots and make the dressing.

- 2 **cups water**
- **Salt**
- 1 **cup bulgur**
- ¼ **cup fresh mint leaves**
- ¼ **cup Italian parsley leaves**
- ¼ **cup lemon juice**
- 1 **teaspoon grated lemon peel**
- 2 **tablespoons olive oil**
- 4 **green onions, cut into 1½-inch lengths**
- 1 **large cucumber (about 10 oz.), peeled, seeded, and chopped**
- 2 **medium-size carrots (about 6 oz. *total*), grated**
- **Pepper**
- **Romaine lettuce leaves, rinsed and crisped**
- 2 **medium-size firm-ripe tomatoes (about 12 oz. *total*), cut into wedges**

1. In a 3-quart pan, bring water to a boil over high heat. Add salt to taste (about ½ teaspoon and bulgur. Reduce heat to a simmer; cover and cook for 15 minutes. Uncover; fluff bulgur with a fork.

2. While bulgur is cooking, combine mint, parsley, lemon juice, lemon peel, oil, and onions in a food processor or blender. Whirl until smoothly puréed. Stir dressing into bulgur along with cucumber and carrots; mix well. Season to taste with salt and pepper.

3. To serve, line a platter or individual plates with lettuce leaves. Spoon bulgur mixture atop lettuce and garnish with tomatoes.

MAKES 6 SERVINGS.

PER SERVING: 150 calories, 5 g total fat, 1 g saturated fat, 0 mg cholesterol, 23 mg sodium, 25 g carbohydrates, 6 g fiber, 4 g protein, 36 mg calcium, 1 mg iron

Couscous Salad with Garbanzos & Feta Cheese

20 MINUTES

Here's a great choice for a warm-weather lunch or dinner: since there's a minimum of cooking, your kitchen stays nice and cool. Serve with flatbreads or lahvosh and a sliced cucumber salad.

- ⅔ **cup water**
- ⅔ **cup couscous**
- 3 **tablespoons lemon juice**
- 2 **tablespoons extra-virgin olive oil**
- **Salt and pepper**
- 1 **can (about 15 oz.) garbanzo beans, rinsed and drained**
- 2 **stalks celery, chopped**
- 1 **medium-size tomato (about 6 oz.), seeded and chopped**
- 4 **green onions, thinly sliced**
- **Romaine lettuce leaves, rinsed and crisped**
- ½ **cup crumbled feta cheese**

1. In a medium-size pan, bring water to a boil over high heat. Stir in couscous; then cover tightly and let stand until all water has been absorbed (about 5 minutes).

2. Meanwhile, in a small jar with a tight-fitting lid, combine lemon juice, oil, and salt and pepper to taste; shake until well blended.

3. Fluff couscous with a fork, then transfer to a large bowl; add beans, celery, tomato, and onions. Pour in dressing; toss to mix.

4. To serve, line a platter with lettuce leaves; spoon couscous mixture atop lettuce. Sprinkle with cheese.

MAKES 6 SERVINGS.

PER SERVING: 205 calories, 8 g total fat, 2 g saturated fat, 10 mg cholesterol, 218 mg sodium, 26 g carbohydrates, 3 g fiber, 7 g protein, 88 mg calcium, 1 mg iron

Moroccan Spiced Couscous with Root Vegetables

20 MINUTES

Couscous goes beautifully with pungent spices and quick-cooked sliced root vegetables—carrots, parsnips, and turnips. Make sure all the vegetables are fresh, with tight skins and good color. To round out the meal, offer steamed Swiss chard or kale and warm whole wheat pocket breads.

2 tablespoons vegetable oil

1 medium-size onion (about 6 oz.), chopped

2 medium-size carrots (about 6 oz. *total*), thinly sliced

2 medium-size parsnips (about 8 oz. *total*), thinly sliced

1 medium-size turnip (about 4 oz.), cut into quarters and thinly sliced

2¼ cups vegetable broth or water

½ teaspoon ground cumin

¼ teaspoon ground cinnamon

¼ teaspoon ground ginger

⅛ teaspoon ground saffron

1 can (about 15 oz.) fava or butter beans, rinsed and drained

½ cup dried currants

Salt and pepper

1⅓ cups couscous

1. Heat oil in a 3- to 4-quart pan over high heat. Add onion, carrots, parsnips, and turnip; cook, stirring often, until onion is tender to bite (about 3 minutes). Add ¼ cup of the broth; reduce heat, cover, and simmer until carrots and parsnips are tender to bite (3 to 4 more minutes).

2. Stir in cumin, cinnamon, ginger, saffron, beans, currants, and remaining 2 cups broth. Season to taste with salt and pepper. Bring to a boil. Stir in couscous; then cover tightly, remove from heat, and let stand until all liquid has been absorbed (about 5 minutes). Fluff with a fork before serving.

MAKES 6 SERVINGS.

PER SERVING: 348 calories, 6 g total fat, 1 g saturated fat, 0 mg cholesterol, 640 mg sodium, 67 g carbohydrates, 9 g fiber, 11 g protein, 81 mg calcium, 3 mg iron

Moroccan Spiced Couscous with Root Vegetables

Roasted Polenta with Broccoli & Fontina

30 MINUTES

Prepared polenta is a versatile and easy-to-use product—just heat it and top it with a sauce or, as here, with stir-fried vegetables. Serve with a loaf of Italian bread and a salad of garbanzos and ripe olives.

1½ **pounds prepared polenta roll, cut crosswise into ½-inch-thick slices**

2 **tablespoons olive oil**

3 **cloves garlic, minced or pressed**

2 **large red or yellow bell peppers (or one of each), about 1 lb.** *total,* **seeded and cut into 1-inch chunks**

6 **cups broccoli flowerets**

¼ **cup water**

Salt and black pepper

1 **cup (about 4 oz.) shredded fontina or mozzarella cheese**

1 **teaspoon grated lemon peel**

2 **tablespoons shredded fresh basil**

1. Arrange polenta slices on a lightly oiled ovenproof platter or in a shallow baking pan. Bake in a 500° oven until heated through (about 15 minutes).

2. Meanwhile, heat oil in a wide frying pan over high heat. Add garlic, bell peppers, and broccoli; stir for 1 minute. Add water and bring to a boil; then reduce heat, cover, and simmer until broccoli is tender to bite (3 to 5 minutes). Season to taste with salt and black pepper.

3. If you used a baking pan, transfer polenta slices to a platter. Pour broccoli mixture over polenta; sprinkle with cheese, lemon peel, and basil.

MAKES 4 SERVINGS.

PER SERVING: 380 calories, 17 g total fat, 7 g saturated fat, 33 mg cholesterol, 612 mg sodium, 41 g carbohydrates, 10 g fiber, 18 g protein, 266 mg calcium, 3 mg iron

Roasted Polenta with Broccoli & Fontina

Hoppin' John

25 MINUTES

In the South, hoppin' John—a mixture of black-eyed peas and rice—is a New Year's Day tradition. Here's a fast, trim version of the famous dish, made with quick-cooking brown rice instead of the usual white rice. Serve with braised collards, cornbread, and plenty of hot sauce for seasoning.

1 tablespoon vegetable oil
1 cup chopped red onion
2 stalks celery, chopped
1 large red bell pepper (about 8 oz.), seeded and chopped
½ teaspoon dried thyme
½ teaspoon salt
1 can (about 15 oz.) black-eyed peas or red beans, rinsed and drained
2 cups quick-cooking brown rice
1¾ cups water
Black pepper

1. Heat oil in a 3-quart pan over high heat. Add onion, celery, and bell pepper; cook, stirring often, until vegetables are lightly browned (about 5 minutes).

2. Stir in thyme, salt, black-eyed peas, rice, and water; bring to a boil. Reduce heat, cover, and simmer for 5 minutes; then remove from heat and let stand until rice is tender to bite (about 5 more minutes). Season to taste with black pepper.

MAKES 4 SERVINGS.

PER SERVING: 323 calories, 6 g total fat, 1 g saturated fat, 0 mg cholesterol, 636 mg sodium, 64 g carbohydrates, 4 g fiber, 10 g protein, 49 mg calcium, 2 mg iron

Coconut Curried Red Beans & Rice

30 MINUTES

This rich, filling stew will make even the most dedicated meat-eater very happy! Round out the meal with sliced tomatoes and cucumbers and heated flour tortillas or chapatis. To get the most flavor from your curry powder, make certain it's fresh; if you can't be sure, purchase a new package.

2 teaspoons vegetable oil
1 small onion (about 4 oz.), chopped
2 cloves garlic, minced or pressed
⅛ teaspoon crushed red pepper flakes
1 tablespoon curry powder
1 large red thin-skinned potato (about 8 oz.), scrubbed and cut into ½-inch pieces
1 can (about 14 oz.) unsweetened low-fat coconut milk
1 can (about 15 oz.) red or Great Northern beans, rinsed and drained
1½ cups quick-cooking rice
2 cups packaged triple-washed baby spinach
1 cup frozen peas

1. Heat oil in a 3-quart pan over high heat. Add onion and cook, stirring often, until browned (4 to 5 minutes). Stir in garlic, red pepper flakes, and curry powder; stir for 30 seconds.

2. Add potato and coconut milk and bring to a boil. Then reduce heat and simmer, uncovered, until potato is tender when pierced (about 6 minutes). Stir in beans, rice, spinach, and peas. Bring to a boil. Cover, remove from heat, and let stand until rice is tender to bite and peas and beans are heated through (about 5 minutes).

MAKES 4 SERVINGS.

PER SERVING: 434 calories, 7 g total fat, 4 g saturated fat, 0 mg cholesterol, 238 mg sodium, 69 g carbohydrates, 9 g fiber, 13 g protein, 82 mg calcium, 5 mg iron

Red Bean Tacos with Avocado & Chiles

25 MINUTES

These hearty vegetarian tacos feature a filling of seasoned, mashed red beans. Dress them up with the usual cheese and lettuce, plus a quick salsa made with avocado, mild chiles, and yellow bell pepper. For dessert, slice some juicy oranges or serve scoops of Strawberry-Orange sorbet (page 212).

1 cup chopped red onion

1 can (about 4 oz.) diced green chiles

1 large yellow bell pepper (about 8 oz.), seeded and chopped

1 medium-size avocado (about 6 oz.), pitted, peeled, and chopped

2 teaspoons white wine vinegar

Salt and black pepper

1 can (about 15 oz.) red beans

½ teaspoon dried oregano

½ teaspoon ground cumin

8 taco shells, heated

Chopped romaine lettuce

Shredded jack or mozzarella cheese

1. In a medium-size bowl, combine onion, chiles, bell pepper, avocado, and vinegar. Mix lightly; season to taste with salt and black pepper. Set aside.

2. Drain beans, reserving ¼ cup of the liquid. Rinse beans; then place beans and reserved ¼ cup liquid, oregano, and cumin in a 3-quart pan. Place over medium-high heat and cook, stirring and mashing beans lightly, until hot and bubbling (about 5 minutes).

3. To serve, spoon bean mixture into taco shells. Top with avocado mixture, lettuce, and cheese.

MAKES 4 SERVINGS.

PER SERVING: 307 calories, 15 g total fat, 2 g saturated fat, 0 mg cholesterol, 734 mg sodium, 40 g carbohydrates, 8 g fiber, 8 g protein, 84 mg calcium, 4 mg iron

Red Bean Tacos with Avocado & Chiles

Mean Lean Vegetable Chili

30 MINUTES

Here's a super-quick vegetarian chili with a minimum of added fat. For the best-tasting results, use good-quality canned beans and tomatoes, and make sure your spices are fresh. Cornbread and a green salad round out a great meal.

2 teaspoons vegetable oil

3 large carrots (about 12 oz. *total*), peeled and chopped

1 large onion (about 8 oz.), coarsely chopped

3 cloves garlic, minced or pressed

2 tablespoons chili powder

½ teaspoon dried oregano

½ teaspoon dried thyme

½ teaspoon ground cumin

1 large can (about 28 oz.) crushed tomatoes in purée

1 can (about 15 oz.) *each* black beans, pinto beans, and kidney beans (or use 3 cans of one kind), rinsed and drained

About ½ cup reduced-fat sour cream or plain nonfat yogurt

Thinly sliced green onions

1. In a 4- to 5-quart pan, combine oil, carrots, and chopped onion. Cook over high heat, stirring often, until vegetables begin to soften (about 3 minutes). Add garlic, chili powder, oregano, thyme, and cumin; cook, stirring, for 30 seconds.

2. Add tomatoes and their purée, then beans; bring to a boil. Reduce heat and simmer for about 10 minutes to blend flavors.

3. To serve, ladle into bowls; top with sour cream and green onions.

MAKES 6 TO 8 SERVINGS.

PER SERVING: 212 calories, 4 g total fat, 1 g saturated fat, 6 mg cholesterol, 507 mg sodium, 36 g carbohydrates, 9 g fiber, 10 g protein, 131 mg calcium, 3 mg iron

Lentil & Brown Rice Salad with Walnuts & Parsley

30 MINUTES

Lentils are a great source of protein—and unlike many other legumes, they're quick to cook, since they require no soaking. Make sure you buy them from a reliable source (one with good turnover), since they may take longer to cook if they aren't fresh. Here, lentils and quick-cooking brown rice combine with toasted walnuts, red onion, and carrots in a tempting warm salad. Serve with lightly dressed arugula and your favorite fresh bread.

1	cup lentils
3½	cups water
1	cup quick-cooking brown rice
½	cup walnut halves
½	cup chopped red onion
2	medium-size carrots (about 6 oz. *total*), coarsely shredded
3	tablespoons red wine vinegar
2	tablespoons extra-virgin olive oil
½	teaspoon salt
½	teaspoon pepper
½	cup chopped Italian parsley
	Italian parsley sprigs

1. Sort through lentils, discarding any debris. Rinse and drain lentils; then place in a 2½-quart pan and add 2½ cups of the water. Bring to a boil; then reduce heat, cover, and simmer until lentils are tender to bite (about 25 minutes). Drain well.

2. Meanwhile, cook rice and toast walnuts. To cook rice, bring remaining 1 cup water to a boil in a 2-quart pan; stir in rice and return to a boil. Reduce heat, cover, and simmer for 5 minutes. Then remove from heat and let stand until rice is tender to bite (about 5 minutes). Spoon rice into a large bowl.

3. To toast walnuts, place them in a small frying pan and cook over medium heat until aromatic and light golden (about 5 minutes), shaking pan often. Remove from pan and chop coarsely; add to bowl with rice.

4. To bowl, add onion and carrots. In a small bowl, whisk vinegar, oil, salt, and pepper to blend well; add to bowl along with chopped parsley. Stir in drained lentils and mix well. Garnish with parsley sprigs.

MAKES 4 SERVINGS.

PER SERVING: 484 calories, 16 g total fat, 2 g saturated fat, 0 mg cholesterol, 311 mg sodium, 58 g carbohydrates, 9 g fiber, 18 g protein, 66 mg calcium, x mg iron

Microwave Grains for One

Preparing sing[...]

serving helpings of rice, polenta, barley, or lentils is a difficult task on a traditional stove: [...]

hard to manage such small amounts without cooking the liquid away and burning the grain[...]

lentils. The microwave, however, handles modest quantities quite handily—and even a bit m[...]

quickly than the range top does. The following five recipes all make a simple meal for just o[...]

to complete your menu, add bread and perhaps a wedge of cheese or a vegetable platter.

Polenta with Mascarpone & Toasted Walnuts

15 TO 20 MINUTES

- ½ cup low-fat milk
- ½ cup water
- ¼ cup polenta or yellow cornmeal
- 1 teaspoon extra-virgin olive oil
- Salt and pepper
- 2 tablespoons mascarpone
- 2 tablespoons chopped toasted walnuts
- 1 pear-shaped (Roma-type) tomato, seeded and chopped
- ⅛ teaspoon grated lemon peel

1. In a 1-quart glass measure or bowl, stir together milk, water, polenta, and oil. Season to taste with salt and pepper. Microwave, uncovered, on HIGH (100%) for 7 to 8 minutes or until polenta is tender and liquid has been absorbed; stir once after 3 minutes, then again after 6 minutes.

2. When polenta is done, stir in mascarpone; then spoon polenta onto a plate. Sprinkle with walnuts, tomato, and lemon peel.

MAKES 1 SERVING.

PER SERVING: 455 calories, 29 g total fat, 12 g saturated fat, 33 mg cholesterol, 81 mg sodium, 38 g carbohydrates, 3 g fiber, 11 g protein, 224 mg calcium, 2 mg iron

Lentils with Lemon & Cucumber

25 MINUTES

- ¼ cup lentils
- 1 cup water
- ½ large cucumber (about a 5-oz. piece)
- 1 teaspoon lemon juice
- ½ teaspoon Dijon mustard
- 2 teaspoons extra-virgin olive oil
- Salt and pepper
- 1 large bunch watercress (about 6 oz.)

1. Sort through lentils, discarding any debris. Rinse lentils, drain, and place in a 1-quart glass measure or bowl; add water. Microwave, uncovered, on HIGH (100%) for 3 to 4 minutes or until mixture boils.

2. Cover with plastic wrap or a paper towel and microwave

on MEDIUM (50%) for [...] to 14 more minutes or u[...] lentils are tender to bite.

3. Meanwhile, peel, seed a[...] chop cucumber; set aside. [...] a small bowl, whisk toget[...] lemon juice, mustard, a[...] oil; season to taste with s[...] and pepper. Remove lar[...] leaves and tender sprigs fr[...] watercress; discard coa[...] stems. Rinse watercress, [...] dry, and arrange to cover [...] individual plate.

4. When lentils are do[...] drain them; stir in cucumb[...] then lemon mixture. Spo[...] mixture atop watercress.

MAKES 1 SERVING.

PER SERVING: 284 calories, 10 g total fat, 1 g saturated fat, 0 mg cholesterol, 138 mg sodiu[...] 34 g carbohydrates, 11 g fiber, 18 g protein, 250 mg calcium, 5 mg iron

fron Rice with
natoes

MINUTES

- cup vegetable broth or water
- Pinch of ground saffron
- Pinch of dried thyme
- tablespoons canned diced tomatoes
- cup long-grain white rice
- Salt and pepper
- tablespoons canned navy beans, rinsed and drained
- cup frozen cut green beans

In a 1-quart glass measure bowl, stir together broth, fron, thyme, tomatoes, d rice; season to taste with t (⅛ to ¼ teaspoon) and pper. Microwave, uncov-ed, on HIGH (100%) for to 11 minutes or until most all liquid has been sorbed.

Stir in navy beans and een beans. Microwave, covered, on MEDIUM)%) for 2 to 5 more min-es or until rice and green ans are tender to bite. Let nd for 2 minutes or until liquid has been absorbed.

AKES 1 SERVING.

R SERVING: 246 calories, total fat, 0 g saturated fat, 0 mg olesterol, 1,197 mg sodium, g carbohydrates, 3 g fiber, protein, 55 mg calcium, 3 mg n

---

Barley Risotto

30 MINUTES

- 1 teaspoon extra-virgin olive oil
- 2 tablespoons minced shallots
- 1 medium-size carrot (about 3 oz.), grated
- ¼ cup pearl barley
- ¾ cup vegetable broth or water
- Salt and pepper
- 1 teaspoon chopped Italian parsley

1. In a 1-quart glass measure or bowl, combine oil, shal-lots, and carrot. Microwave, uncovered, on HIGH (100%) for 1 minute. Stir in barley and broth; season to taste with salt (⅛ to ¼ teaspoon) and pepper. Microwave, uncovered, on HIGH (100%) for 3 to 4 minutes or until mixture boils.

2. Cover with plastic wrap or a paper towel and microwave on MEDIUM (50%) for 18 to 20 minutes or until barley is tender to bite. Sprinkle with parsley.

MAKES 1 SERVING.

PER SERVING: 264 calories, 7 g total fat, 1 g saturated fat, 0 mg cholesterol, 782 mg sodium, 47 g carbohydrates, 10 g fiber, 7 g protein, 44 mg calcium, 2 mg iron

---

Brown Rice Salad with Celery, Grapes & Pecans

30 MINUTES

- 1⅓ cups vegetable broth or water
- ¼ cup short-grain brown rice
- ⅓ cup seedless red or green grapes
- 1 small stalk celery
- 2 tablespoons toasted pecan halves
- ½ teaspoon sherry vinegar
- ½ teaspoon balsamic vinegar
- 2 teaspoons extra-virgin olive oil
- Salt and pepper

1. In a 1-quart glass measure or bowl, stir together broth and rice. Microwave, uncov-ered, on HIGH (100%) for 20 minutes or until almost all liquid has been absorbed. Cover with plastic wrap or a paper towel and microwave on MEDIUM (50%) for 2 to 5 more minutes or until rice is tender to bite.

2. While rice is cooking, cut grapes in half lengthwise and place in a medium-size bowl. Thinly slice celery and coarsely chop pecans; add to bowl. Then stir in sherry vinegar, balsamic vinegar, and oil.

3. When rice is done, rinse it with cool water, drain well, and add to bowl. Mix well. Season to taste with salt and pepper.

MAKES 1 SERVING.

PER SERVING: 411 calories, 22 g total fat, 2 g saturated fat, 0 mg cholesterol, 1,358 mg sodium, 53 g carbohydrates, 4 g fiber, 5 g protein, 33 mg calcium, 1 mg iron

Stir-fried Bell Peppers with Coconut Milk & Cashews

20 MINUTES

For variety, you might use toasted almonds in this recipe instead of cashews; if you'd like to boost the protein, stir in some cubed firm tofu. The dish will look prettiest if it's made with fresh, good-looking peppers—choose those with tight, unwrinkled skins and stems still intact. Serve warm chapatis or tortillas alongside.

1½ cups plus ⅓ cup vegetable broth

1 cup couscous

2 teaspoons vegetable oil

1 *each* medium-size red and yellow bell pepper (about 12 oz. *total*), seeded and thinly sliced

1 medium-size red onion (about 6 oz.), cut into wedges

2 cloves garlic, minced or pressed

1 tablespoon curry powder

1 cup unsweetened low-fat coconut milk

½ cup salted roasted cashews

2 tablespoons chopped cilantro

1. In a 2- to 3-quart pan, bring 1½ cups of the broth to a boil over high heat. Stir in couscous; then cover tightly, remove from heat, and let stand until all liquid has been absorbed (about 5 minutes).

2. Meanwhile, heat oil in a wide frying pan or wok over high heat. Add bell peppers, onion, and garlic; cook, stirring often, until edges of vegetables are golden brown (about 5 minutes). Add curry powder and stir for 30 seconds. Add remaining ⅓ cup broth and coconut milk and bring to a simmer; then simmer until peppers are tender to bite (2 to 3 more minutes).

3. To serve, fluff couscous with a fork and spoon onto a platter or into individual bowls; spoon pepper mixture over couscous. Sprinkle with cashews and cilantro.

MAKES 5 SERVINGS.

PER SERVING: 319 calories, 11 g total fat, 3 g saturated fat, 0 mg cholesterol, 472 mg sodium, 44 g carbohydrates, 4 g fiber, 8 g protein, 38 mg calcium, 2 mg iron

Stir-fried Bell Peppers with Coconut Milk & Cashews

Corn Cakes with Corn, Sage & Tomatoes

30 MINUTES

Who doesn't jump at the chance to eat pancakes for dinner? Hot, golden, and crisp, these Tex-Mex corn cakes are everything a pancake should be. Offer crisp baby carrots and celery sticks on the side; serve flan for dessert.

- ¼ cup vegetable oil
- ½ cup chopped red onion
- 1 package (about 10 oz.) frozen corn kernels
- 2 large tomatoes (about 1 lb. *total*), seeded and chopped
- 1 small avocado (about 4 oz.), pitted, peeled, and chopped
- Salt and pepper
- 1½ cups packaged corn muffin mix (about one 8½-oz. package)
- 1 large egg
- 1 cup low-fat milk
- ½ teaspoon dried sage

Corn Cakes with Corn, Sage & Tomatoes

1. Heat 1 tablespoon of the oil in a wide non-stick frying pan over medium-high heat. Add onion and corn; cook, stirring often, until onion is soft (about 3 minutes). Transfer 1 cup of the corn mixture to a medium-size bowl and stir in tomatoes and avocado; season to taste with salt and pepper. Set aside. Transfer remaining corn mixture to a large bowl and add muffin mix, egg, milk, and sage. Stir just until smooth; do not overmix.

2. Wipe frying pan clean with a paper towel; then heat 1 more tablespoon oil in pan over medium-high heat. Add batter in ¼-cup portions, spreading slightly to make 3- to 4-inch pancakes. Cook pancakes, turning once, until golden brown on both sides (6 to 8 minutes); add remaining 2 tablespoons oil to pan as needed to prevent sticking. Serve hot pancakes with corn-avocado mixture.

MAKES 4 SERVINGS.

PER SERVING: 549 calories, 26 g total fat, 6 g saturated fat, 58 mg cholesterol, 569 mg sodium, 70 g carbohydrates, 5 g fiber, 10 g protein, 193 mg calcium, 3 mg iron

Two Potato Hash

25 MINUTES

Hash browns and eggs are classic partners at breakfast–and they're just as delicious at lunch or dinner. These hash browns are a bit out of the ordinary, since they're made with both russet and sweet potatoes. Try them with poached eggs, buttered toast, and steamed green beans.

2 tablespoons vegetable oil

1 large yellow onion (about 8 oz.), chopped

1 very large russet potato (about 12 oz.), peeled and cut into ½-inch cubes

1 large sweet potato (about 12 oz.), peeled and cut into ½-inch cubes

1 teaspoon crumbled dried rosemary

¾ cup water

½ teaspoon Worcestershire sauce

   Salt and pepper

1. Heat oil in a wide nonstick frying pan over high heat. Add onion, russet potato, and sweet potato; cook, stirring often, until vegetables are browned (about 8 minutes).

2. Add rosemary and water. Stir to scrape browned bits free from pan bottom; then reduce heat, cover, and simmer until potatoes are tender to bite (about 5 minutes). Stir in Worcestershire sauce; season to taste with salt and pepper.

MAKES 4 SERVINGS.

PER SERVING: 209 calories, 7 g total fat, 1 g saturated fat, 0 mg cholesterol, 23 mg sodium, 34 g carbohydrates, 4 g fiber, 3 g protein, 28 mg calcium, 1 mg iron

Teriyaki Tofu with Eggplant

20 MINUTES

Inspired by the flavors of Japan, this dish features firm tofu, cubes of tender eggplant, and bright green peas in a sweet teriyaki sauce. Serve over hot white or brown rice.

2 tablespoons vegetable oil

1 large eggplant (about 1½ lbs.), peeled and cut into ½-inch pieces

½ cup water

1 clove garlic, finely chopped

1 teaspoon grated fresh ginger

¼ cup reduced-sodium soy sauce

3 tablespoons mirin

1 tablespoon firmly packed brown sugar

2 teaspoons cornstarch

1 package (about 12 oz.) extra-firm tofu, drained and cut into ½-inch cubes

1 cup frozen peas

4 green onions, thinly sliced

1. Heat oil in a wide frying pan or wok over high heat. Add eggplant and water. Cover and cook until eggplant is tender when pierced (5 to 6 minutes).

2. Stir in garlic and ginger and cook for 1 more minute. In a small bowl, stir together soy sauce, mirin, sugar, and cornstarch; add to frying pan along with tofu and peas. Bring to a boil; then reduce heat and simmer until sauce is slightly thickened and tofu is heated through (about 2 minutes). Sprinkle with onions.

MAKES 4 SERVINGS.

PER SERVING: 272 calories, 12 g total fat, 1 g saturated fat, 0 mg cholesterol, 659 mg sodium, 26 g carbohydrates, 4 g fiber, 15 g protein, 115 mg calcium, 3 mg iron

Asparagus with Tofu-Mushroom Sauce

20 TO 25 MINUTES

Fresh asparagus in the market means spring is on its way. Here's one delicious way to prepare the tender spears: simmer them until just tender, then top with a gingery sauce of tofu and crimini mushrooms. Serve with fluffy rice; offer oranges and fortune cookies for dessert.

1 pound crimini mushrooms or regular button mushrooms

2 teaspoons grated fresh ginger

1 teaspoon Oriental sesame oil

1 tablespoon reduced-sodium soy sauce

2 tablespoons oyster sauce (or 1 more tablespoon reduced-sodium soy sauce)

1 package (about 12 oz.) extra-firm tofu, drained and cut into ½-inch cubes

2½ pounds asparagus

6 green onions, thinly sliced

1. Trim and discard stems from mushrooms; then whirl mushrooms in a food processor until finely chopped. Transfer mushrooms to a wide frying pan; add ginger. Cook over high heat, stirring often, until mushrooms have released their liquid (about 5 minutes). Stir in oil, soy sauce, oyster sauce, and tofu. Reduce heat and simmer until tofu is heated through (1 to 2 minutes).

2. Meanwhile, bring about 1 inch water to a boil in a wide frying pan over high heat. Snap off and discard tough ends of asparagus; then add asparagus to boiling water and cook, uncovered, until just tender when pierced (3 to 5 minutes).

3. Drain asparagus and arrange on individual plates. Spoon mushroom sauce over asparagus. Sprinkle with onions.

MAKES 6 SERVINGS.

PER SERVING: 129 calories, 5 g total fat, 1 g saturated fat, 0 mg cholesterol, 353 mg sodium, 12 g carbohydrates, 3 g fiber, 14 g protein, 75 mg calcium, 3 mg iron

Widely available in supermarkets all over the country, frozen veggie burgers are a staple for many vegetarians. Choose your favorite brand for this recipe, then dress them up with a cilantro-chile mayonnaise, jack cheese, lettuce, avocado, and onions. (If raw red onions are too strong for your taste, soak the slices in cold water for a few minutes before using.)

½ cup reduced-fat mayonnaise

1 can (about 4 oz.) diced green chiles

3 tablespoons chopped cilantro

1 loaf (12 to 16 oz.) ciabatta or Italian bread, cut crosswise into 4 pieces

4 frozen veggie or garden burgers (about 3 oz. *each*)

8 thin slices jack cheese (about 4 oz. *total*), *each* about 2½ inches square

Romaine lettuce leaves, rinsed and crisped

4 thin slices red onion

1 large avocado (about 8 oz.), pitted, peeled, and cut lengthwise into 16 slices

1. In a small bowl, stir together mayonnaise, chiles, and cilantro. Set aside.

2. Split each piece of bread horizontally. Then arrange bread, cut sides up, on a large baking sheet. Broil about 3 inches below heat until golden (about 2 minutes). Remove to individual plates. Spread cut surfaces of bottom halves of bread with mayonnaise mixture, using about half of it.

3. Arrange veggie burgers on baking sheet; broil about 3 inches below heat, turning once, until hot through and golden on both sides (4 to 6 minutes). Top each burger with 2 slices of cheese. Continue to broil until cheese is melted (about 2 more minutes).

4. Cover bottom halves of bread with lettuce leaves; then top each piece with a burger, an onion slice, 4 avocado slices, and a fourth of the remaining mayonnaise mixture. Add top halves of bread and serve hot.

MAKES 4 SERVINGS.

PER SERVING: 667 calories, 28 g total fat, 9 g saturated fat, 30 mg cholesterol, 1,500 mg sodium, 69 g carbohydrates, 9 g fiber, 34 g protein, 376 mg calcium, 6 mg iron

Tex-Mex Veggie Burgers

Yellow Pepper Pizzas

0 MINUTES

A wonderful combination of tomatoes, yellow bell pepper, and smoked and plain mozzarella cheese tops these attractive pizzas. (If you can't find smoked mozzarella, simply use the plain variety.) Alongside, you might serve marinated green beans, ripe olives, and cold beer.

1 tablespoon olive oil

1 large yellow bell pepper (about 8 oz.), seeded and thinly sliced

¼ cup water

2 cloves garlic, minced or pressed

½ teaspoon dried oregano

1 teaspoon grated orange peel

2 medium-size pear-shaped (Roma-type) tomatoes (about 4 oz. *total*), seeded and chopped

4 packaged small baked pizza crusts (*each* about 6 inches in diameter)

½ cup shredded mozzarella cheese

1 cup (about 4 oz.) shredded smoked mozzarella cheese

1. Heat oil in a wide frying pan over high heat. Add bell pepper and cook, stirring often, until browned (about 3 minutes). Add water and stir to scrape browned bits free from pan bottom; then cook for 2 minutes. Stir in garlic, oregano, orange peel, and tomatoes. Cook, stirring, for 1 more minute.

2. Arrange pizza crusts on 1 or 2 baking sheets. Top crusts equally with pepper mixture and sprinkle with cheeses. Bake in a 450° oven until cheese is melted and topping is hot (10 to 12 minutes).

MAKES 4 SERVINGS.

PER SERVING: 557 calories, 24 g total fat, 9 g saturated fat, 41 mg cholesterol, 456 mg sodium, 69 g carbohydrates, 7 g fiber, 15 g protein, 314 mg calcium, 3 mg iron

Zucchini Ricotta Pizzas

30 MINUTES

Packaged baked pizza crusts make this entrée especially quick and easy to prepare. Complete the meal with a crisp salad of torn romaine lettuce tossed with lemon juice and olive oil. (If your market doesn't carry pasta-style tomatoes, you may use diced tomatoes instead.)

1 can (about 14½ oz.) chunky pasta-style tomatoes

1 cup (about 8 oz.) part-skim ricotta cheese

¼ teaspoon ground cumin

4 packaged small baked pizza crusts (*each* about 6 inches in diameter)

1 small zucchini (about 4 oz.), grated

1½ cups (about 6 oz.) shredded part-skim mozzarella cheese

¼ cup grated Parmesan cheese

6 calamata olives, pitted and chopped

1. Place a fine strainer in the sink; pour tomatoes into strainer and let drain. In a small bowl, stir together ricotta cheese and cumin.

2. Arrange pizza crusts on 1 or 2 baking sheets; top equally with ricotta mixture, spreading it almost to edge of crusts. Top evenly with drained tomatoes, zucchini, mozzarella cheese, Parmesan cheese, and olives.

3. Bake pizzas in a 450° oven until mozzarella cheese is melted and lightly browned (12 to 15 minutes).

MAKES 4 SERVINGS.

PER SERVING: 654 calories, 25 g total fat, 11 g saturated fat, 48 mg cholesterol, 1,096 mg sodium, 78 g carbohydrates, 6 g fiber, 27 g protein, 614 mg calcium, 3 mg iron

Spiced Spinach & Potatoes

25 MINUTES

Baby spinach is tender and very flavorful—and when you buy it prewashed, it couldn't b[...] simpler to use. Here, the leaves are combined with browned potatoes and Indian spices f[...] a satisfying entrée. Serve with plain yogurt and warm poppadums.

2 tablespoons vegetable oil

1 medium-size onion (about 6 oz.), chopped

About 1½ pounds russet potatoes, peeled and cut into ½-inch cubes

2 cloves garlic, minced or pressed

2 teaspoons ground coriander

½ teaspoon ground ginger

½ cup water

5 cups packaged triple-washed baby spinach

Salt and ground red pepper (cayenne)

1. Heat oil in a wide frying pan over high hea[...] Add onion and potatoes; cook, stirring often, until potatoes are well browned all over (abou[...] 10 minutes). Add garlic, coriander, and ginger stir for 30 seconds. Add water. Reduce heat, cover, and simmer until potatoes are tender to bite (about 5 minutes).

2. Add spinach and stir until wilted (about 2 minutes). Season to taste with salt and red pepper.

MAKES 4 SERVINGS.

PER SERVING: 219 calories, 7 g total fat, 1 g saturated fat, 0 mg cholesterol, 69 mg sodium, 34 g carbohydrates, 5 g fiber, 6 g protein, 83 mg calcium 3 mg iron

Egg & Asparagus Gratins

Grated lemon peel gives a lovely flavor to both asparagus and eggs in these easy gratins. If you have wide, shallow ramekins, use them; if not, make the gratins in custard cups and increase the baking time by a few minutes. Serve with whole wheat toast and a bowl of cherry tomatoes.

12 asparagus spears

8 large eggs

¼ cup whipping cream

1 teaspoon grated lemon peel

Salt and ground red pepper (cayenne)

½ cup grated Parmesan cheese

1. In a wide frying pan, bring about 1 inch water to a boil over high heat. Meanwhile, snap off and discard tough ends of asparagus; then cut spears into 1-inch pieces. Add asparagus to boiling water and cook, uncovered, until just tender when pierced (3 to 5 minutes). Drain well.

2. Divide asparagus among 4 well-buttered 4- to 5-inch-wide ovenproof dishes. Carefully break 2 eggs over asparagus in each dish. Spoon 1 tablespoon of the cream over eggs in each dish. Then sprinkle eggs evenly with lemon peel and sprinkle with salt and red pepper to taste.

3. Set dishes on a baking sheet and bake in a 450° oven until eggs are done to your liking (5 to 7 minutes for firm whites and soft yolks). Sprinkle evenly with cheese and bake for 1 more minute. Serve at once.

MAKES 4 SERVINGS.

PER SERVING: 265 calories, 20 g total fat, 9 g saturated fat, 455 mg cholesterol, 338 mg sodium, 4 g carbohydrates, 0 g fiber, 18 g protein, 208 mg calcium, 2 mg iron

Apple & Cheese Omelet

30 MINUTES

Our variation on a classic French jelly omelet combines sweet and savory in one pan. Use crisp, tart apples; Granny Smiths and Newtown Pippins are both good choices. Make a quick salad of packaged prewashed baby spinach; serve poppy seed rolls on the side.

3 tablespoons unsalted butter or margarine

2 large tart apples (about 1 lb. *total*), peeled, cored, and thinly sliced

1 small onion (about 4 oz.), finely chopped

¼ teaspoon dried thyme

8 large eggs

2 tablespoons water

Salt and pepper

1 cup (about 4 oz.) shredded sharp Cheddar cheese

3 tablespoons all-fruit style apricot spread

1. Melt 1 tablespoon of the butter in a wide nonstick omelet pan or frying pan over medium-high heat. Stir in apples, onion, and thyme; cook, stirring often, just until apples begin to brown (6 to 8 minutes). Remove to a plate and keep warm. Wipe pan clean with a paper towel.

2. In a medium-size bowl, beat eggs and water to blend; sprinkle in salt and pepper to taste. In omelet pan, melt remaining 2 tablespoons butter over medium heat. Pour in eggs and cook, gently lifting cooked portions with a wide spatula to let uncooked eggs flow underneath, until omelet is softly set. Remove from heat.

3. Spoon two-thirds of the apple mixture down center of omelet; sprinkle with ⅔ cup of the cheese. Top evenly with apricot spread. Fold a third of omelet over filling; slide unfolded edge onto a serving plate, then flip folded portion over top. Spoon remaining apple mixture over omelet and sprinkle with remaining ⅓ cup cheese. Serve at once.

MAKES 4 SERVINGS.

PER SERVING: 424 calories, 28 g total fat, 14 g saturated fat, 478 mg cholesterol, 304 mg sodium, 23 g carbohydrates, 2 g fiber, 20 g protein, 266 mg calcium, 2 mg iron

Artichoke Hearts Frittata

25 MINUTES

Though they are a bit expensive, frozen artichoke hearts are wonderful for special occasions. In this frittata, they're teamed with fresh mint and roasted red peppers. To complete the menu, make a watercress salad and warm up wedges of focaccia.

- 2 tablespoons olive oil
- 1 large onion (about 8 oz.), chopped
- 1 package (about 9 oz.) frozen artichoke hearts, thawed and drained
- ⅓ cup drained, chopped bottled roasted red peppers
- ¼ cup chopped fresh mint or parsley
- 8 large eggs
- ½ cup grated Parmesan cheese
- Salt and pepper

1. In a wide nonstick frying pan with an oven-proof handle, heat 1 tablespoon of the oil over high heat. Add onion and artichokes; cook, stirring often, for 1 minute. Then cover and cook until artichokes are tender to bite (3 to 4 more minutes). Stir in roasted peppers and mint; transfer to a bowl and keep warm. Wipe frying pan clean with a paper towel.

2. In a medium-size bowl, beat eggs to blend; beat in ¼ cup of the cheese and sprinkle in salt and pepper to taste. Heat remaining 1 tablespoon oil in frying pan over medium heat. Pour in eggs and cook without stirring until bottom is set. Then, with a wide spatula, lift cooked portion gently all around sides of pan to let uncooked eggs flow underneath. When eggs are almost set, spread artichoke mixture over them.

3. Sprinkle with remaining ¼ cup cheese; broil about 6 inches below heat until eggs are firm to the touch and lightly browned (about 5 minutes). Serve at once; cut into wedges to serve.

MAKES 6 SERVINGS.

PER SERVING: 205 calories, 14 g total fat, 4 g saturated fat, 289 mg cholesterol, 248 mg sodium, 9 g carbohydrates, 4 g fiber, 13 g protein, 144 mg calcium, 2 mg iron

Italian Tomatoes & Eggs

20 MINUTES

These Mediterranean-inspired eggs make a perfect summer supper. Find the ripest, most flavorful tomatoes you can and splurge on a fresh goat cheese. Serve with toasted crusty bread, an assortment of olives, and a plain green salad.

- 4 medium-size firm-ripe tomatoes (about 1½ lbs. *total*), seeded and chopped
- Salt
- 2 tablespoons olive oil
- 1 pound sliced mushrooms
- 8 large eggs
- Pepper
- ½ cup crumbled goat cheese, such as Montrachet
- 1 tablespoon snipped chives

1. Place a fine strainer in the sink. Place tomatoes in strainer; sprinkle with ½ teaspoon salt.

2. Heat oil in a wide frying pan over high heat. Add mushrooms and cook, stirring often, until mushrooms are soft and liquid has evaporated (about 5 minutes). Add drained tomatoes and stir until heated through (about 1 minute).

3. With a spoon, make 8 depressions in tomato mixture; carefully break an egg into each. Sprinkle lightly with salt and pepper. Reduce heat to low, cover, and cook until eggs are done to your liking (3 to 4 minutes for firm whites and soft yolks). Sprinkle with cheese and chives and serve at once.

MAKES 4 TO 6 SERVINGS.

PER SERVING: 264 calories, 18 g total fat, 6 g saturated fat, 351 mg cholesterol, 293 mg sodium, 11 g carbohydrates, 3 g fiber, 16 g protein, 86 mg calcium, 3 mg iron

Black Bean Hummus with Carrot Slaw

20 MINUTES

Traditional hummus is made with garbanzo beans and lots of olive oil. This trimmer version is based on canned black beans instead—and it entirely omits the oil, though it does call for the usual tahini (sesame seed paste). Serve it in pocket breads, topped with a sprightly carrot slaw. To speed preparation, shred the carrots first in your food processor; then change the blade to make the hummus.

Carrot Slaw (below)

2 **cans (about 15 oz. *each*) black beans**

¼ **cup tahini**

2 **tablespoons lemon juice**

1 **clove garlic, chopped**

Salt and ground red pepper (cayenne)

4 **whole wheat pocket breads (*each* 6 to 7 inches in diameter)**

Chopped romaine lettuce

CARROT SLAW

12 **ounces carrots, shredded**

2 **tablespoons lime juice**

1 **teaspoon sugar**

2 **tablespoons chopped cilantro**

1 **teaspoon vegetable oil**

Salt and crushed red pepper flakes

1. Prepare Carrot Slaw.

2. Drain beans, reserving 2 tablespoons of the liquid. Rinse beans and drain again; then place in a food processor and add the reserved 2 tablespoons bean liquid, tahini, lemon juice, and garlic. Whirl until smooth. Season to taste with salt and ground red pepper.

3. To serve, line pocket breads with lettuce, then spoon in hummus. Serve with Carrot Slaw.

MAKES 4 SERVINGS.

CARROT SLAW

In a large bowl, combine carrots, lime juice, sugar, cilantro, and oil. Season to taste with salt and red pepper flakes.

PER SERVING: 455 calories, 12 g total fat, 2 g saturated fat, 0 mg cholesterol, 889 mg sodium, 73 g carbohydrates, 18 g fiber, 19 g protein, 154 mg calcium, 5 mg iron

Rotelle with Broccoli

Part-skim ricotta cheese, lightly scented with lemon and seasoned with spicy red pepper flakes, makes a rich, creamy sauce for broccoli and pasta corkscrews. Serve the dish with warm Italian bread drizzled with extra-virgin olive oil.

12 ounces dried rotelle or other pasta shapes
2 tablespoons olive oil
¼ teaspoon crushed red pepper flakes
2 cloves garlic, minced or pressed
6 cups broccoli flowerets
¼ cup water
1 teaspoon grated lemon peel
1½ cups (about 12 oz.) part-skim ricotta cheese
Grated Romano or Parmesan cheese

1. In a 5- to 6-quart pan, bring about 3 quarts water to a boil over high heat; stir in pasta and cook, uncovered, until just tender to bite (about 10 minutes). Or cook pasta according to package directions.

2. Meanwhile, heat oil in a wide frying pan over medium-high heat. Add red pepper flakes, garlic, and broccoli; cook, stirring often, until broccoli starts to turn bright green (about 1 minute). Add the ¼ cup water and bring to a boil; then reduce heat, cover, and simmer until broccoli is tender-crisp to bite (3 to 5 minutes). Remove from heat.

3. Drain pasta well and pour into a large bowl. Add broccoli mixture, lemon peel, and ricotta cheese; toss to mix. Spoon onto a platter or individual plates and offer Romano cheese to add to taste.

MAKES 4 SERVINGS.

PER SERVING: 566 calories, 17 g total fat, 6 g saturated fat, 29 mg cholesterol, 204 mg sodium, 79 g carbohydrates, 8 g fiber, 28 g protein, 363 mg calcium, 5 mg iron

Spaghetti with Zucchini Carbonara

This all-vegetable variation on popular spaghetti carbonara is perfectly simple—just grated zucchini, eggs, cheese, pasta, and plenty of garlic and pepper for seasoning. (Grate the zucchini in the food processor and the job will be done in no time flat.) Serve with hot, crusty peasant bread; offer scoops of gelato for dessert.

1 pound dried spaghetti, linguine, or other pasta strands
2 tablespoons olive oil
3 cloves garlic, peeled
2 pounds zucchini, grated
4 large eggs, lightly beaten
¼ cup low-fat milk
1 cup (about 3 oz.) shredded or grated Parmesan cheese
Salt and coarsely ground pepper

1. In a 6- to 8-quart pan, bring about 4 quarts water to a boil over high heat; stir in pasta and cook, uncovered, until just tender to bite (10 to 12 minutes). Or cook pasta according to package directions.

2. Meanwhile, heat oil in a wide frying pan over medium-high heat. Gently crush garlic with the flat of a knife; add to oil. Cook until garlic turns golden (about 1 minute); then remove garlic from pan. Add zucchini and cook, stirring often, until tender to bite (about 3 minutes). Remove from heat.

3. Drain pasta well and return to cooking pan. In a bowl, beat eggs and milk to blend; add egg mixture and zucchini to pasta. Over low heat, toss mixture until egg clings to pasta and forms a creamy sauce. Add cheese and toss to mix; season to taste with salt and pepper.

MAKES 4 TO 6 SERVINGS.

PER SERVING: 556 calories, 17 g total fat, 6 g saturated fat, 184 mg cholesterol, 385 mg sodium, 75 g carbohydrates, 3 g fiber, 26 g protein, 315 mg calcium, 5 mg iron

Shells with Cauliflower, Saffron & Sun-dried Tomato Sauce

30 MINUTES

Chopped fresh cauliflower in an unusual saffron-seasoned dried tomato sauce makes a rich topping for pasta shells. Serve with lemon-seasoned steamed zucchini and plenty of sour dough bread.

1 cauliflower (about 2 lbs.)

1 pound dried small pasta shells

2 tablespoons olive oil

2 cloves garlic, minced or pressed

⅛ to ¼ teaspoon crushed red pepper flakes

Pinch of ground saffron

½ cup water

½ cup sun-dried tomato bits or prepared sun-dried tomato tapenade

Grated Romano cheese

1. Remove stem from cauliflower; rinse cauliflower and finely chop.

2. Meanwhile, bring about 4 quarts water to a boil in a 6- to 8-quart pan over high heat; stir in pasta and cook, uncovered, until just tender to bite (8 to 10 minutes). Or cook pasta according to package directions.

3. While pasta is cooking, heat oil in a wide frying pan over medium-high heat. Add garlic and red pepper flakes and cook, stirring often, for 1 minute. Add cauliflower, saffron, and the

½ cup water. Bring to a boil; then reduce heat, cover, and simmer until cauliflower is very tender to bite (5 to 6 minutes). Stir in tomato bits; remove from heat.

4. Drain pasta well, reserving ⅔ cup of the cooking water. Pour pasta and reserved cooking water back into cooking pan; then pour in cauliflower sauce. Simmer over medium-high heat, stirring, until water has been absorbed (2 to 3 minutes). Spoon onto a platter or individual plates. Offer cheese to add to taste.

MAKES 4 TO 6 SERVINGS.

PER SERVING: 502 calories, 15 g total fat, 1 g saturated fat, 0 mg cholesterol, 658 mg sodium, 77 g carbohydrates, 7 g fiber, 15 g protein, 71 mg calcium, 5 mg iron

Pasta with Grilled Eggplant & Pesto

25 MINUTES

Grilled eggplant and pesto go together beautifully—and purchased pesto makes this dish a snap to assemble. Serve with warm focaccia and sliced ripe red and yellow tomatoes.

1 **pound dried penne or rigatoni**

2 **large eggplants (about 1½ lbs. *each*), unpeeled, cut lengthwise into ½-inch slices**

2 **tablespoons olive oil**

Salt and pepper

1 **jar (about 7 oz.) pesto**

Shredded Parmesan cheese

1. In a 6- to 8-quart pan, bring about 4 quarts water to a boil over high heat; stir in pasta and cook, uncovered, until just tender to bite (10 to 12 minutes). Or cook pasta according to package directions.

2. Meanwhile, arrange eggplant slices on a lightly oiled grill 4 to 6 inches above a solid bed of hot coals (you can hold your hand at grill level for only 2 to 3 seconds) or over high heat on a gas grill. Brush eggplant with oil; sprinkle with salt and pepper. Close lid on gas grill. (Or arrange eggplant on a rack in a broiler pan, brush with oil, and broil about 3 inches below heat.) Grill or broil eggplant, turning once, until well browned on both sides and tender when pierced (4 to 6 minutes). Remove to a cutting board and chop coarsely. Transfer to a large bowl.

3. Drain pasta well and pour into bowl with eggplant. Add pesto and toss to mix. Spoon onto a platter or individual plates; offer cheese to add to taste.

MAKES 4 TO 6 SERVINGS.

PER SERVING: 667 calories, 28 g total fat, 4 g saturated fat, 7 mg cholesterol, 318 mg sodium, 88 g carbohydrates, 6 g fiber, 19 g protein, 217 mg calcium, 7 mg iron

Chapter Eight

DESSERTS

◀ *Previous page: Quick Napoleons (page 225)*

Sparkling Berries

5 TO 10 MINUTES

Utterly simple, this dazzling dessert is a showcase for perfectly ripe and sweet seasonal berries.

- **2 cups strawberries, fraises des bois, raspberries, or blackberries**
- **2 cups chilled sparkling muscat wine**

1. Hull berries, if necessary.

2. Divide berries equally among 4 stemmed glasses (about ¾-cup size). Slowly fill each glass with wine. Sip wine first; then eat berries with a spoon.

MAKES 4 SERVINGS.

PER SERVING: 206 calories, 0 g total fat, 0 g saturated fat, 0 mg cholesterol, 12 mg sodium, 19 g carbohydrates, 2 g fiber, 0 g protein, 20 mg calcium, 1 mg iron

Vin Santo–Peach Splashes

5 MINUTES

Like Sparkling Berries (above) this refreshing treat is part drink, part dessert. If you like, use about 8 ounces of ripe apricots, pitted and sliced, in place of the peach.

- **1 large ripe peach (about 8 oz.), peeled, pitted, and sliced**
- **1 to 1½ cups chilled Vin Santo, late-harvest gewürztraminer, or late-harvest Johannisberg Riesling**

1. Divide peach slices equally among 4 stemmed glasses (about ½-cup size). Slowly pour wine into each glass over peaches. Sip wine first; then eat peaches with a spoon.

MAKES 4 SERVINGS.

PER SERVING: 69 calories, 0 g total fat, 0 g saturated fat, 0 mg cholesterol, 4 mg sodium, 5 g carbohydrates, 1 g fiber, 0 g protein, 9 mg calcium, 0 mg iron

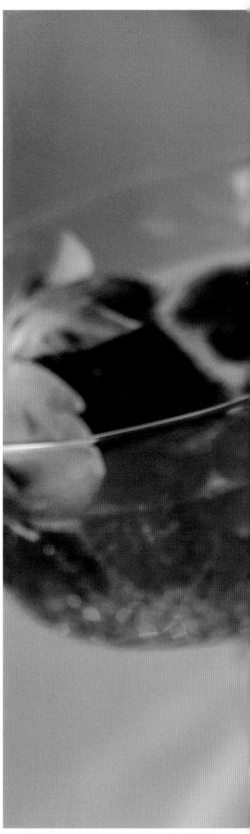

Sparkling Berries, Vin Santo–Peach Splashes

Zabaglione

Three simple ingredients—eggs, sugar, and wine—ma[ke] *zabaglione,* one of the world's great desserts. To prepare it, you simply combine everything [in] a round-bottomed zabaglione pan (or in a double boiler set over simmering water) and wh[isk] to create a luscious thick, hot foam. As the recipes here show, zabaglione is delicious ma[de] with various wines. It's versatile, too; you can serve it as is (with a little whipped cream, if y[ou] like) or spoon it over your choice of fresh fruit. Always serve zabaglione as soon as it's do[ne;] if left to stand, it will collapse and separate.

Warm Fruit Gratin with Zabaglione

20 MINUTES

> **About 5 cups fresh fruit, such as hulled straw-berries, blueberries, or sliced peaches (or use a combination)**
>
> **3 large eggs**
>
> **6 tablespoons granulated sugar**
>
> **2 tablespoons fruity white wine, such as Johannisberg Riesling**
>
> **2 tablespoons powdered sugar**
>
> **2 tablespoons sliced almonds**

1. Divide fruit among 4 to 6 about 6-inch-wide, shallow ovenproof bowls. Position broiler rack so top of fruit will be about 4 inches below heat. Set bowls aside.

2. In a 2½- to 3-quart round-bottomed zabaglione pan or in the top of a double boiler, combine eggs, granulated sugar, and wine. Whisk until frothy. Place zabaglione pan directly over medium-high gas heat or high electric heat; place double boiler top over simmering water. Whisk vigorously just until mixture holds a slight peak when whisk is lifted and no liquid remains in pan bottom (3 to 5 minutes).

3. Immediately pour zabaglione equally over fruit in bowls (it continues to thicken). Dust with powdered sugar and sprinkle with almonds. Broil until golden brown (about 1 minute). Serve at once.

MAKES 4 TO 6 SERVINGS.

PER SERVING: 199 calories, 5 g total fat, 1 g saturated fat, 128 mg cholesterol, 42 mg sodium, 36 g carbohydrates, 3 g fiber, 5 g protein, 34 mg calcium, 1 mg iron

Late-harvest Zabaglione

15 MINUTES

> **3 to 4 tablespoons black raspberry–flavored liqueur or crème de cassis (optional)**
>
> **½ cup whipping cream**
>
> **4 large egg yolks**
>
> **4 to 6 tablespoons late-harvest wine, such as Riesling, gewürz-traminer, or chenin blanc; or a muscat wine such as Muscat Canelli or Essensia**
>
> **1 to 2 tablespoons sugar**

1. If using liqueur, pour it equally into 4 stemmed glasses (about ¾-cup size). In a small bowl, whip cream until it holds soft peaks; spoon whipped cream equally atop liqueur. Set aside.

2. In a 2½- to 3-quart rou[nd-] bottomed zabaglione pa[n or] in the top of a double bo[iler,] combine egg yolks, wine, [and] 1 tablespoon of the su[gar.] Whisk until frothy. [Place] zabaglione pan directly [over] medium-high gas heat [or] high electric heat; set do[uble] boiler top over simme[ring] water. Whisk vigorously [just] until mixture holds a sl[ight] peak when whisk is li[fted] and no liquid remains in [pan] bottom (3 to 4 minut[es.)] Remove from heat and t[aste] quickly; whisk in 1 m[ore] tablespoon sugar, if desire[d.]

3. Immediately pour za[ba-] glione into glasses (it con[tin-] ues to thicken) and serve.

MAKES 4 SERVINGS.

PER SERVING: 177 calories, 14 g total fat, 7 g saturated fat, 246 mg cholesterol, 18 mg sodium, 6 g carbohydrates, 0 g fiber, 3 g protein, 45 mg calciu[m,] 1 mg iron

t Wine Foam with
awberries

MINUTES

- **cup whipping cream**
- **to 16 large strawberries, hulled**
- **large egg yolks**
- **tablespoons sugar**
- **cup port**
- **Thin strands of lemon peel (optional)**

In a small bowl, whip am until it holds soft ks. Spoon whipped cream ually into 4 stemmed sses (about ½-cup size). 3 or 4 strawberries, hulled l down, in each glass.

In a 2½- to 3-quart round-tomed zabaglione pan or the top of a double boiler, nbine egg yolks, sugar, and t. Whisk until frothy. Place aglione pan directly over edium-high gas heat or h electric heat; place dou-boiler top over simmering ter. Whisk vigorously just til mixture holds a slight ak when whisk is lifted and liquid remains in pan bot-n (3 to 5 minutes).

Immediately pour warm aglione equally over ber-s in glasses (it continues to cken). Garnish with lemon el, if desired, and serve at ce.

AKES 4 SERVINGS.

R SERVING: 203 calories, g total fat, 7 g saturated fat, 3 mg cholesterol, 18 mg lium, 14 g carbohydrates, 0 g er, 3 g protein, 41 mg calcium, ng iron

Port Wine Foam with Strawberries

Strawberry-Orange Sorbet

25 MINUTES

Just three ingredients—frozen strawberries, frozen orange juice concentrate, and a little sugar—go into this refreshing sorbet. Whip it up in 5 minutes or so, then let your ice cream freezer finish the work for you.

- **6 to 8 cups frozen unsweetened strawberries**
- **1 small can (about 6 oz.) frozen orange juice concentrate**
- **2 to 3 tablespoons sugar**

1. In a blender or food processor, combine strawberries, orange juice concentrate, and sugar. Whirl until puréed.

2. Pour strawberry mixture into container of a 1-quart or larger ice cream maker. Freeze according to manufacturer's instructions until softly frozen (15 to 20 minutes). Serve; or, if made ahead, store in freezer in an airtight container for up to 1 week.

MAKES 3 TO 4 CUPS (ABOUT 4 SERVINGS).

PER SERVING: 191 calories, 0 g total fat, 0 g saturated fat, 0 mg cholesterol, 7 mg sodium, 48 g carbohydrates, 0 g fiber, 2 g protein, 56 mg calcium, 2 mg iron

Mango Fool

20 MINUTES

A fool is a popular English dessert, a summertime favorite that's nothing more than mashed fresh fruit folded into whipped cream. For a leaner version, replace all or part of the cream with plain yogurt.

- **2 pounds ripe mangoes**
- **½ cup sugar**
- **2 teaspoons grated lime peel**
- **1 cup whipping cream or about 1½ cups plain nonfat yogurt**
- **1 teaspoon orange-flavored liqueur (optional)**

1. Peel mangoes; cut fruit from pits in chunks. In a large bowl, combine mangoes, sugar, and 1 teaspoon of the lime peel. Mash with a fork until mangoes are coarsely crushed and sugar is completely dissolved. Set aside.

2. In a medium-size bowl, combine cream and liqueur (if used); whip until stiff. Fold cream into mango mixture.

3. To serve, spoon mango fool into individual bowls; sprinkle with remaining 1 teaspoon lime peel.

MAKES 6 SERVINGS.

PER SERVING: 251 calories, 13 g total fat, 8 g saturated fat, 44 mg cholesterol, 16 mg sodium, 36 g carbohydrates, 1 g fiber, 1 g protein, 39 mg calcium, 0 mg iron

Wine & Berry Compote

20 MINUTES

The best way to enjoy ripe summer berries may be to eat them warm from the vine—but the next best thing just might be this old-fashioned compote. Drench your choice of fresh berries in a vanilla-scented red wine syrup, then spoon them over ice cream.

- 1 cup dry red wine
- 1 cup water
- ¾ cup sugar
- 6 tablespoons lemon juice
- 1 vanilla bean, split lengthwise (or 1 teaspoon vanilla extract)
- 4 to 6 cups mixed berries, such as hulled strawberries, raspberries, blackberries, blueberries, gooseberries, and red currants (choose 3 or 4 kinds)
- 1½ to 2 pints vanilla ice cream
  Fresh mint leaves

1. In a 4- to 5-quart pan, combine wine, water, sugar, lemon juice, and vanilla bean (if used). Bring to a boil over high heat, stirring until sugar is dissolved; then boil, uncovered, stirring occasionally, until reduced to 1¼ cups. If using vanilla extract, stir in at this point. Remove from heat.

2. Remove vanilla bean from pan and scrape seeds into syrup. Rinse bean and let dry; save to reuse. (At this point, you may let syrup cool, then cover and refrigerate for up to 3 weeks. Reheat to a simmer before continuing.)

3. Gently stir berries into hot syrup; let cool slightly.

4. For each serving, place a scoop of ice cream in a dessert bowl or on a rimmed plate. Spoon berries and syrup around ice cream. Garnish with mint leaves.

MAKES 6 TO 8 SERVINGS.

PER SERVING: 260 calories, 8 g total fat, 4 g saturated fat, 29 mg cholesterol, 59 mg sodium, 47 g carbohydrates, 2 g fiber, 3 g protein, 105 mg calcium, 1 mg iron

s with Orange
ueur &
scarpone

TO **15** MINUTES

For dessert or a luscious breakfast treat, serve split fresh figs with rich, creamy mascarpone and a sprinkling of toasted pine nuts.

1 tablespoon pine nuts

8 medium-large to large ripe figs
(¾ to 1 lb. *total*)

2 tablespoons orange-flavored liqueur
(or 1 tablespoon frozen orange juice
concentrate, thawed)

6 to 8 ounces mascarpone, at room
temperature

Mint sprigs (optional)

1. Toast pine nuts in a small frying pan over medium heat until golden (about 5 minutes), shaking pan often. Pour out of pan and set aside.

2. Trim tip from stem of each fig, if desired; then cut figs in half lengthwise. Arrange 4

halves on each of 4 individual plates. Drizzle figs with liqueur (or brush lightly with orange juice concentrate).

3. In center of each plate, mound a fourth of the mascarpone; shape it into a cone with a spatula, if desired. Sprinkle mascarpone evenly with pine nuts; garnish with mint sprigs, if desired. Eat figs and cheese with a fork.

MAKES 4 SERVINGS.

PER SERVING: 321 calories, 23 g total fat, 15 g saturated fat, 41 mg cholesterol, 26 mg sodium, 23 g carbohydrates, 3 g fiber, 5 g protein, 135 mg calcium, 1 mg iron

xed Berry
fle with
und Cake &
mon Curd

MINUTES

Trifle, a deservedly famous English dessert, is usually made with liquor-soaked sponge cake or ladyfingers layered with custard, fruits, and whipped cream. This quick version calls for purchased pound cake and both fresh and frozen berries; whipped cream combined with a jar of lemon curd makes a luscious, citrusy filling.

8 ounces frozen unsweetened raspberries

½ cup granulated sugar

1 loaf (11 to 12 oz.) frozen pound
cake, thawed and cut crosswise into
⅓-inch-thick slices

3½ cups mixed fresh berries, such as
blueberries, raspberries, strawberries
(hulled and sliced), and blackberries

1 cup whipping cream

1 jar (about 6½ oz.) lemon curd

Powdered sugar

1. In a 1½-quart pan, combine frozen raspberries and ¼ cup of the granulated sugar. Stir over medium heat until berries are soft and sugar is dissolved (about 5 minutes). Remove from heat. Using a heavy wooden spoon, rub raspberry mixture through a fine strainer into a medium-size bowl. Set aside to cool.

2. Cover bottom of a 2-quart glass bowl or trifle dish with about a third of the pound cake slices. Set remaining cake slices aside.

3. In a large bowl, mix 3 cups of the fresh berries with 2 tablespoons of the granulated sugar.

4. In a medium-size bowl, whip cream with remaining 2 tablespoons granulated sugar until it holds soft peaks. Fold in lemon curd.

5. Spoon 1 cup of the sweetened fresh berries over cake in bowl. Top with a third of the raspberry purée and a third of the cream–lemon curd mixture. Repeat layers 2 more times, using remaining cake, sweetened fresh berries, raspberry purée, and cream mixture; finish with cream mixture. Top trifle with remaining ½ cup unsweetened fresh berries and dust with powdered sugar.

MAKES 4 TO 6 SERVINGS.

PER SERVING: 640 calories, 31 g total fat, 17 g saturated fat, 203 mg cholesterol, 318 mg sodium, 93 g carbohydrates, 3 g fiber, 8 g protein, 87 mg calcium, 2 mg iron

Assorted Citrus with Honeyed Yogurt

25 MINUTES

Bright, translucent fresh orange and grapefruit segments and candied peel make a lovely jewel-like topping for vanilla frozen yogurt.

> 1 medium-size pink grapefruit
>
> 1 large orange (about 8 oz.)
>
> 2 cups water
>
> ¼ cup orange-flavored liqueur
>
> 1½ tablespoons honey
>
> 1½ tablespoons sugar
>
> About 1 quart vanilla nonfat frozen yogurt

1. With a sharp knife or a vegetable peeler, cut peel (colored part only) from grapefruit and orange. Cut peel into very thin shreds, place in a 1- to 1½-quart pan, and add 1 cup of the water. Bring to a boil over high heat; then boil, uncovered, for 2 minutes. Drain. Repeat with remaining 1 cup water. Drain well, return to pan, and set aside.

2. Cut off and discard all white membrane from outside of grapefruit and orange. Holding grapefruit and orange over a bowl to catch juice, cut between membranes to release segments into bowl; also squeeze juice from membranes into bowl. Drain juice from bowl into a glass measure; add water, if needed, to make ½ cup. Set aside. Stir 3 tablespoons of the liqueur into citrus segments.

3. To drained peel in pan, add the ½ cup citrus juice, honey, and sugar. Bring to a boil over high heat; boil, uncovered, stirring occasionally, until peel is translucent and syrup is reduced to 2 tablespoons (5 to 8 minutes). Remove from heat. Stir in remaining 1 table-spoon liqueur.

4. To serve, scoop frozen yogurt equally into 6 individual bowls. Spoon citrus segments over yogurt; top with peel-syrup mixture.

MAKES 6 SERVINGS.

PER SERVING: 216 calories, 0 g total fat, 0 g saturated fat, 0 mg cholesterol, 60 mg sodium, 47 g carbohydrates, 1 g fiber, 3 g protein, 153 mg calcium, 0 mg iron

Ginger & Orange Poached Pears

30 MINUTES

Here's a stunning dessert for an autumn menu. The pears take on the rich, tawny color—and the ginger-nipped flavor—of the port in which they are simmered.

> 2 cups port
>
> ½ cup sugar
>
> 2 teaspoons grated orange peel
>
> 1 tablespoon minced crystallized ginger
>
> 4 d'Anjou, Bartlett, Bosc, or Comice pears; or 6 to 8 Forelle, Winter Nellis, or Seckel pears (about 2 lbs. *total*)
>
> 1 tablespoon lemon juice

1. In a 2- to 3-quart pan, combine port, sugar, orange peel, and ginger. Stir over medium-high heat until sugar is dissolved; then bring mixture to a boil. Meanwhile, peel, halve, and core pears.

2. Reduce heat so port mixture simmers; place pears in port mixture, cut side down. Cover and cook until very tender when pierced (about 15 minutes). With a slotted spoon, transfer pears to a wide bowl or platter. Set aside.

3. Bring cooking liquid to a boil over high heat; then boil, uncovered, until thickened and reduced to about ½ cup (10 to 12 minutes). Stir in lemon juice; then pour syrup evenly over pears. Serve warm or at room temperature.

MAKES 4 SERVINGS.

PER SERVING: 293 calories, 1 g total fat, 0 g saturated fat, 0 mg cholesterol, 14 mg sodium, 75 g carbohydrates, 5 g fiber, 1 g protein, 44 mg calcium, 2 mg iron

Ginger & Orange Poached Pears

Peach-Blueberry Crackle

15 MINUTES

Lending drama to simple fresh fruit, strands of melted sugar form a glistening net ove sweetened sliced peaches and blueberries. To caramelize the sugar, simply heat it in a fry ing pan until it melts and takes on a delicate amber color; once it's poured over the fruit, takes just a few minutes to turn crisp and brittle.

2 **large firm-ripe peaches (about 1 lb.** *total***)**

¾ **cup sugar**

1 **teaspoon grated lemon peel**

1 **tablespoon lemon juice**

½ **teaspoon almond extract**

¼ **cup orange-flavored liqueur**

¼ **cup blueberries**

1 **tablespoon water**

1. Peel, halve, and pit peaches; cut each half into 4 wedges. Place peaches in a large bowl and sprinkle with ¼ cup of the sugar, lemon peel, lemon juice, almond extract, and liqueur. Add blueberries and toss gently to mix. Transfer to a rimmed platter.

2. Place water and remaining ½ cup sugar in a wide regular or nonstick frying pan. Heat over medium-high heat, tilting and shaking pan frequently, until sugar melts and turns a pale amber color (about 8 minutes); watch carefully to avoid scorching. Drizzle sugar syrup evenly over fruit; let cool slightly, then serve.

MAKES 4 SERVINGS.

PER SERVING: 231 calories, 0 g total fat, 0 g saturated fat, 0 mg cholesterol, 2 mg sodium, 53 g carbohydrates, 2 g fiber, 1 g protein, 6 mg calcium, 0 mg iron

Peach-Blueberry Crackle

Chocolate Pots de Crème

30 MINUTES

Rich and chocolaty, these elegant individual desserts are a lovely ending to a simple mea[...] Assemble them in just minutes, then chill; by the time dinner is over, they'll be ready to serv[...] Lidded pot de crème cups make for an especially nice presentation, but any ramekins [...] custard cups will do.

1 **cup semisweet chocolate chips**
2 **tablespoons sugar**
   Pinch of salt
1 **large egg**
1 **teaspoon vanilla**
¾ **cup milk**
   Sweetened whipping cream
   Chocolate curls (optional)

1. In a food processor or blender, whirl chocolate chips until coarsely chopped. Add sugar, salt, egg, and vanilla. Set aside.

2. In a 1-cup glass measure, microwave milk on HIGH (100%) for 2 minutes or until it begins to bubble at edges. With processor or blender running, gradually add scalded milk, whirling on high speed until mixture is smoot[...] (about 1 minute).

3. Pour chocolate mixture into 6 ramekins (about ½-cup size) and refrigerate until cool and slightly thicker (about 25 minutes); for a firmer desert, refrigerate for 45 minutes to 1 hour.

4. To serve, top pots de crème with whipped cream and, if desired, chocolate curls.

MAKES 6 SERVINGS.

PER SERVING: 184 calories, 10 g total fat, 6 g saturated fat, 40 mg cholesterol, 51 mg sodium, 24 g carbohydrates, 0 g fiber, 3 g protein, 50 mg calcium, 1 mg iron

Chocolate Pots de Crème

This variation on the classic Italian sweet makes a special dessert after a holiday meal. Ladyfingers are soaked in an orange-rum syrup, then topped with chestnut spread, tart yogurt lightened with whipped cream—and a thick sprinkling of dark chocolate curls for crunchy contrast.

  1 **cup water**

  ½ **cup sugar**

  2 **teaspoons finely shredded orange peel**

  6 **tablespoons rum or orange juice**

12 **ounces double ladyfingers; or 1 loaf (11 to 12 oz.) frozen pound cake, thawed**

  1 **can (about 17½ oz.) or 1½ cups sweetened chestnut spread**

  1 **cup whipping cream**

  2 **cups plain nonfat yogurt (or reduced-fat or regular sour cream)**

  3 **to 4 ounces semisweet chocolate**

  3 **or 4 crosswise slices peeled orange or tangerine (optional)**

1. In a 1- to 1½-quart pan, combine water, sugar, and orange peel. Bring to a boil over high heat; then boil, uncovered, until reduced to ¾ cup. Let cool slightly; stir in ¼ cup of the rum.

2. Split ladyfingers or thinly slice pound cake. Arrange ladyfinger halves or cake slices side by side, overlapping as needed, to cover a rimmed platter or very shallow bowl 14 to 15 inches wide; leave a 1-inch-wide bare area between ladyfingers and edge of platter.

3. In a small bowl, stir together chestnut spread, remaining 2 tablespoons rum, and 2 tablespoons of the orange-rum syrup. Pour remaining orange-rum syrup over ladyfingers to moisten evenly. Gently spread chestnut mixture over ladyfingers, leaving 1 inch uncovered at outside edge.

4. In a medium-size bowl, whip cream until stiff; whisk in yogurt. Swirl cream mixture over chestnut spread and most of the exposed ladyfinger rim.

5. Draw a vegetable peeler firmly across chocolate to make curls (or finely chop chocolate with a knife or in a food processor). Scatter chocolate over cream mixture. Serve at once; or cover airtight (without touching topping) and refrigerate for up to 24 hours. Garnish with orange slices before serving, if desired.

MAKES 10 TO 12 SERVINGS.

PER SERVING: 341 calories, 12 g total fat, 7 g saturated fat, 138 mg cholesterol, 85 mg sodium, 46 g carbohydrates, 2 g fiber, 6 g protein, 115 mg calcium, 1 mg iron

Oranges in Brandy

15 MINUTES

For a light, aromatic close to a rich meal, serve prunes and fresh orange segments soaked in a coriander-spiced syrup of orange juice and brandy.

   6 **large oranges (about 4¾ lbs. *total*)**
   1 **tablespoon grated orange peel**
  ½ **cup sugar**
   1 **teaspoon coriander seeds, crushed**
   1 **cup water**
1½ **cups moist-pack pitted prunes**
   1 **cup plum brandy or regular brandy**

1. With a sharp knife, cut peel and all white membrane from oranges. Then, holding oranges over a bowl to catch juice, cut between membranes to release segments into bowl; also squeeze juice from membranes into bowl. Drain juice from bowl into a 1½- to 2-quart pan. Set orange segments aside.

2. To pan, add grated orange peel, sugar, coriander seeds, and water. Stir over high heat until sugar is dissolved. Add prunes; reduce heat, cover, and simmer for 5 minutes. Remove from heat and add brandy. Let cool until slightly warm.

3. Gently mix orange segments with prunes and syrup. Serve; or, if made ahead, cover and refrigerate for up to 24 hours.

MAKES 8 TO 10 SERVINGS.

PER SERVING: 263 calories, 1 g total fat, 0 g saturated fat, 0 mg cholesterol, 1 mg sodium, 57 g carbohydrates, 6 g fiber, 2 g protein, 93 mg calcium, 1 mg iron

Meringue Berries with Orange-Ginger Sauce

15 MINUTES

Drizzled with liqueur and topped with a fluffy cloud of meringue, your favorite berries make a dramatic summer dessert. As soon as the meringue is browned, pour a ginger-accented fresh orange sauce around the fruit, then serve.

1½ **tablespoons cornstarch**
   1 **cup granulated sugar**
   1 **cup orange juice**
   3 **thin slices fresh ginger**
   3 **tablespoons lemon juice**
   2 **cups hulled strawberries, raspberries, or blackberries (or use a combination)**
   2 **tablespoons currant-flavored, black raspberry–flavored, or orange-flavored liqueur**
   3 **large egg whites**
  ¼ **teaspoon cream of tartar**
   1 **teaspoon vanilla**
   1 **tablespoon powdered sugar**

1. To prepare orange-ginger sauce, combine cornstarch and ½ cup of the granulated sugar in a 1- to 1½-quart pan; stir to mix well. Stir in orange juice; add ginger. Bring to a boil over high heat (about 2 minutes), stirring constantly; sauce will thicken slightly. Remove from heat. Remove and discard ginger; stir in lemon juice. Set aside.

2. Arrange berries close together in a single layer on a rimmed, ovenproof 10- to 12-inch platter. Spoon liqueur evenly over berries.

3. In a large bowl, beat egg whites and cream of tartar with an electric mixer on high speed until frothy. Gradually add remaining ½ cup granulated sugar, beating until meringue holds stiff peaks. Beat in vanilla.

4. Mound meringue over berries, leaving a 1- to 2-inch-wide border of berries uncovered. Sift powdered sugar evenly over meringue. Broil 6 inches below heat until lightly browned (about 3 minutes). Pour orange-ginger sauce around berries on platter and serve at once.

MAKES 6 SERVINGS.

PER SERVING: 202 calories, 0 g total fat, 0 g saturated fat, 0 mg cholesterol, 31 mg sodium, 47 g carbohydrates, 1 g fiber, 2 g protein, 13 mg calcium, 0 mg iron

Fila & Puff Pastry

Purchased puff pastry and fila (you'll a[lso] see it spelled "fillo" and "phyllo") let you turn out impressive desserts in a hurry: fruit-fil[led] tartlets and napoleons; sugar-crusted, buttery *palmiers;* even delicate "cannoli" filled w[ith] cherries and ricotta cheese.

Fila is sold refrigerated or frozen, usually in 1-pound packages of 18 to 20 sheets; thaw [the] frozen pastry before using. And always work with fila a portion at a time, keeping the she[ets] you aren't using tightly covered with plastic wrap to prevent them from drying out. Puff pas[try] is typically sold frozen, two sheets to a package. Thaw it before using.

Palmiers

25 MINUTES

About 2 cups granulated sugar

1 sheet frozen puff pastry (from a 17¼-oz. package), thawed

1. Sprinkle a work surface generously with sugar. Unfold pastry sheet and place it on sugar; roll out lightly to make a rectangle about 10 by 12 inches. Fold pastry in thirds (as you would fold a letter) to form a rectangle about 4 by 10 inches. Then fold this rectangle in half lengthwise.

2. Cut folded pastry crosswise into slices about ½ inch thick. Roll each slice in sugar to coat and turn cut side up. Bend the 2 ends of each slice outward, so slice looks something like a tulip. Place slices on a parchment-lined baking sheet.

3. Bake in a 450° oven until pastries are golden on bottom (about 6 minutes). Using a spatula, turn pastries over; sprinkle with sugar. Continue to bake until nicely caramelized on bottom (3 to 4 more minutes). Transfer to racks to cool.

MAKES ABOUT 20 PASTRIES.

PER PASTRY: 145 calories, 5 g total fat, 1 g saturated fat, 0 mg cholesterol, 31 mg sodium, 25 g carbohydrates, 0 g fiber, 1 g protein, 1 mg calcium, 0 mg iron

Sour Cherry "Cannoli" with Ricotta & Orange

30 MINUTES

1 can (about 1 lb.) pitted tart cherries

¼ cup ricotta cheese

1 tablespoon granulated sugar

2 teaspoons kirsch (optional)

2 teaspoons grated orange peel

16 sheets fila pastry (about 12 oz. *total***), each** 12 to 14 inches wide by about 18 inches long

¼ cup butter or margarine, melted

1. Drain cherries, reserving 1 tablespoon of the juice. Set cherries aside. In a small bowl, combine reserved 1 tablespoon cherry juice, ricotta cheese, sugar, kirsch (if used), and 1 teaspoon of the orange peel. Set aside.

2. Work with 2 sheets of fila at a time, keeping remainder tightly covered to prevent drying. Lay one sheet of fila flat on a work surface; brush lightly with butter. Lay a second sheet on top of the first; brush lightly with butter. Spread an eighth of the ricotta mixture 3 inche[s] from a short side; top with [an] eighth of the cherries. [From] short side of fila closes[t to] filling over filling; then [fold] in the 2 long sides, over[lap]ping one over the other. [Fold] filled end of pastry over its[elf] toward opposite short [end,] then continue to fold it over end until you re[ach] opposite end. Place resul[ting] fila packet, seam side do[wn,] on a lightly oiled large bak[ing] sheet.

3. Repeat to make 7 m[ore] packets, using remaining [fila] sheets, butter (reserve 1[½] teaspoons for brushing [tops] of packets), ricotta mixt[ure,] and cherries.

4. Cut an "X" in center [of] each packet; gently bend [the] edges back. Brush pack[ets] lightly with butter. Bake i[n a] 350° oven until golden bro[wn] (about 15 minutes). Trans[fer] to individual plates; garn[ish] with remaining 1 teaspo[on] orange peel.

MAKES 8 SERVINGS.

PER SERVING: 255 calories, 10 g total fat, 5 g saturated fat, 19 mg cholesterol, 274 mg sodium, 37 g carbohydrates, 0 [g] fiber, 4 g protein, 29 mg calciu[m,] 2 mg iron

...berry-Peach Cobbler ... Fila Crust

... INUTES

- ... sheets fila pastry (about 2½ oz. *total*), *each* 12 to 14 inches wide by about 18 inches long
- ... tablespoons butter or margarine, melted
- ... tablespoons all-purpose flour
- ... tablespoons grated orange peel
- ... teaspoon ground cardamom
- ... cup plus 2 tablespoons sugar
- ... pounds firm-ripe peaches, peeled, pitted, and quartered
- ... cups raspberries
- Vanilla ice cream

... Cut fila sheets in half ... wise. Then stack halved ... ets on a work surface, ... shing each piece lightly ... butter before adding the ...; you will have a stack of ... ayers. Using a 2-inch- ... nd plain or fluted cookie cutter, cut 8 circles from stacked fila sheets. If edges of cutter are not sharp enough to cut through all pastry layers, cut around cutter and through pastry with a sharp paring knife. Transfer stacked fila circles to a lightly buttered baking sheet. Bake in a 350° oven until golden (about 10 minutes).

2. Meanwhile, in an oval 2½-quart casserole, combine flour, orange peel, cardamom, and sugar. Mix well. Stir in peaches and raspberries. Bake, uncovered, in a 350° oven until fruit juices are bubbly (about 15 minutes). Serve hot, warm, or at room temperature.

3. To serve, carefully arrange baked fila circles atop fruit mixture. Serve at once, spooning into bowls. Top with ice cream.

MAKES 8 SERVINGS.

PER SERVING: 207 calories, 4 g total fat, 2 g saturated fat, 9 mg cholesterol, 77 mg sodium, 43 g carbohydrates, 3 g fiber, 2 g protein, 17 mg calcium, 1 mg iron

Quick Napoleons

30 MINUTES

Pictured on page 206

- 6 sheets fila pastry (about 5 oz. *total*), *each* 12 to 14 inches wide by about 18 inches long
- 2 tablespoons butter or margarine, melted
- 1½ cups whipping cream
- ¼ cup granulated sugar
- 1 cup blueberries
- 2 teaspoons grated lemon peel
- Powdered sugar

1. Stack fila sheets on a work surface, brushing each sheet lightly with butter before adding the next. Cut stack crosswise into 4 equal strips; then cut lengthwise into 2-inch-wide strips. You will have a total of 24 to 28 pieces, each about 2 by 4½ inches. Using a wide spatula, transfer pieces to lightly buttered baking sheets, arranging them slightly apart. Bake in a 350° oven until golden brown (10 to 15 minutes). Let cool slightly.

2. While pastry is baking, in a medium-size bowl, whip cream with 2 tablespoons of the granulated sugar until it holds soft peaks. Set aside. Also combine blueberries, remaining 2 tablespoons granulated sugar, and lemon peel in a small frying pan; stir over medium heat until sugar is completely dissolved (5 to 6 minutes). Remove from heat.

3. To make napoleons, you will need 18 of the baked pastry pieces; reserve remaining pieces for other uses. Spoon whipped cream atop 6 of the pastry pieces, using half the cream; top with some of the berry mixture. Top with 6 more pastry pieces; add remaining whipped cream and berries, dividing evenly. Top with remaining 6 pastry pieces and dust generously with powdered sugar.

MAKES 6 SERVINGS.

PER SERVING: 313 calories, 24 g total fat, 14 g saturated fat, 78 mg cholesterol, 153 mg sodium, 23 g carbohydrates, 1 g fiber, 3 g protein, 47 mg calcium, 1 mg iron

...ffed Tartlets with Fresh Berries

... MINUTES

- ... sheet frozen puff pastry (from a 17¼-oz. package), thawed
- ... cup blueberries
- ... cup raspberries
- ... tablespoons sugar
- ... teaspoon grated orange peel
- Sweetened whipped cream

1. Unfold pastry and place on a work surface; roll out lightly to make a rectangle about 10 by 12 inches. Cut pastry into rounds, using a 1½-inch cookie cutter with a fluted edge (you should have about 30 rounds). Pierce each round in several places with a fork to prevent pastry from puffing too much during baking.

2. Arrange pastry rounds on a parchment-lined baking sheet. Bake in a 350° oven until lightly browned (15 to 20 minutes).

3. Meanwhile, in a medium-size bowl, mix blueberries, raspberries, sugar, and orange peel. Let stand while pastries are baking so berries will absorb sugar.

4. Arrange warm baked pastry rounds on a platter; place a spoonful of the berry mixture in center of each pastry. Serve warm, topped with whipped cream.

MAKES ABOUT 2½ DOZEN TARTLETS.

PER TARTLET: 51 calories, 3 g total fat, 0 g saturated fat, 0 mg cholesterol, 20 mg sodium, 5 g carbohydrates, 0 g fiber, 1 g protein, 2 mg calcium, 0 mg iron

Hot Papaya Sundaes

25 MINUTES

Papaya halves baked with rum, lime, and honey make edible bowls for tangy frozen yogurt. Save the syrup from the baking dish to serve as a topping for the dessert.

2 medium-size firm-ripe papayas (about 1 lb. *each*)

1 tablespoon butter or margarine, melted

½ teaspoon finely shredded lime peel

⅓ cup rum or water

¼ cup lime juice

3 tablespoons honey

1 pint orange-flavored nonfat frozen yogurt

1. Cut papayas in half lengthwise and remove seeds.

2. In a 9- by 13-inch baking dish, combine butter, lime peel, rum, lime juice, and honey. Place papaya halves, cut side down, in pan.

3. Bake in a 375° oven until papayas are hot and sauce begins to bubble (about 15 minutes). Transfer hot papaya halves, cut side up, to 4 individual plates. Let cool for about 5 minutes, then fill each papaya half with a scoop of frozen yogurt. Pour pan juices into a small pitcher or bowl; pour over fruit and yogurt to taste.

MAKES 4 SERVINGS.

PER SERVING: 279 calories, 3 g total fat, 2 g saturated fat, 8 mg cholesterol, 92 mg sodium, 50 g carbohydrates, 1 g fiber, 5 g protein, 235 mg calcium, 1 mg iron

Broiled Pineapple with Vanilla Ice Cream & Pecans

MINUTES

Three delicious layers—a broiled pineapple slice, a scoop of vanilla ice cream, and a cloak of warm caramel sauce—add up to a simple dessert that's elegant enough for company. Sprinkle the sauce with toasted pecans for crunch.

- 1 pint vanilla ice cream
- 1 container (about 20 oz.) sliced peeled, cored fresh pineapple (about 6 slices)
- 1 jar (about 11 oz.) caramel sauce or caramel ice cream topping
- 1 cup toasted pecan halves

1. Scoop ice cream into 6 balls; place balls in a metal pan and place in freezer.

2. Place pineapple slices in a shallow 10- by 15-inch baking pan. Broil about 3 inches below heat until tinged with brown (5 to 7 minutes). Turn slices over; broil until tinged with brown on other side (4 to 5 more minutes).

3. Meanwhile, scrape caramel sauce from jar into a 1-quart pan. Stir occasionally over medium heat until pourable.

4. To serve, arrange one pineapple slice on each of 6 individual plates; let cool slightly. Top each slice with a scoop of ice cream. Drizzle with warm caramel sauce and sprinkle with pecans.

MAKES 6 SERVINGS.

PER SERVING: 386 calories, 17 g total fat, 4 g saturated fat, 19 mg cholesterol, 218 mg sodium, 60 g carbohydrates, 2 g fiber, 4 g protein, 97 mg calcium, 1 mg iron

Strawberry Ricotta Tart with Ginger Crust

TO 20 MINUTES

This elegant, strawberry-topped no-bake cheesecake is simple to make. If you like, prepare the gingersnap crust ahead of time, then spoon in the filling and add the fruit just before serving.

- 25 packaged gingersnap cookies (*each* about 2 inches in diameter)
- ⅓ cup butter or margarine, melted
- 2 cups (about 1 lb.) part-skim ricotta cheese
- ½ cup powdered sugar
- 1 teaspoon vanilla
- 2 cups strawberries, hulled and halved

1. In a food processor, whirl cookies until crushed (you should have about 2 cups crumbs). Add butter and pulse until mixture holds together (about 15 seconds). Press mixture over bottom and sides of an 8-inch tart pan with a removable rim. Bake in a 350° oven for 8 minutes. Set aside to cool.

2. In a medium-size bowl, combine ricotta cheese, sugar, and vanilla. Beat with an electric mixer on low speed until smooth.

3. Spread cheese mixture evenly in crust. Remove pan rim and set tart on a serving plate; arrange strawberries over filling.

MAKES 6 SERVINGS.

PER SERVING: 375 calories, 19 g total fat, 11 g saturated fat, 51 mg cholesterol, 417 mg sodium, 40 g carbohydrates, 2 g fiber, 10 g protein, 237 mg calcium, 2 mg iron

Strawberry-Rhubarb Crumble with Cinnamon Oatmeal Topping

30 MINUTES

The classic combination of fresh strawberries and rhubarb is as delicious in a fruit crumble as it is in the traditional springtime pie. This crumble features a spicy, buttery oatmeal topping; serve it with whipped cream or vanilla ice cream, if you like.

⅓ cup firmly packed brown sugar

2 tablespoons all-purpose flour

¾ teaspoon ground cinnamon

3 cups strawberries, hulled and quartered

1 cup ¼-inch pieces fresh rhubarb

1 tablespoon lemon juice

1 cup quick-cooking rolled oats

¼ cup firmly packed brown sugar

¼ teaspoon ground ginger

3 tablespoons butter or margarine, melted

Sweetened whipped cream or vanilla ice cream (optional)

1. In a shallow 8-inch-wide casserole, stir together the ⅓ cup sugar, flour, and ½ teaspoon of the cinnamon. Add strawberries, rhubarb, and lemon juice; mix well.

2. In a medium-size bowl, stir together oats, the ¼ cup sugar, remaining ¼ teaspoon cinnamon, ginger, and butter. Sprinkle evenly over fruit mixture.

3. Bake in a 375° oven until fruit is bubbly and topping is golden brown (about 25 minutes). Serve hot, warm, or cool. To serve, spoon into bowls; top with whipped cream, if desired.

MAKES 6 SERVINGS.

PER SERVING: 221 calories, 7 g total fat, 4 g saturated fat, 16 mg cholesterol, 70 mg sodium, 38 g carbohydrates, 3 g fiber, 3 g protein, 59 mg calcium, 2 mg iron

Strawberry-Rhubarb Crumble with Cinnamon Oatmeal Topping

[Sal]zburger [No]ckerln

MINUTES

Light and billowy, this famous Austrian dessert is surprisingly easy to prepare. It makes a dramatic offering when presented warm and golden from the oven.

- 1 ounce semisweet chocolate
- 4 large egg whites
- ¼ cup sugar
- 3 large egg yolks
- 4 teaspoons all-purpose flour
- 1 tablespoon butter or margarine
  Unsweetened cocoa

1. Draw a vegetable peeler firmly across chocolate to cut it into thin shavings. Set chocolate shavings aside.

2. In a large bowl, beat egg whites with an electric mixer on high speed until they hold soft peaks. Gradually add sugar, beating until mixture holds very stiff peaks. Set aside.

3. Place egg yolks in a small bowl. With same beaters, beat egg yolks on high speed until very light in color and slightly thickened. Gradually add flour, beating until mixture is thick and well blended. Fold yolk mixture into whites, blending lightly but thoroughly.

4. In a shallow, heatproof, oval or rectangular 2-quart pan, melt butter directly over medium heat. Then heap egg mixture into pan, making 6 equal mounds. Bake in a 350° oven until top is pale brown (10 to 12 minutes). Sprinkle with chocolate shavings and dust lightly with cocoa.

MAKES 6 SERVINGS.

PER SERVING: 119 calories, 6 g total fat, 3 g saturated fat, 111 mg cholesterol, 60 mg sodium, 13 g carbohydrates, 0 g fiber, 4 g protein, 15 mg calcium, 1 mg iron

[Zi]nfandel Port [C]ookies

5 TO 20 MINUTES

Covered with a snowy powdered sugar coating, these richly flavored no-bake cookies are easy to whip up in your food processor. They keep well in the refrigerator or freezer.

- 1 package (about 12 oz.) vanilla wafers
- ½ cup unsweetened cocoa
- 1 cup pecan halves
- ¼ cup dark corn syrup
- ½ cup Zinfandel port or other port
  About ½ cup powdered sugar

1. In a food processor, combine vanilla wafers, cocoa, and pecans. Whirl until wafers are reduced to fine crumbs; then pulse for several seconds. Add corn syrup and port. Whirl just until well blended.

2. Using your hands, shape dough into 1-inch balls; roll each ball in powdered sugar. If made ahead, package airtight and refrigerate for up to 1 month or freeze for up to 2 months. If desired, roll in powdered sugar again just before serving.

MAKES ABOUT 4 DOZEN COOKIES.

PER COOKIE: 62 calories, 3 g total fat, 0 g saturated fat, 0 mg cholesterol, 31 mg sodium, 9 g carbohydrates, 0 g fiber, 1 g protein, 6 mg calcium, 0 mg iron

Chocolate Chip Cookie Bars

30 MINUTES

This streamlined version of an all-time favorite includes rolled oats for chewiness and apple sauce for moist texture. To speed preparation, we spread the dough in a square pan and cut it into bars after baking, but you can bake it as drop cookies if you wish (drop the dough o baking sheets by rounded teaspoonfuls and bake for about 10 minutes).

- 2 **tablespoons butter or margarine, at room temperature**
- 2 **tablespoons vegetable oil**
- 1 **cup firmly packed dark brown sugar**
- 1 **large egg**
- ½ **cup unsweetened applesauce**
- 1 **teaspoon vanilla**
- 1 **teaspoon baking powder**
- ½ **teaspoon baking soda**
- ½ **teaspoon salt**
- 1½ **cups all-purpose flour**
- 2 **cups regular rolled oats**
- 1 **cup semisweet chocolate chips**
  About 2 tablespoons granulated sugar

1. In a large bowl, beat butter, oil, and brown sugar with an electric mixer until smooth. Add egg, applesauce, and vanilla; beat until blended. Beat in baking powder, baking soda, salt, and flour until smooth. Scrape down side of bowl; then stir in oats and chocolate chips. Bake dough right away; if it is allowed to stand, cookies will be dry.

2. Spread dough evenly in a lightly oiled 8-inch-square baking pan. Sprinkle evenly with granulated sugar. Bake in a 350° oven until pale golden (about 15 minutes). Let cool briefly on a rack; then cut into 1- by 4-inch bars. Serve warm or cool.

MAKES 16 COOKIES.

PER COOKIE: 222 calories, 8 g total fat, 3 g saturated fat, 17 mg cholesterol, 156 mg sodium, 38 g carbohydrates, 2 g fiber, 3 g protein, 41 mg calcium, 2 mg iron

Espresso White Chocolate Chip Cookies

30 MINUTES

Studded with white chocolate chips, these dark chocolate cookies are flavored with finely ground coffee. Let the cookies cool completely before removing them from the baking sheet; while warm, they tend to be quite tender.

- 1 **ounce unsweetened chocolate, chopped**
- ¼ **cup butter or margarine, diced**
- 1 **tablespoon finely ground coffee beans**
- ½ **cup sugar**
- ¾ **cup all-purpose flour**
- 1 **teaspoon baking powder**
- 2 **tablespoons milk**
- 1 **teaspoon vanilla**
- ¼ **cup sweetened shredded coconut**
- ¼ **cup white chocolate chips**

1. Combine unsweetened chocolate, butter, and ground coffee in the top of a double boiler set over simmering water; stir often until mixture is smoothly melted. Or place ingredients in a microwave-safe bowl and microwave on MEDIUM (50%), stirring at 30-second intervals, until smoothly melted.

2. In a bowl, stir together sugar, flour, and baking powder. Add chocolate mixture, milk, vanilla, coconut, and white chocolate chips; stir to mix well. Shape dough into 24 equal-size balls. Set balls about 3 inches apart on lightly oiled baking sheets. With your palm, flatten balls to about ¼ inch thick.

3. Bake in a 350° oven until cookies feel firm at edges when lightly touched (10 to 12 minutes). Let cool for at least 10 minutes on baking sheets; then, using a wide spatula, transfer to racks to cool. If made ahead, cover airtight and refrigerate for up to 5 days; freeze for longer storage.

MAKES 2 DOZEN COOKIES.

PER COOKIE: 75 calories, 4 g total fat, 2 g saturated fat, 6 mg cholesterol, 46 mg sodium, 10 g carbohydrates, 0 g fiber, 1 g protein, 18 mg calcium, 0 mg iron

Fabulous Fritters with Apricot Sauce

30 MINUTES

Here's a dessert or brunch specialty that makes the most of summer fruit. Each crisp, golden fritter hides a delicious surprise: a plump, sweet-tart fresh blackberry. Serve the fritters atop a fresh apricot sauce embellished with a little crème fraîche or sour cream.

- 3 **pounds apricots, pitted and sliced**
- ¾ **cup water**
- ⅔ **cup plus 2 teaspoons granulated sugar**
- ¼ **teaspoon baking powder**
- ¼ **cup all-purpose flour**
- 1 **large egg white**
- 2 **tablespoons milk**
- ½ **teaspoon vanilla**
  Vegetable oil
- 24 **to 30 large blackberries (1½ to 2 cups)**
- ¼ **cup crème fraîche or sour cream**
  Powdered sugar

1. Place apricots, water, and ⅔ cup of the granulated sugar in a medium-size pan over medium-high heat. Bring to a simmer, stirring occasionally; then continue to simmer, stirring occasionally, until fruit falls apart. Remove from heat, cover, and set aside.

2. While fruit is cooking, prepare batter: in a medium-size bowl, stir together baking powder, remaining 2 teaspoons granulated sugar, flour, egg white, milk, and vanilla.

3. In a wok or deep, narrow 1- to 1½-quart pan, heat about 1 inch oil to 360° to 370°F on a deep-frying thermometer. Drop berries into fritter batter; turn gently to coat. With a fork, lift batter-coated berries, one at a time, from batter; drop into hot oil (do not crowd pan). Cook, turning often, until fritters are golden brown all over (1 to 1½ minutes). Remove from pan with a slotted spoon and arrange in a single layer on paper towels on a wide heat-proof platter. Keep cooked fritters warm in a 150° oven until all have been cooked.

4. To serve, spoon cooked apricots equally into 6 individual wide, shallow bowls. In a cup, stir crème fraîche until smooth and thin; then spoon a dollop onto apricots in each bowl. Draw the tip of a knife through crème fraîche to make decorative swirls. Arrange fritters equally atop apricots in each bowl. Serve at once; offer powdered sugar to add to taste.

MAKES 6 SERVINGS.

PER SERVING: 341 calories, 12 g total fat, 3 g saturated fat, 9 mg cholesterol, 41 mg sodium, 58 g carbohydrates, 5 g fiber, 5 g protein, 83 mg calcium, 2 mg iron

Common-sense Quick Cooking

★ Remember, you don't have to do it all. You can take advantage of prepared foods and still personalize your menus. Go ahead and microwave a roll of ready-cooked polenta, but make your own Italian sausage and mushroom sauce to serve over it. The next time, you might cook the polenta from scratch, then serve it with a sauce from the supermarket refrigerator case.

★ As you shop, be aware of the resources around you. Keep your eyes open for new products you can put to imaginative use in your kitchen.

★ Cooks who enjoy food seasoned and cooked to their own tastes aren't likely to accept completely prepared foods. Rather than searching for a frozen entrée that measures up to memories of traditional cooking, learn to identify the cuts of meat and poultry that can be cooked to your taste in a short time.

★ Choose convenience foods selectively. You may never come across a bottled salad dressing that tastes as good on crisp greens as your own homemade vinaigrette. But perhaps you can find one that makes a fine quick marinade for grilled meats. If you want to make a pie without fussing with pastry, try different forms—frozen, refrigerated, packaged mix—until you find one to your liking. If you don't care for quick-cooking rice, cook the standard kind in 20 minutes (or less) while you prepare the rest of your dinner.

★ Read labels. If you're trying to avoid excessive fat, you've probably already learned to sort out the numbers that matter to you. If you prefer to avoid preservatives and additives, look at several forms of the same product and choose the one containing the fewest such ingredients.

★ Supermarket produce sections are becoming an increasingly good source of quick-cooking ingredients. Today it's no trick to find peeled pineapple, sliced mushrooms, shredded carrots, prewashed spinach and salad greens, and broccoli flowerets. Tomorrow, who knows?

★ Look for recipes with relatively short ingredient lists: the fewer things you have to take out of the pantry or refrigerator, the sooner you can begin cooking.

★ Thinner cuts of meat cook faster. By pounding steaks, chops, boneless chicken breasts, or turkey breast slices, you can make them thin enough to cook in 5 minutes or less. Trim and discard any excess fat; then place the pieces of meat between two pieces of plastic wrap. Using a heavy, flat-sided mallet, pound the meat all over to about ¼ inch thick (don't pound so hard that you tear the meat). Now you're ready to sauté or grill in a jiffy.

★ To avoid waste, wrap cheese tightly in plastic wrap and store it in the refrigerator (many varieties keep for several weeks). If you use shredded cheese often, prepare it with your food processor, then keep it refrigerated in a tightly covered container or plastic bag.

★ When you cook pasta, your first step should be to heat the water; it takes time for a large quantity of water to come to a rolling boil. If the water boils before you're ready, reduce the heat to keep it at a simmer; then increase the heat again just before cooking the pasta.

★ Here's one exception to the rule about saving time by shopping ahead: wait to buy seafood until the day you plan to cook it. Uncooked seafood doesn't keep well, and freshness pays off in good flavor.

★ Recognizing when seafood is done is essential to cooking it well. When overcooked, fish and shellfish rapidly lose flavor and moisture. Most recipes tell you to cook fish until it's "just opaque but still moist in thickest part." To test, cut into the thickest part, since thinner parts may seem done while thicker portions are still uncooked inside. As a general rule, allow 8 to 10 minutes of cooking time per inch of thickness for fish cooked by any method other than microwaving.

★ A dollop or slice of seasoned butter, either homemade or from the dairy case, adds flavor interest to grilled or broiled meats, poultry, and seafood. Consider adding fresh herbs such as chopped parsley, cilantro, basil, tarragon, or dill, accented by lemon juice and spices such as pepper, chili powder, or ground cumin.

Convenience from the Supermarket

You'll find ready-to-use foods in every section of the supermarket where you do most of your shopping. Here, listed by department, are a few you might like to include in your meals.

PRODUCE
Miniature "baby-cut" peeled carrots
Shredded carrots
Sliced mushrooms
Triple-washed spinach
Coleslaw mix
Shredded red cabbage
Broccoli flowerets
Baby lettuce mix (mesclun)
Romaine hearts
Peeled, sliced pineapple
Melon balls
Asian pastas such as egg roll wrappers, Chinese-style noodles
Polenta rolls, plain and seasoned
Tofu

MEATS
Beef steaks (flank, cube, strip or market, culotte, top sirloin, skirt, fillet, top round)
Beef cut for fajitas, fondue, or kebabs
Tri-tip roast
Pork tenderloin
Pork chops (boneless; smoked)
Lamb chops (loin, rib, sirloin, round bone, shoulder)
Rack of lamb
Lamb sirloin
Veal scaloppine and cutlets
Veal chops (loin, rib)
Ground meat (beef, lamb, veal)
Sausages (raw and fully cooked)

QUICK-COOKING POULTRY
Chicken breasts (bone in; boneless, skinless)

Chicken thighs (boneless, skinless)
Chicken drummettes
Turkey breast (tenderloins and cutlets)
Ground turkey
Chicken and turkey sausages (with various seasonings)
Smoked turkey sausage

FRESH SEAFOOD
Trout (whole; boneless)
Fish fillets
Fish steaks
Salmon burgers
Cooked whole crab; crabmeat
Oysters
Clams
Mussels
Shrimp (shelled, deveined cooked or raw)
Scallops (bay and sea)
Calamari steaks

REFRIGERATED
Flavored butters
Juices and nectars
Crème fraîche
Mascarpone
Doughs (pizza crust, breadsticks, biscuits, pie crusts)
Pasta (plain, flavored, filled, gnocchi)
Pasta sauces

FROZEN
Vegetables (including tiny onions, chopped onions, Swiss chard, hash browns, mashed potatoes, cooked squash, herbs, creamed spinach)
Berries

Filled pasta
Sauces (such as pesto)
Stocks (veal, fish, chicken, beef, vegetable)
Pastry (pie crusts, puff pastry, fila pastry)
Breads (bagels, soft pretzels, bread dough)
Pound cake

DELICATESSEN
Rotisserie roast chicken
Smoked chicken, turkey
Smoked salmon, trout
Prosciutto
Pancetta
Roast beef
Guacamole
Salsas
Specialty olives (green cracked, Niçoise, calamata, oil-cured black ripe)

GROCERY
Baked pizza crusts
Packaged croutons
Bread crumbs, panko
Roasted red peppers
Dried tomatoes in oil
Pasta sauces (in jars, cans)
Caponata
Tapenade
Chutney
Oils (olive, walnut, avocado)
Vinegars (balsamic; flavored types such as raspberry)
Rice (basmati, arborio, jasmine)
Polenta
Canned beans (garbanzos, black, red kidney, cannellini, pinto, fava, red)
Asian cooking sauces
Tahini

A Well-stocked Pantry

Creating an appetizing meal in minutes depends on a well-stocked kitchen. Start with the following list of often-used staple foods; then add your family's favorites to it.

PANTRY SHELF

Many of these foods should be refrigerated after opening.

Canned tomatoes
Tomato sauce
Tomato paste
Tuna
Anchovy fillets
Canned green chiles
Canned and marinated
  artichoke hearts
Canned beans (black, red
  kidney, cannellini, gar-
  banzo, pink or pinto)
Olives (whole and sliced
  ripe, calamata, pimento-
  stuffed green)
Roasted red peppers
Apricot jam
Major Grey's chutney
Honey
Maple syrup
Mild-flavored molasses
Light corn syrup
Peanut butter
Soy sauce
Worcestershire sauce
Liquid hot pepper seasoning
Canned broth
Canned unsweetened
  coconut milk
Solid vegetable shortening
Vegetable oil
Olive oil
Oriental sesame oil
Vinegar (distilled white,
  cider, red and white wine,
  balsamic, rice)
Rice (long-grain white;
  arborio or other short-
  grain white; quick-cooking)
Couscous
Lentils
Pasta (your favorite shapes)
All-purpose flour
Sugar (granulated, brown,
  powdered)
Salt
Baking powder
Baking soda
Vanilla and almond extracts
Cornstarch

Yellow cornmeal, polenta
Rolled oats
Raisins and other dried fruit
Semisweet chocolate chips
Unsweetened cocoa

LIQUOR CABINET

Dry red and white wine
Dry sherry
Brandy
Rum
Orange-flavored liqueur;
  other flavored liqueurs

PRODUCE BIN

These don't need refrigeration, but keep them in a cool, dark, dry place.

Garlic
Onions (yellow and red)
Shallots
Russet potatoes

REFRIGERATOR

Milk
Whipping cream
Sour cream
Plain yogurt
Butter or margarine
Cheese (Parmesan,
  Cheddar, feta, blue-
  veined, jack, ricotta)
Eggs
Mayonnaise
Catsup
Dijon mustard
Salsa
Hoisin sauce
Dill pickles
Capers
Prepared horseradish
Lemons, oranges
Salad greens
Bell peppers
Carrots
Celery
Green onions
Parsley
Thin-skinned potatoes
Fresh ginger
Nuts (pine nuts, almonds,
  cashews, pecans, walnuts)

FREEZER

Keep out-of-season fruits and vegetables in the freezer, so you'll have them when needed. Breads also keep best when frozen, unless you use them very quickly.

Ice cream or frozen yogurt
Raspberries, blueberries,
  cranberries
Orange juice concentrate
Tiny peas
Corn kernels
Chopped spinach
Breads
Bread crumbs
Tortillas (flour, corn)

SPICE AND HERB SHELVES

Allspice (ground and whole)
Basil (dried)
Bay leaves (dried)
Caraway seeds
Chili powder
Cinnamon (ground and
  sticks)
Cloves (ground and whole)
Crushed red pepper flakes
Cumin (ground)
Curry powder
Dill weed (dried)
Ginger (ground and
  crystallized)
Ground red pepper
  (cayenne)
Herbes de Provence
Marjoram (dried)
Mustard (dry and seeds)
Nutmeg (ground and whole)
Oregano (dried)
Paprika
Pepper (ground white and
  black; black peppercorns)
Rosemary (dried)
Sage (dried)
Sesame seeds
Tarragon (dried)
Thyme (dried)